PRAISE FOR THE WORK OF JAY MILBRANDT

"C. S. Lewis spoke of the counsel of the past as 'the clean sea breeze of the centuries.' Jay Milbrandt turns us fully into those breezes with his stirring retelling of the Pilgrim story. How desperately we need both the historian's craft and heroic tale found in these pages."

—STEPHEN MANSFIELD, *NEW YORK TIMES* BESTSELLING AUTHOR

"Weaving together religious conviction, moral fortitude, and adventure narrative, *They Came for Freedom* is a gripping story of faith and survival. Jay Milbrandt reminds us of this important piece of world history and how it shaped the founding of our nation. This remarkable work is a gripping reminder of why our families gather together every November to give thanks for all that we have and for those who have come before us."

—KENNETH W. STARR, FORMER US SOLICITOR
GENERAL AND FEDERAL JUDGE

"Just brilliant—history so alive you feel it and so profound you can't miss the importance of it. Jay has done it again."

—JOHNNIE MOORE, FOUNDER, THE KAIROS COMPANY

"A spectacular, ground-breaking, well-researched, splendidly told, and thoroughly gripping story."

—ERIC METAXAS, *NEW YORK TIMES* BESTSELLING
AUTHOR OF *BONHOEFFER* AND *MIRACLES*

"Milbrandt's portrait is like an old masterpiece cleaned of its dust and grime—a burning inspiration to all who know the link between the Gospel, mission, justice, and freedom."

—OS GUINNESS, AUTHOR OF *THE CALL*

"Milbrandt illuminates Livingstone's extraordinary story with great energy and clarity."

"Reads like a thriller . . . Enables the reader to obtain a glimpse into the faith which enabled [Livingstone] to make a unique contribution to the abolition of the slave trade in East Africa."

"A moving read and cautionary tale for anyone who cares about today's fight to end slavery."

"A fast and fascinating read: once you start, you won't want to put it down."

"Livingstone's commitment to the abolition of slavery changed the course of Africa. Through his life, we learn much about ourselves and God."

"Reminds us of God's goodness and grace."

"Will resonate and inspire activists, abolitionists, and explorers for years to come."

"At a time when missionaries past and present are too often carica-
tured and disdained, it is refreshing to read this gripping study of
David Livingstone."

—Paul Marshall, Senior Fellow at Hudson Institute's
Center for Religious Freedom and author of *Persecuted*

"The story of David Livingstone needed to be told, and Jay does not
disappoint. He is bold and brilliant."

—Suzan Johnson Cook, 3rd US Ambassador at
Large for International Religious Freedom

"David Livingstone was a great man, a great explorer, a great freedom
fighter, and a spiritual man. Livingstone remains an example of exceptional courage and leadership for the modern world."

—Azarias Ruberwa, former Vice President, DR
Congo and board member, Mercy Ships

"An adventure-packed biography of one man's courage and persistence
that finally broke the back of the slave trade and brought the influence
of Christianity to the African continent."

—Alan Terwilleger, President, the Chuck
Colson Center for Christian Worldview

"Livingstone's story is powerful—a triumph of humanity, faith, and
dignity. This is a must-read for anyone with African interests."

—Ron Tschetter, former Director, US Peace Corps

"Fascinating and very well written! It's the story of a determined and
tenacious human being with frailties common to us all. . . . An inspiration for us to selflessly invest into the lives of our fellow beings!"

—Kadita "A.T." Tshibaka, board member and former
President and CEO, Opportunity International

"I struggle to think of any Livingstone biographies that provide as much information about the east coast slave trade."

—ALISON RITCHIE, PROPERTY MANAGER, DAVID LIVINGSTONE CENTRE IN SCOTLAND

"Impressively researched and compellingly written . . . Whether you enjoy adventure or history, or are seeking spiritual inspiration as well as insights into the epic struggle to end the slave trade, this is a must-read."

—BENEDICT ROGERS, HUMAN RIGHTS ADVOCATE AND JOURNALIST, CHRISTIAN SOLIDARITY WORLDWIDE, AND AUTHOR OF *ON THE SIDE OF ANGELS*

"It is hard not to compare David Livingstone with another Victorian era opponent of slavery, William Wilberforce. I suspect each would be surprised to know that there are more slaves today in the world than when they lived. Their work needs to be continued."

—ROBERT F. COCHRAN, JR., LOUIS D. BRANDEIS PROFESSOR OF LAW AND DIRECTOR, HERBERT AND ELINOR NOOTBAAR INSTITUTE ON LAW, RELIGION, AND ETHICS AT PEPPERDINE UNIVERSITY SCHOOL OF LAW

"Combines the adventure of Sir Ernest Shackleton with the passionate opposition to the slave trade of William Wilberforce."

—JAY BARNES, PRESIDENT, BETHEL UNIVERSITY

THEY CAME FOR
FREEDOM

OTHER BOOKS BY JAY MILBRANDT

The Daring Heart of David Livingstone: Exile, African
Slavery, and the Publicity Stunt That Saved Millions
Go and Do: Daring to Change the World One Story at a Time
A Twist of Innovation
The Intercountry Adoption Debate: Dialogues Across Disciplines

THEY CAME FOR
FREEDOM

THE FORGOTTEN, EPIC ADVENTURE
OF THE PILGRIMS

JAY MILBRANDT

NELSON
BOOKS

An Imprint of Thomas Nelson

Published in Nashville, Tennessee, by Nelson Books, an imprint of Thomas Nelson. Nelson Books and Thomas Nelson are registered trademarks of HarperCollins Christian Publishing, Inc.

Published in association with Yates & Yates, www.yates2.com

Thomas Nelson titles may be purchased in bulk for educational, business, fund-raising, or sales promotional use. For information, please e-mail SpecialMarkets@ThomasNelson.com.

Any Internet addresses, phone numbers, or company or product information printed in this book are offered as a resource and are not intended in any way to be or to imply an endorsement by Thomas Nelson, nor does Thomas Nelson vouch for the existence, content, or services of these sites, phone numbers, companies, or products beyond the life of this book.

Scripture quotations marked ESV are taken from the ESV® Bible (The Holy Bible, English Standard Version®), copyright © 2001 by Crossway, a publishing ministry of Good News Publishers. Used by permission. All rights reserved.

Scripture quotations marked NASB are taken from the New American Standard Bible®, Copyright © 1960, 1962, 1963, 1968, 1971, 1972, 1973, 1975, 1977, 1995 by The Lockman Foundation. Used by permission. (www.Lockman.org)

Scripture quotations marked GENEVA BIBLE are taken from The Geneva Bible.

ISBN 978-0-7180-3785-7 (HC)
ISBN 978-0-7180-3786-4 (eBook)

Library of Congress Cataloging-in-Publication Data
Names: Milbrandt, Jay, 1982- author.
Title: They came for freedom : the forgotten, epic adventure of the pilgrims / Jay Milbrandt.
Description: Nashville, Tennessee : Nelson Books, an imprint of Thomas Nelson, 2017. |
Includes bibliographical references.
Identifiers: LCCN 2017005053 | ISBN 9780718037857
Subjects: LCSH: Pilgrims (New Plymouth Colony) | Massachusetts--History--
New Plymouth, 1620-1691. | Mayflower (Ship)
Classification: LCC F68 .M64 2017 | DDC 974.4/02--dc23 LC record available
at https://lccn.loc.gov/2017005053

Printed in the United States of America

17 18 19 20 21 LSC 10 9 8 7 6 5 4 3 2 1

For Lilly Ami

All these died in faith, and received not the promises, but saw them afar off, and believed them, and received them thankfully, and confessed that they were strangers and pilgrims on the earth.

For they that say such things, declare plainly, that they seek a country.

And if they had been mindful of that country, from whence they came out, they had leisure to have returned.

But now they desire a better, that is an heavenly: wherefore God is not ashamed of them to be called their God: for he hath prepared for them a city.

—Hebrews 11:13–16 (geneva bible)

Contents

Author's Note

For as many times as we have heard the Pilgrims' story, it remains complex—more than I had imagined when I started. As with most history makers, the men and women who set out on the *Mayflower* voyage had little sense of the monumental, culture-shaping event they had undertaken.

For as many people as this story involves, we have relatively few sources of detail. When a group is gripped in a life-or-death struggle for survival, chronicling daily matters is not necessarily one's primary quest. Thankfully, however, we had two men with the foresight to leave parts of the story for generations to come. William Bradford and Edward Winslow, our best sources on the Pilgrim story, were both generally prolific writers.[1] Bradford documented the happenings of the Pilgrims in great detail. For their work, we are grateful.

Such sources, however, can be biased. In this case, both men had a purpose to their writing: attracting their friends and families to join them in the New World. Thus, retelling the Pilgrim story involves a great deal of discernment and an appreciation for setting. As often as I can, I will let the Pilgrims speak for themselves. Still, as with many testimonies, there are two versions—and also the truth.

When I write about history, my chief intention is impartiality. I make it my foremost goal to leave out bias. As a lawyer, I try to approach history with some application of an evidentiary standard. I do my best to corroborate stories and present the facts. Broadly, I believe we are receiving the truth from these sources. Bradford appears to be chronicling a history of Plymouth Colony to preserve it for future generations. Winslow, a burgeoning diplomat, appears to be using his writings as a tool for building his platform in Europe and promoting Plymouth Colony. His work requires a more discerning eye. Bradford, in particular, had little reason to hide what happened. Their European counterparts would have viewed even the worst of their offenses inconsequentially.

I also avoid conjecture except for a few places in Squanto's early story where some speculation is required. I am careful to footnote any statements where I am suspicious of the truth or where mild speculation is made to fill gaps. In those footnotes, you will find a detailed account of why I made certain decisions, possible alternatives, and critical research. These instances are very few, but documented for the reader's further exploration.

There are many questions still to be asked about the Pilgrims, and many moral dilemmas to be waged. From past experience with writing about history, I am often asked for my opinion on controversial questions or characters. Throughout the content of this book, I do all I can to leave out my perspective. I prefer to let the characters speak for themselves and allow readers to craft their own conclusions.

Preface

W hy are we here, and where did we come from?"
Since the dawn of humankind, we have asked ourselves these important questions. Every faith, culture, and
philosophy has crafted an answer, or set of answers, to explain
human existence.

Our pluralistic world has come to exist with several, often
competing, explanations. Billions of faithful believers find their
answers in Scripture, with interpretations sometimes leaving
us at odds. Various Eastern religious traditions have conceived
of a circular vortex of life through hierarchy and virtue while
animistic cultures have found answers in nature, ancestry, and
story. Even today's most intelligent thinkers continue to wrestle
with these questions, including theoretical physicist Stephen
Hawking who points to spontaneous creation.

Despite their breadth, these inquiries continue to be the
more curious questions of our time. The History Channel can
draw record audiences by asking whether Jesus truly existed,
Hawking can sell out auditoriums for his lectures, and an article

on science increasingly proving the existence of God can set a *Wall Street Journal* reading record.

The struggle to answer the macroscale "Why does life exist?" query is mirrored by intimations in more grounded puzzles: Why do I live in this state or in this town? Why do I belong to this church? What is my place in this community?

The nation, about whose founding this book is written, regularly asks itself a similar set of questions: Why does America exist? What should we value? What is our role in the world?

As I write this book, the people of the United States are asking themselves if America is exceptional, as we have many times told ourselves. We are deciding whether cultures, races, and religions can ever truly coexist here in this two-hundred-year-old experiment. For some, this melting pot has begun to feel full. A national debate has arisen over whether our nation should continue to serve as a refuge for the world's oppressed, abandoned, and disenfranchised.

This book seeks to shed light on this question. This is an attempt to paint a portrait of one of the most foundational stories for our country, the groundwork on which much of our culture and history are built, and a story that we recognize nationally every November.

Indeed, this is a time when our nation is wrestling with pluralism. We face deep-seated racial tension in our streets and entrenched political battles at our polls. We are testing identity questions in our bathrooms and religious questions in courtrooms. We are asking whether America is a Christian nation and to what extent we should tolerate contradictory ideas. These are debates that rage in our media and over dinner.

Perhaps now, at an inflection point in our nation's history, is a time to revisit the Pilgrim quest. For the Pilgrims, religious toleration was their beacon, their North Star. They pursued it relentlessly and took on one of history's most daring escapes. Their story is also paradoxical. While they craved freedom of worship, they abhorred anyone who brought a different brand of religion to New Plymouth. Their lighthouse became a blinding light and eventually their undoing.

The latter part of the story—their undoing—has received little attention. We tell stories as we want them to be, and modernly, the Pilgrim story has swirled in legend and myth. As such, the "Pilgrim" has become an enduring, reverent icon. We buy Pilgrim costumes in browns and whites adorned with huge buckles and amusing hats. Our children cut Pilgrim figures out of craft paper in school. And, in one of our nation's most hallowed anthems, "My Country, 'Tis of Thee," we are reminded that America is the "land of the pilgrims' pride."[1]

We have come to misunderstand and commercialize their story, thereby relegating the Pilgrims to a quaint, backward people of American folklore. They were anything but. By embarking on a death-defying, forward-looking adventure that would come to reshape the world, theirs is a story of sacrifice, risk, and survival. But it is also a cautionary tale. It is admonitory in that experiments in freedom sometimes breed the opposite.

The Plymouth experiment was, ultimately, a failure. It survived (only barely), took controversial action toward its Indian neighbors, practiced excessive religious intolerance, and eventually chose abandonment over impending dissolution. Despite all this, the Pilgrims became curiously associated with the founding of America. Yet they were not the first to reach America—by the time the Pilgrims arrived, explorers had charted America's coasts and established outposts from Maine to Florida, and settlers had made permanent homes in Jamestown.

Why, then, do we give so much credit to the Pilgrims? Why do we today view the title "Pilgrim" with reverence and honor?

Why, every November, do we recognize the Pilgrim vision in word and imagery as a bastion of freedom and self-government?

Despite their many shortcoming and failures, the Pilgrims stood as the model to our nation's founding fathers. At times when our nation was facing seemingly insurmountable challenges, the "Pilgrim Fathers" offered an example of steadfast, enduring faith, and they made radical experiments in civil government that continue to shape our nation hundreds of years later.

In the face of hardship, the Pilgrims exercised incredible faith. At a time when news from the New World often comprised messages about death and failure, the Pilgrims chose to cross the Atlantic on a brave adventure. They knew that not all their party would survive, but perhaps they underestimated how many would perish the first winter. Even with the opportunity to return to England, they stayed. They endured several hard years, and when it appeared they may not survive, they prayed, asking for God's grace. Their Harvest Festival—a celebration of God's gifts to them—set the stage for our Thanksgiving centuries later.

Many years after the Pilgrims' arrival, the founding fathers looked for signs of God's hand in the forging of a new nation. The Pilgrim fathers provided inspiration.

In a letter to the Town of Plymouth in 1766, leading up to the Revolutionary War, Samuel Adams, John Ruddock, and John Hancock wrote, "To the Inhabitants of the Town of Plymouth . . . That the Spirit of our venerable Fore-Fathers may revive and be diffused through every Community in this Land . . . is the fervent wish."[2]

Indeed, the Pilgrims broke new ground in uncharted territory. With their Mayflower Compact, the Pilgrims had proffered a radical new form of civil authority—self-government. Many consider it to be the predecessor to a modern constitution and a building block for the foundation of American democracy.

Nearly two hundred years after the signing of the Mayflower Compact, John Quincy Adams would say of it, "It was the first example in modern times of social compact or system of government instituted by voluntary agreement conformably to the laws of nature, by men of equal rights and about to establish their community in a new country."[3]

Out of this new model of self-government, the Pilgrims firmly established the rule of law. For a tumultuous group still lightly tethered to European monarchy, they created a remarkably orderly society. They instituted a system of land records, again a revolutionary feat in a time when aristocracies largely controlled European land and limited individual ownership rights. The Pilgrims further determined that land should descend to all children of a family, not solely the eldest son. In 1636, they codified a document tantamount to a bill of rights, a precursor to one of America's foundational documents a little more than 150 years later.

The Pilgrims effectively separated church and state. In direct response to the English theocracy they fled, they imagined a society where the church would not dictate how they would be governed, and vice versa. To those ends, they chose nonclergy for their government offices and distinct decision-making processes. They took legal recognition of marriage out of the church and made it a civil function. These were brave new ideas.

The chronicles of the Pilgrims could quickly fill volumes—and indeed they do. Books have focused exclusively on the *Mayflower* voyage, life in Plymouth, and many decades of important history after. Among the cast of characters on the *Mayflower*, each passenger lived an adventure of epic proportions. This cannot all be told here.

I chose to write this book because I wanted to understand the Pilgrims' quest for religious freedom. I could not find such a book. This story starts long before the Pilgrims arrived in the New World and even long before they conceived of the *Mayflower* voyage.

I opened this book with the question: *Why am I here?*

We will each have our own answer, but mine is this: I am here because I am a thirteenth-generation, one might say, illegal immigrant. My ancestors arrived in North America on a boat named the *Mayflower*, with dubious permission and questionable intent. One was arguably a mercenary who shed blood in the name of his cause; the other, an indentured servant with a hot temper.

But I am also here because of an aspiring idea. There was a notion, however small the seed may have been, of a freer world. This was an idea so worthy of living for that it was worth dying for. And so, the Pilgrims embarked upon one of history's greatest, most daring, and most misunderstood adventures of all time.

This is their story.

Prologue

FALL 1644
NEW ENGLAND

Their great experiment began to crumble. They had left Europe to preserve a precious religious identity, but now its remnants could scarcely be seen. Disillusion and discontent had afflicted its body. Vice and restlessness had infected its youth. The flame that once burned boldly enough to send them into a courageous, improbable adventure had now dwindled to a slight flicker.

Thirty-one years had passed since "the Pilgrims," as they would become known, had landed on the shores of the New World in search of freedom. They had crafted an epic escape to "New Plymouth"—a natural harbor turned humble womb for their fledgling church—and a new beginning for a faithful identity. The colony had survived its arduous exodus from England, but only barely. Famine, disease, and war had all threatened their feeble existence. Against all odds, they executed a plan that by most accounts appeared ludicrous.

But now the Pilgrims faced perhaps their greatest challenge of all—preserving everything for which they had fought and for which the best of them had given their fortunes and their lives. The Pilgrims' uncertain experiment in freedom had succeeded by the mere fact that they stayed alive. They persevered by clinging to an ideology: simple, unadulterated worship and a modest agrarian lifestyle. They had fled intolerance, but now, as New England blossomed with activity and diversity, they faced their latest challenge: coexistence. These religious Separatists had become the minority in a land becoming overrun by Puritans, purveyors, and pagans. The future troubled New Plymouth's elders.

William Bradford, the Pilgrims' faithful leader, sat by the fire in a corner of his small home.[1] A kettle hung by chain over the blaze, boiling water for dinner. Bradford was an old man now at fifty-eight. His hair draped to his shoulders and mustache turned up at the corners of his mouth. It had grayed long before, over the course of many exhausting years. He was Plymouth Colony's Solomon, its wise philosopher-king who ruled with a just and thoughtful hand and was always willing to surrender his power.

Bradford had fled England as a teenager with the first wave of Pilgrims. He had sacrificed family and fortune not only to join them, but also to further a faith system he believed to be true and right. He had dreamed of a pure, undefiled life for his faithful companions. They could worship without the oversight of the state, emulate the early church of the New Testament, and recreate the basic simplicities of a rural English hamlet.

Elected governor at age thirty-one, and still in office twenty years later, Bradford had witnessed colossal changes during his tenure as commander in chief of the colony. His steady hand had guided them through turmoil and sorrow, misery and celebration.

Bradford saw God's plan in their suffering. He had believed from their earliest moments together that the Pilgrims were

God's chosen people with special providence for their time on earth. But he had also begun to doubt.

Now, as an old man, he wondered whether indeed God had held a special purpose for them. The fledgling colony found itself at a watershed moment. Their intention was to start a refuge of the righteous, free from the vice and oppression of England. But, alas, New Plymouth had a new enemy. The Pilgrims' quiet plantation in New England had been overrun by adventurers, merchants, and religious pluralists. Their children took note— and began to leave in droves.

Two years earlier, Bradford began documenting his concerns:

Marvelous it may be to see and consider how some kind of wickedness did grow and breake forth here in a land where the same was . . . severely punished. . . . And yet all this could not suppress the breaking out of sundry notori- ous sins, . . . especially drunkenness and uncleaness; not only incontinencie between persons unmarried, for which many both men and women have been punished sharply enough, but some married persons also. But that which is worse, even sodomy and buggery, (things fearful to name) have broke forth in this land, oftener than once. I say it may justly be marveled at, and cause us to fear and tremble at the consideration of our corrupte natures, which are so hardly bridled, subdued, and mortified; nay, cannot by any other means but the powerful worke and grace of God's spirit. But (besides this) one reason may be, that the Devil may carry a greater spite against the churches of Christ and the gospell here, by how much the more they indea[v]our to preserve holiness and purity amongst them, and strictly punisheth the contrary when it ariseth either in church or common- wealth . . . I would rather thinke thus, than that Satan hath more power in these heathen lands, as some have thought, than in more Christian nations, especially over God's servants in them.[2]

Bradford stepped out of his house onto Plymouth Colony's main dirt road, the artery of the small colony. He had a gathering to attend on Burial Hill, the site of Plymouth's fort. The square two-story wooden structure rose like a turret above the town—their lookout for native attacks and new ships on the bay. The small fort not only provided protection but also served as the colony's meeting house and church. Surrounded by a nine-foot-tall stockade, Plymouth was its own bubble in a wild, hostile world. For Bradford, it felt like the evil beyond Plymouth's walls had launched a Trojan horse in the colony's youth.

Bradford had served as the colony's historian, documenting its life and times from their departure from England. He would shape future generations' understanding of the Pilgrims' lives and motives. But the degradation of Plymouth was painful. He could hardly chronicle the colony any longer. His always-quick pen slowly came to a withering halt. His narrative went silent—unfinished perhaps. Instead of continuing Plymouth's biography, Bradford looked back, chronicling a list of the *Mayflower*'s passengers and updating their legacies.

He still found solace in writing, turning to poetry as an outlet for his lamentations.

> From my years young in days of youth,
> God did make known to me his truth,
> And call'd me from my native place
> For to enjoy the means of grace.
> In wilderness he did me guide,
> And in strange lands for me provide.

In fears and wants, though weal and woe,
A pilgrim, past I to and fro:
Oft left of them whom I did trust;
How vain it is to rest on dust!
A man of sorrows I have been,
And many changes I have seen.
Wars, wants, peace, plenty, have I known;
And some advanc'd, others thrown down.

My days are spent, old age is come,
My strength it fails, my glass near run:
Now I will wait, when work is done,
Until my happy change shall come,
When from my labours I shall rest,
With Christ above for to be blest.[3]

Bradford was deeply concerned about the future of New Plymouth. In the thirty-one years since the Pilgrims arrived, an entire generation had been born and raised in Plymouth with no connection to their journey or heritage in England. He knew this generation would soon assume leadership—but only if New Plymouth could retain them.

He had called together a group of young men of the colony and gathered a group of elders from the New Plymouth church, "ancient men," as he styled them. The elders needed to pass along their history and their heritage—their purpose. Like the great dialogues of Socrates with the youth of Athens, Bradford would record the testimony for generations to come.

Bradford walked slowly up Burial Hill toward the meeting house. The village had grown considerably since they built the small fortress—it had since served as garrison, infirmary, and winter refuge. Tall, narrow wooden buildings now lined the street.

Their thatched roofs rustled in the breeze as smoke from their fires drifted out from the chimneys. The meeting house would be a tight fit—Bradford expected a crowd, as several generations of men gathered together for what Bradford believed to be one of New Plymouth's most critical conferences.

The young men of New Plymouth opened the meeting.[4] A speaker for the young men began:

> Gentlemen, you were pleased to appoint us this time to confer with you, and to propound such questions . . . in some things wherein we are ignorant. Our first request, therefore, is, to know your minds concerning the true and simple meaning of those of *The Separation*, as they are termed, when they say the Church of England is . . . no true Church.[5]

They did not call themselves "Pilgrims," but "Separatists." They found the high church, government-infused theocracy of the Church of England not only repulsive, but sinful. Following the apostle Paul's admonition to "come out from among them, and be separate," they did so, separating unlawfully from the Anglican Church in the late sixteenth century. They founded a Separatist church, modest and modeled after the early Christian church of the gospel.

Speaking for the elders, Bradford told the young men:

> They speak of it as . . . a National Church, combined together of all in the land promiscuously under the hierarchical government of archbishops, their courts and canons, so far different from the primitive pattern in the Gospels. . . . [T]he churches and chief of the ministers here hold that the National Church . . . is not alloweable according to the primitive order of the Gospel.

A young man spoke up.

"We desire to know how many have been put to death for this cause," he asked, "and what manner of persons they were, and what occasions were taken against them by bringing them to their end."

"We know certainly of six that were publicly executed, besides such as died in prisons," Bradford replied. "Mr. Henry Barrow [and] Mr. Greenwood . . . suffered at Tyburn."

"Did any of you know Mr. Barrow?" probed another young man. "If we may be so bold to ask, for we would willingly know what his life and conversation; because some, we perceive, have him in precious esteem, and others can scarcely name him without some note of obloquy and dislike."

"We have not seen his person," Bradford replied, "but some of us have been well acquainted with those that knew him familiarly. . . . He was a gentleman of good worth and a flourishing courtier in his time, and . . . he was sometimes a student at Cambridge and the Inns of Court, and accomplished with strong parts."

Bradford continued to tell them Barrow's story.

"Walking in London, one Lord's-day, with one of his companions, [Barrow] heard a preacher at his sermon very loud, as they passed by the church."

Something caught Barrow's attention, Bradford explained, and he wanted to go inside and listen. His companion could not understand why he would want "to hear a man talk."

Barrow could not quiet his curiosity, so he slipped into the church and sat down. He had dutifully fulfilled the strict mandates of the Church of England, as required by law. The church had left him with rules, but no moral compass, and he had overindulged himself in London's opulence. He felt more at home in London's drinking parlors and gambling houses than he did in a church.

Before Bradford could continue the story, an elder of the

Plymouth church interjected:

"[T]he minister was vehement in reproving sin . . . things as [Barrow] was guilty of, so as God set it home to his soul, and began to work his repentance."

"For he was so stricken as he could not be quiet," Bradford added, ". . . with diligent reading and meditation, God brought peace to his soul and conscience, after much humiliation of heart and reformation of life; so he left the Court, and retired himself to a private life, sometime in the country, and sometime in the city, giving himself to study and reading of the Scripture, and other good works, very diligently. And being missed at Court by his consorts and acquaintance, it was quickly bruited abroad that Barrow was turned Puritan."

In fact, Barrow had not joined the Puritans—those who wanted to remain in the Church of England, intending to purify it from within. Instead, Barrow chose to join those who had left the church—Separatists.

Barrow's absence in London did not go unnoticed. A man of his stature could not simply disappear. His abrupt departure from the high life of London and his subsequent "conversation" generated gossip, but also serious conversation. His prominence brought the Separatist movement not only new life, but legitimacy.

"We can further affirm from those that well knew him," an elder continued to tell the young men of New Plymouth, "that he was very comfortable to the poor and those in distress in their sufferings; and when he saw he must die, he gave a stock for the relief of the poor of the church, which was of good help to them in their banished condition afterwards."

"We cannot but marvel," the young men replied, "that such a man should be [hated] by so many."[6]

"It is not much to be marveled at," Bradford answered, "for he was most plain in discovering the cruelty, fraud, and hypocrisy of the enemies of the truth, and searching into the corruptions of the time, which made him abhorred of them."

The young and old men continued for a long while. They further discussed Barrow's life, the theology of Separatism, and its interactions with various churches. The hour grew late and the men needed to return to their work or families. The conversation had ended only for the night. They would meet again.

"Having thus far satisfied all your demands," an elder concluded, "we shall here break off this conference for this time, desiring the Lord to make you grow up in grace and wisdom and the true fear of God, that in all faithfulness and humility you may serve him in your generations."

"Gentlemen," the young men responded, "we humbly thank you for your pains with us and respect unto us . . . and herewith do humbly take our leave."

Part One —————————————————

FAITH

Chapter One

The Clink

NOVEMBER 19, 1586[1]
LONDON, ENGLAND

The cold November air stung at Henry Barrow's face and hands. He walked hurriedly across London's rugged streets just east of the Thames. In a narrow alley, he made a sharp left, down a half-flight of stone steps and up to a fortified gate. He rapped his knuckles against the icy iron door, then waited for the warden.

This was Sunday—the Lord's Day—and Barrow had arrived at this prison door to visit his friend, the Reverend John Greenwood. With the warden's permission, Barrow stepped inside the iron gate and walked into the bowels of this torturous edifice. *Clink*—the lock fastened behind him. This sound had become synonymous with the prison: "The Clink" it was named—a medieval jail so notorious it would forever lend its title to prisons the world over.

Barrow followed the dark, narrow corridors to Greenwood's cell. Every step on the stone floor made a crunching sound. Lice, fleas—a living carpet covered its cold surfaces and infested the prison. Its dark corridors were lit only by candles, and the shadows hid stories rarely spoken beyond these walls. Its prisoners received the basic staples only through an underground market of bribes and corrupt jailers. Beds and blankets necessitated payments. Food arrived by similar means. The prison itself provided no meals. Prisoners begged, calling out into the city through the Clink's iron fence for a compassionate passerby to leave a morsel of food. For enough money, a man could be unshackled and walk freely. The poor would simply starve. A brothel, too, operated freely within the prison confines.

The prison walls seemed to bear down on Barrow like the suffocating prison of the Church of England beyond them. The state church was his Clink. He could hear London bustling beyond the Clink's stone ramparts. Yet knowing his faith could put him behind bars at any moment, he felt no more a free man than Greenwood.

The friendship these two men shared was an unlikely one. While both attended colleges at Cambridge University, their paths diverged considerably. Greenwood had studied theology. After graduating from Corpus Christi College, he took orders in the Church of England. However, he quickly became disenchanted with the church's rules and structure.

The English government had created the national church—the Church of England—in 1534 when the pope refused to recognize the annulment of a marriage between Henry VIII and Catherine of Aragon. The English Reformation ensued as the Church of England broke away from Rome and created its own doctrine.

In 1558, the "Act of Uniformity" standardized expectations for both laypeople and clergy. The act required all churches to follow the *Book of Common Prayer*, a structured regimen for the content and order of religious services. Further, worshippers could not gather without the presence of a licensed bishop.

For the citizens of England, the act made attendance mandatory—or face punishment. Fines for a one-week lapse in church attendance: twelve pence.[2] Routine absence and seditious activity could amount to imprisonment, or even death.

Greenwood found these legalistic practices unscriptural and renounced the Church of England altogether. He soon found his convictions welcomed among a growing movement of fellow dissenters who wanted to worship outside the confines of the Church of England. The bishops branded them "Separatists." The brethren of the movement, however, preferred "Congregationalists," and sometimes "Brownists" in honor of the father of the movement.

As a young preacher in the late 1570s, Robert Browne began to believe that the Church of England had divorced itself from the truer principles of the early church. He spoke out zealously, spreading his ideas and planting churches based on his beliefs. His books laid out the principles for these congregations and went so far as to recommend civil disobedience against the Church of England, rather than waiting in vain for the approval of church reforms.[3] The state quickly saw him as a threat. By the end of his life in 1633, Browne had been committed to thirty-two prisons, and he had started a movement, inspiring men like Barrow and Greenwood.

Greenwood's departure from the pulpit of the Church of England evoked the ire of its bishops. That he withdrew to join this subversive movement made his offense even more punishable. He quickly rose to leadership among the Separatists, leveraging his academic credentials to add theological depth to their cause. Eventually his influence became too much for the bishops. They had him arrested and thrown into jail.

Greenwood suffered in chains nearly six months before receiving a formal examination. The state viewed his crimes significant enough to warrant some of its most prominent law-givers. For his long-overdue inquisition, he came before the lord chief justice of England, the archbishop of Canterbury, and the bishops of London, among other clergy and noblemen at London Palace.

The commission began by requiring Greenwood to lay his hand upon a Bible to take an oath. He refused. He would swear by the name of God—the author of truth—"but not by, or upon a book."[4] That book—the Bishops' Bible—was, to Greenwood, an abomination.

Greenwood's examination covered the *Book of Common Prayer*, his views of marriage, his opinion of the Church of England, and the supremacy of the queen. The panel imposed lengthy questions of theology but allowed him only short, simple answers.

"No prattling—answer only directly—yea or nay," the panel reminded him regularly.[5] They left no room for explanation, no space for debate.

They asked if church congregations should follow the *Book of Common Prayer*.

"Christ and his apostles prayed in other words, according to their present necessity," Greenwood replied. "[The queen is] supreme magistrate over all persons, to punish the evil and defend the good. Christ only is head of the church, and his laws may no man alter."

The examiners found Greenwood's answers vile, warranting a stiff penalty. The panel condemned him to the Clink. There could be, perhaps, no worse punishment short of death.

Barrow had much to risk by visiting his friend in the notorious prison, yet their friendship and cause had grown deep enough that Barrow believed the risk to be justified.

Barrow had enjoyed a lifestyle much different from Greenwood's. Whereas Greenwood was a student of theology, Barrow studied law. He was accomplished, energetic, and ambitious. He lived at the center of London life, and together with the rising stars of the nation a golden path lay before him. He had grown up in a wealthy family and received a Cambridge University education. After graduation, he became a member of the honorable society of Gray's Inn and practiced in Queen Elizabeth's court. Due to his family's prominence, along with his own merits, Barrow became well known. Yet his youthful enthusiasm and affluence gave way to vice—drinking and gambling. Impulsive, passionate, and fearless, he overindulged, and where debauchery and excess found their audience among London's young and elite, he fit right in.

Barrow's lifestyle made him an unexpected disciple of the Separatist movement, a discreet, conservative, careful minority. A man of his stature and constitution did not forgo the Church of England. Attendance was reported, and absence punishable—a likely death sentence for a career in the public eye. Even if Barrow could conceal his interest, he could not hide his separation long. If inconspicuous Greenwood had been caught, then surely Barrow's participation would not go unnoticed.

Perhaps Barrow's passion and impulse initially attracted him to the Separatist movement, but Greenwood's counterculture faith captured him. Greenwood's convictions and influence significantly shaped Barrow's theology, and their friendship blossomed at secret gatherings of Separatists.

Fifteen minutes into Barrow's visit to the Clink, the warden returned to Greenwood's cell. He came not for Greenwood, but for Barrow.

"[W]ith commandment from the Lord's Grace so to do," the warden told him as he placed Barrow under arrest. He showed no warrant and gave no cause.

Soon two government messengers arrived carrying a *lettre de cachet*—orders imposing punishment without trial or appeal. Barrow refused to acknowledge it.

⤺⧓⤻

Barrow stood before John Whitgift, the archbishop of Canterbury, the highest official of the Church of England. A sturdy man, both in countenance and constitution, Whitgift had solemn brown eyes, jet-black hair, and a thin, graying beard. His features complemented his dark complexion and grave personality.

Whitgift demanded to know why Barrow had refused to receive and obey his letter.

"Because I was under arrest and imprisoned without warrant," Barrow replied, "and therefore it was too late to bring the letter."[6]

Whitgift had gained the reputation of a tyrannical, self-centered priest. He had achieved authority as he climbed up the church hierarchy, receiving prestigious professorships and eventually the vice-chancellory of Trinity College. He had an aggressive vision for the Church of England. He wanted religious uniformity across England—uniformity in theology and practice consistent, most importantly, with his own beliefs. His resolve to standardize the national church placed him frequently at odds with many religious leaders and even at the center of controversy.

Whitgift took great lengths to bring down—even put to death—those who opposed his vision. He hated Puritans who sought to cleanse the Church of England of its trappings of Roman Catholicism. He needed the hierarchical vestiges of Catholicism, and its supremacy of authority, to maintain his place of power and prominence. If the Puritans presented a threat, then the Separatists, who wanted to see the Church of England disappear altogether, spoke utter heresy.

Barrow suspected what Whitgift wanted from this hearing. The archbishop hoped to prove Barrow had denounced the Church of England, or simply force him to admit it. Barrow, however, knew Whitgift's evidence would be circumstantial at best and trusted that none of his Separatist friends would testify against him.

The archbishop called for a Bible. When it arrived, Barrow refused to swear on it, just as Greenwood had done.

"Mr. Barrow refused to swear upon a book," Archbishop Whitgift directed for the recorder, then proceeded with his examination.[7]

"It is reported, that you come not to church, are disobedient to Her Majesty, and say there is no true church in England," Archbishop Whitgift began. "What say you?"

"These are reports," Barrow replied. "When you have produced your testimony, I will answer."

"Well, when were you at church?" Whitgift asked.

"That is nothing to you," said Barrow.

"You are a schismatic, a recusant, and a seditious person," Whitgift barked.

"Say what you will of me," Barrow responded, "I freely forgive you."

"I care not for your forgiveness."

"But if you offend me, you ought to seek it," Barrow said, "whilst you are in the way with me."

"When were you at church?" Whitgift continued with the examination.

"I have answered that already," Barrow said. "It belongeth not to you."

"It belongeth to us," Whitgift replied, "and I will not only meddle with you, but arraign you before me as an heretic."

"You shall do no more than God will," Barrow rejoined. "Err I may; but an heretic I will never be."

"Will you hereafter come to church?" Whitgift continued, composing himself.

"Future things are in the Lord's hands," Barrow replied. "If I do not, you have a law."

"Have you spoken this of the Church of England?" Whitgift asked.

"When you have produced your witness," Barrow said, "I will answer."

"Upon your oath, I will believe you," Whitgift responded.

"But I will not accuse myself," Barrow said.

"You are lawless," Whitgift retorted.

"I had rather you produced your witness," Barrow said.

"What occupation are you of?" Whitgift asked, changing the subject.

"I am a Christian," Barrow replied.

"So are we all," said Whitgift.

"I deny that," Barrow said confidently.

Finally, Whitgift made him an offer: Barrow would be set free if he attended the Church of England and agreed to return if Whitgift wanted a further examination. Barrow still refused.

The archbishop closed the examination, ordering Barrow to prison.

∾⧸⧹∾

During eight months of mostly solitary confinement, Barrow underwent two more examinations before Archbishop Whitgift and a commission of governmental authorities. In May 1587, he and Greenwood were released on bail.

Freshly released from prison, Barrow and Greenwood immediately returned to their secret Sunday evening meeting of twenty-two men and women. Sometimes they met in the woods or in barns; other times they risked gathering in private residences. They would pray and read from the Geneva Bible—a translation unauthorized by the government.[8] They did not follow the *Book of Common Prayer*; they had no ordained bishop present.

The attendees came from diverse backgrounds, sharing little in common except disgust for the national church. The circle included Nicholas Crane, a minister ordained by the bishop of London, who had effectively renounced his priesthood. Margret Maynerd, an elderly widow, regularly joined them—she had not attended the Church of England in ten years, publicly condemned it, and notably said there was no true church in England at all. The group included Catherine Unwen, a twenty-nine-year-old widow who had refused the Church of England's requirement of infant baptism for her son. He was now eleven years old.[9]

The group warmly welcomed back Barrow and Greenwood. This week, shortly after their release, the group met in a small home on the north bank of the Thames River under the towering shadow of St. Paul's Cathedral. The meeting proceeded as normal with prayer and Bible readings.

Suddenly the sheriff of London burst into the house, stopping the meeting. He had uncovered the secret meeting after acting on a tip from a servant of one of the attendees.

The sheriff proceeded to arrest the group, returning Barrow to prison and scattering the rest throughout various London jails. After his arrest visiting Greenwood, Barrow had learned to survive in confinement, but his prominence and family connections afforded him comforts unavailable to his Separatist colleagues. For many of them, the suffering was too much. Maynerd, the elderly widow, and two other members of the group shortly died of the infections rampant in the squalid prison conditions. The chancellor to the bishop of London forced the baptism of Unwen's son, and out of fear of further punishment, she ran away upon release.

After nearly a year of waiting, Barrow received attention again. On March 18, 1588, officials from Whitehall Palace summoned Barrow to its courts. Officials took him to the lord chancellor's chamber and placed him in the withdrawing room. He found himself seated with twelve of his friends whom the sheriff had arrested at their worship gathering. None could speak as they waited to be called, one by one, into the lord's chamber.

Eventually they called for Barrow. Court officials paraded him into the chamber and forced him to kneel before a large table. Across the table sat Archbishop Whitgift and the bishop of London, cloaked in their pontificalibus, as well as the lord chancellor and Lord Treasurer Burghley.

Barrow knew of Lord Treasurer Burghley, and he wondered if he might bring a dose of sympathy to the matter. William Burghley had begun his career in Parliament in his early twenties, gaining a reputation as an intelligent, artful, and industrious politician. As an aid to Queen Elizabeth, he managed her royal affairs well, earning her confidence and becoming an indispensable adviser to her. Their relationship placed him on a trajectory for her special appointments, eventually the lord treasurer.[10]

Burghley's friendship with the queen and his artful politicking transformed the role of lord treasurer from financial overseer to the most powerful nonroyal in England—effectively de facto prime minister. Burghley also possessed a more temperate disposition toward religious nonconformists. First and foremost, he sought to protect the Crown, but as long as religious nonconformists were loyal to the Crown, Burghley felt they should be allowed to worship discreetly. As soon as they posed a threat to the queen, of course, he would support action against them.

Barrow distinguished administrative officials, like Lord

Treasurer Burghley, from religious officials, like Archbishop Whitgift. Even if he disagreed with their politics, he respected administrative officials and treated them with courtesy. Religious leaders, however, he regarded as hypocrites and would not tolerate or give much consideration.

"Why are you in prison, Barrow?" Lord Treasurer Burghley opened the hearing.

"I am in prison, my lord," Barrow replied, "upon the statute made for recusants," using a term to describe those who refused to comply with religious regulation.

"Why will you not come to church?" the lord treasurer inquired.

"My whole desire is to come to the church of God."

"I see thou art a fantastical fellow," the lord treasurer replied. "But why not come to our churches?"

"My lord, the causes are great and many," Barrow continued, "because all the wicked in the land are received unto the Communion; you have a false and Antichristian ministry set over your church; you do not worship God aright, but in an idolatrous and a superstitious manner; and your church is not governed by the Testament of Christ, but by the Romish Courts Canons."

"Here is matter enough, indeed," the lord treasurer replied. "I perceive thou takest delight to be an author of this new religion."

"I never heard such stuff in all my life," the lord chancellor agreed.

"[Barrow] was a sower of errors," Archbishop Whitgift interjected, "and therefore I committed him."

"You indeed committed me half a year, close prisoner in the Gatehouse," Barrow replied, "and I never until now, understood the cause, neither do I yet know what errors they are; show them—"

"You complained to us of injustice," the lord treasurer inquired, "wherein have you received wrong?"

"By being imprisoned, my lord, without due trial," Barrow replied.

"You said that you were condemned upon the statute," said the lord treasurer.

"Unjustly, my lord," Barrow said, "that statute was not made for us."

"There must be stricter laws made for you?" the lord treasurer asked.

"Oh, my lord," Barrow replied, ". . . we have suffered enough."

"Indeed," said the lord treasurer, "you look as though you have a troubled conscience."[11]

"No, my lord, I praise God for it," Barrow replied, "but it is an awful thing, that the sword of our prince should thus be drawn against her faithful subjects."

"The queen's sword is not yet drawn against Mr. Barrow and his fellow prisoners," the lord treasurer explained.

"We have been long confined in close prison."

"Have you not had a hearing?" the lord treasurer asked.[12]

"Several have been with them, whom they mocked," the bishop of London interjected.

"We have mocked no man," said Barrow. "Miserable physicians are you all. We desired a public hearing, that all might know our opinions, and wherein we err."

"You shall have no such hearing," the archbishop bellowed. "You have published too much already; and, therefore, I committed you close prisoners."

"But contrary to the law," Barrow said.

"On such occasions it may be done by law," the lord treasurer insisted. "Have you any learning?"

"The Lord knows I am ignorant. I have no learning to boast of. But this I know, that you are void of all true learning and godliness."

"See the spirit of this man," snapped one of the lords.

"I have matter to call you before me as an *heretic*," the archbishop bellowed.

"Err I may; but heretic, by the grace of God, I will never be."

Lord Treasurer Burghley brought the conversation back to points of theology.

"Do you not hold, that it is unlawful to enact a law for ministers to live by tithes, and that the people be required to pay them?" he asked Barrow.

"My lord, such laws are abrogated and unlawful."

"You would have the minister live upon something," Burghley stated. "What should he live of?"

"Wholly of alms, as Christ hath ordained, and as he and his apostles lived," Barrow replied.

"How if the people will not give?" the lord treasurer asked.

"Such are not the people of God."

"But what shall the ministers do, in the meantime?"

"Not stand as minister to such, neither take the goods of the profane," Barrow responded.

"Where can you show me, from Scripture, that ministers ought not live by tithes?"

"Hebrews 7:12; Galatians 6:6," Barrow said. "In the one place tithes are abrogated; in the other, another kind of provision is made for ministers. The words of the former text are these: 'For the priesthood being changed, there is made necessity a change also for the law.' And you cannot deny that tithes were a part of that law: as Numbers 18."

"Wouldst you have the minister to have all my goods?" the lord treasurer asked in jest.

"No, my lord, but I would have you not withhold your goods in helping him," Barrow responded. "Neither rich nor poor are exempted from this duty."

"Ministers are not now called priests?" the lord treasurer asked, prodding Barrow for more.

"If they receive tithes, they are priests," Barrow responded. "They are called priests in the law."

"What is a presbyter, I pray thee?" the bishop of London asked.

"An elder."

"What, in age only?" inquired the bishop.

"No," Barrow replied. "Timothy was a young man."

"Presbyter is Latin for a priest," the bishop told him.

"It is no Latin word, but derived from the Greek and signifies the same as the Greek word does, which is elder."

"Do you not know those two men?" the chancellor asked Barrow, pointing at the bishop and archbishop.

"Yes, my lord, I have cause to know them."

"Is not this the bishop of London?" the chancellor inquired.

"I know him for no bishop, my lord."

"What is he then?" the chancellor wondered.

"His name is Aylmer, my lord," Barrow said. "The Lord pardon my fault, that I did not lay him open as a wolf, a bloody persecutor, and an apostate."

"What is that man?" the lord chancellor then asked Barrow, pointing to the archbishop of Canterbury.

"He is a monster, a miserable compound; I know not what to make of him," an emboldened Barrow replied. "[H]e is neither ecclesiastical nor civil, but that second beast spoken of in Revelation."

"Where is that place?" inquired the lord treasurer. "Show it."

Barrow began to read from Revelation 13: "Then I saw a second beast, coming out of the earth. It had two horns like a lamb, but it spoke like a dragon."[13]

Barrow turned to the second chapter of 2 Thessalonians:

"Who opposeth and exalteth himself above all that is called God, or that is worshipped; so that he as God sitteth in the temple of God, showing himself that he is God."

The archbishop rose in fury. "Will you suffer him, my lords?"[14]

With no objection to his request, a prison guard grabbed Barrow, plucking him up from his knees. Barrow pled to Lord Treasurer Burghley for freedom as the guard dragged him out of the room. He received no reply.

The Church of England anticipated that Barrow's imprisonment would suppress the Separatist movement. Incarceration had broken Robert Browne, the father of their movement. After serving more than thirty prison sentences and leaving England in exile, Browne eventually recanted his Separatist ideas and returned to England as an Anglican priest. The commission assumed that, eventually, incarceration would break Barrow as well.

Despite their efforts, in the weeks and months following his tribunal, Barrow became the mascot of Separatism. His noble resistance began to take on a life of its own with many Separatists now identifying as "Barrowists." Even Francis Bacon, the famous English philosopher and jurist who introduced the scientific method, wrote of Barrow. If not for Barrow, Bacon noted, these "silly" movements might long ago have "breathed out."[15]

❧

The walls of Newgate Prison formed tall, imposing ramparts around Henry Barrow. Even when his imprisonment began in 1586, Newgate could be considered an old jail. In 1128, King Henry II ordered a dungeon and guard tower built into the old Roman wall that once surrounded London, forming Newgate Prison. Although the prison had received several expansions, its conditions rarely improved, rivaling only the horrific squalor of the Clink. Between sadistic jailers and the rampant spread of "jail fever"—typhus transmitted by lice and fleas—only one in four prisoners survived to their execution day.

Reverend Greenwood could tell a similar saga from his many years in prison. Through the regular course of transfers and hearings, the companions reunited at Newgate. To pass their time in prison, the men wrote voraciously. Although the prisons prohibited writing, friends smuggled scraps of paper and writing materials into Newgate when they brought food to the prisoners. Barrow and Greenwood smuggled their writings out the same way—when they could avoid the frequent strip searches for contraband.

Outside the gates, their friends transcribed the notes or sent them directly to a printer in Holland. Barrow's and Greenwood's writings soon were smuggled back into England for circulation to the Separatist community. Barrow labored through this tedious communication apparatus to publish two books from behind bars, continuing to stoke the fire of Separatism and deepen the growing body of theological thought for the movement.

Their lengthy detention was intended to serve the state's goal of quietly defusing the Separatist movement by removing its prominent leaders. Despite isolating Barrow and Greenwood and avoiding a public trial, Separatism continued to grow, fueled in part by their writings and affliction. Eventually the bishops caught wind of these publications.

More than six years had passed since Barrow's tribunal before the lord treasurer's council. On March 23, 1593, guards came to the cells of Barrow and Greenwood. They escorted the men out of Newgate and next door to the Old Bailey for trial. This time the government possessed an official indictment: "for writing and publishing sundry seditious books and pamphlets, tending to the slander of the queen and government, contrary to the statute of 23 of Elizabeth."[16]

The jury quickly returned its verdict: guilty. The sentence: death.

According to custom, they would be executed the next day.

Barrow's attorney immediately wrote an appeal directly to Queen Elizabeth. She would know Barrow, if not from his recent fame, then she might recall that he served as an attorney in her court.

"[I]f her majesty's pleasure should be to have execution deferred," Barrow's attorney wrote, "it might be known this night, and order given accordingly, otherwise the direction given by the judges in open court will prevail."[17]

The men prayed for an answer.

Barrow and Greenwood had become well-known revolutionaries challenging English institutions. Thus, the government feared their execution might invite more than sympathy; it might make them martyrs. The English prosecution worked quickly to avoid a deferral or attract unnecessary attention. They would execute the men at an unusual hour. Darkness would provide cover and government officials would be in bed.

During the early hours of March 24, prison guards retrieved Barrow and Greenwood from their cells and took them to the condemned room. With the sun still far from rising, the tall arched windows let in only moonlight. The guards worked by candlelight, striking off their iron shackles and tying their hands with rope.

Barrow's and Greenwood's families had been summoned for customary good-byes and embraces. A hush fell over the somber room as the prison chaplain, the ordinary of Newgate, read the men their final rites with black coffins at their side. Traditionally the bells of St. Sepulchre Church would begin to toll, signifying an impending execution. But this execution was too early—and too clandestine.

With ropes tied and the ordinary's work complete, the guards backed a horse and cart up to the prison door. Barrow and Greenwood watched, knowing they had only a few precious hours remaining.

As the condemned men stepped on board the cart, a messenger arrived with an urgent letter. The courier handed the letter to the guards: official orders from Queen Elizabeth. She had granted Barrow and Greenwood reprieve, temporarily staying their execution. Obligated to follow the queen's orders, the guards ordered the men off the cart and replaced their iron shackles.

As the men waited at Newgate Prison under the fragile liberty of their temporary stay, clergy leaders from the Church of England began visiting them in their cells. The bishops had sent them. With Queen Elizabeth now personally involved in the matter, the church leaders felt a formal renunciation of Separatism from Barrow and Greenwood might protect their interests. The leaders directed Puritan-leaning clergy to assuage them. One by one, these clergy leaders met with Barrow and Greenwood, pleading for the men to recant. Even their lawyer joined, lobbying for a change of heart to save their lives.

Despite the efforts by many, the men would not be shaken.

"We had been well nigh six years in their prisons," Barrow wrote that night, "never refused, but always humbly desired of [the bishops a] Christian hearing . . . but could never obtain it at their hands. . . . That our time now was short in this world, neither were we to bestow it unto controversies, so much as unto more profitable and comfortable considerations."[18]

Once again, Barrow and Greenwood submitted a written petition to the queen and her council of lords.

"[I]n a land where no papist was touched for religion by

death," they wrote, "the blood of these protestants, who perfectly concurred in the faith professed by the realm, should be shed for ecclesiastical opinions merely."[19]

One week later, on March 31, Barrow and Greenwood were once again led out of their dungeon and into the condemned room for its ceremonial practices. As the men stepped onto the cart, they looked around for another messenger. None appeared.

With Barrow and Greenwood in the horse-drawn cart, the prison gates opened onto the dark, still streets of London. The three-mile journey from Newgate to the gallows of the Tyburn Tree could take as long as three hours. At this early hour, before the massive crowds of heckling spectators could assemble, the trip would go much faster.

Prominently placed in the intersection of two major roads, by design the Tyburn Tree could not be overlooked. The "tree"—erected wooden gallows—exemplified the rule of the Crown. To all who entered London, it symbolically bellowed that the law would prevail. For those who called London home, it loomed over them as a reminder of the firm, heavy hand of justice.

The gallows of the Tyburn Tree also employed novel engineering. Three tall legs supported a triangular crown of thick beams, appearing as a three-legged stool from a distance. It was designed to be sturdy, supporting the weight and force of mass executions. In one execution, as many as twenty-four prisoners could be simultaneously hung from its beams.

"The drop" had served as a reverent event, a hallowed symbol of justice. In recent years, however, it had become a circus-like attraction. Crowds would begin gathering in the afternoon, first near Newgate Prison, then along the entire route to the Tyburn Tree. For Londoners, watching an execution might be part of a holiday excursion. For peasants across England, witnessing one might be a once-in-a-lifetime experience.

By the thousands, spectators would line the streets, hang out of windows, and watch from crowded balconies. The people jeered and taunted the condemned as they rolled along the streets. Their jailers would adorn them with flamboyant costumes to further aggrandize the spectacle, and the crowd would respond raucously, hurling food and excrement.

To keep the masses at bay, the city marshal would escort the prison cart, flanked by a convoy of armed guards on horseback. They would not prevent the mockery, only keep the cart moving and thwart occasional vigilante rescue attempts.

If the condemned stood strong through the onslaught, they would receive cheers and applause from the crowd—a "good dying," as it was commonly known. For those who showed weakness, the mockery swelled.

At the Tyburn Tree, the execution event grew to an aggressive commercial venture. Competition for the best seats was so strong that the nearby village of Tyburn erected a grandstand and charged for access to the gallery. Even the executioner joined the spectacle, cutting the offending rope into small pieces to sell as souvenirs.

The most eager observers among the crowd were the anatomists. A past papal decree inherited by England prevented the dissection of the human body and convinced people that to be resurrected to life after death, the body must remain intact for burial. Despite a lifting of the formal ban in England, licenses and quotas still limited the profession, and families still decried its defilement. Professional and amateur scientists hoping to further their understanding of the human body turned to body snatching and grave robbing. Occasionally large fights would break out at the Tyburn Tree as families and anatomists fought for possession of the corpse.

Barrow's and Greenwood's predawn execution was intended to avoid the theatrics. Execution ceremonies customarily took place at four o'clock in the afternoon—this one might be finished by seven o'clock in the morning. Undoubtedly, crowds would gather, but not as large or as unruly.

When Barrow and Greenwood arrived at the Tyburn Tree, their horse-drawn cart came to a halt under the towering timbers of the gallows. The executioner placed ropes around their necks and prepared for an immediate event. A crowd, indeed, had assembled, and in the tradition of condemned men's final speeches, they were granted time to speak a few words.

Barrow and Greenwood expressed their loyalty to the queen and the state but protested their charge.

"[We] had no malicious or evil intent toward any of these; or towards any person in the world," they said. "Let fall any word or sentence that had caused offence, or had any appearance of irreverence . . . and humbly besought pardon of the same, of all thus offended."[20]

The apology proceeded into a sermon, as the men spoke in turns.

Have "obedience and hearty love of [your] prince and magistrates, and even to lay down [your] lives in their defense against all enemies; yea, at their hands to receive meekly and patiently death itself, or any punishment they should inflict, whether justly or unjustly."

"Walk orderly, quietly and peaceably in [your] respective callings, and in the holy fear and true worship of God."

"And, as to the books written by [us] . . . receive nothing contained in them except they should find sound proof of the same in the Holy Scriptures."[21]

Then Barrow and Greenwood began to pray.

A large crowd had gathered, and its mood grew somber as the people listened. Instead of the usual mockery, sobs could be heard emanating from the multitude.

Suddenly a messenger appeared. The crowd parted as he walked up to the base of the Tyburn Tree and handed a letter to the executioner. As they awaited the executioner's response, a hush fell over the people, leaving only the voices of the condemned men, who continued to pray aloud. The executioner examined the letter and then, turning to Barrow and Greenwood, immediately removed the nooses from their necks. They had received a second reprieve.

"Amen, and amen," Greenwood ended his prayer. "And now, O most gracious Father, King of kings, who holdest the hearts of princes in thine own hands, what shall we render unto thee for thy most signal mercy unto this realm, in bestowing upon us a queen, who doth plentifully, daily imitate thee in mercy!"[22]

The crowd burst forth in shouts of joy as the horse-drawn cart pulled away from the Tyburn Tree. All the way back to Newgate Prison, people gathered in the streets to witness the extraordinary turn of events and shower the men with applause.

This time the unexpected reprieve had not come from Queen Elizabeth. In fact, the queen had never received the men's petition. Much to the queen's dismay, Archbishop Whitgift had secretly intercepted her mail and destroyed their letter.

Lord Treasurer Burghley had intervened to secure Barrow's and Greenwood's second reprieve. Barrow's arguments at the hearing convinced him to grant the temporary stay of another week.

Lord Treasurer Burghley had not finished with a mere stay of the execution. He took a further step, seeking a permanent absolution of their conviction. He appealed to his colleagues on the council, but even after several rounds of arguments, he found no benevolence among the clergy. The lord treasurer could do nothing more to avert the "malice of the bishops."

Immediately upon the expiration of the lord treasurer's reprieve at Tyburn Tree, Archbishop Whitgift took personal oversight of the matter. With the queen traveling away from London, he carefully orchestrated the jailers at Newgate Prison. Early in the morning of April 6, 1593, guards pulled Barrow and Greenwood from their cells. They were led, yet again, to the condemned room, unshackled, and tied for execution. The jailers dressed them in costume and placed them in horse-drawn carts for the long ride to the Tyburn Tree.

At the tree, the cart was driven under the gallows and the nooses placed around their necks. Barrow and Greenwood once again addressed the growing crowd, prayed for the queen, and bid each other farewell.

Crack! At the executioner's command, the driver whipped the horses and the cart pulled away.

Barrow and Greenwood dropped onto their ropes.

Chapter Two

The Slave

APRIL 1603
NORTH AMERICA

We behold very good groves and woods replenished with tall oaks, beeches, pine trees, fir trees, hazels, witch hazels, and maples," wrote a European explorer as he sailed into Cape Cod. "We saw here all sundry sorts of beasts, as stag, deer, bear, wolves, foxes, lynx, and dogs with sharp noses."[1]

North America teemed with life, particularly along its coastline.

Not far from the ship's course, the Patuxet people lived near a sheltered harbor on the west side of Cape Cod. The bay provided sustenance, rather than trade, for the tribe of only a few hundred. What they could not make or grow, they acquired through trade with neighboring tribes. They fished the bay and hunted in the woods. In the clearings, they planted maize, tobacco, pumpkins, and cucumbers. In the fields, they foraged for wild peas, strawberries, gooseberries, and huckleberries.

As the warm spring breezes drifted ashore from the Atlantic Ocean, two large objects gracefully rose on the watery horizon. Slowly they floated into the bay at Patuxet, which had a natural breakwater, a deep channel entrance, and surrounding hills for visual advantage.

The Patuxet men retrieved their bows and gathered on the bay's sandy shore to watch the incoming boats—not native canoes, but ships from another land. Although unusual and mysterious, the sight was not remarkable. For nearly a century, Spanish, Portuguese, French, and English boats had explored the Atlantic Coast of North America, sometimes for map-making and other times for fishing. Occasionally the sailors traded with the tribes along the coast, and other times they shipwrecked, giving the people along the coast a glimpse of the "palefaces."

The boats had names inscribed on their hulls: *Speedwell* and *Discoverer*. As the vessels approached shore, they dwarfed the Patuxets' tiny canoes. The flagship *Speedwell* measured in at fifty tons and carried thirty men. At half its size, twenty-six tons and thirteen men, the bark *Discoverer* still loomed as a behemoth. The canoes off Patuxet, a mere seventeen feet long and four wide, paled in comparison. Their vessels, shaped from large tree trunks patiently hollowed out with fire and hand tools, bobbed on the water like small specks at the foot of a giant.

Among the men, witnessing the spectacle stood a teenage Patuxet boy.[2] At fourteen years old, Squanto was thin and quiet.[3] Born at Patuxet, he was left an orphan at the untimely death of his low-caste parents. The tribe cared for him, but he inherited his parents' class. He would be bound to his place, mostly in service to the elite.

The sight of the *Speedwell* and the *Discoverer* was remarkable. Squanto had only heard stories of these seemingly once-in-a-lifetime encounters with palefaces.

The previous spring, Squanto had nearly witnessed another arrival—a European expedition anchored on the east side of

Cape Cod, landing on its shore. One young Indian boy had made contact with the men: Europeans. The men were searching for something peculiar—a plant. When they failed to find it on the Cape, they promptly departed. Squanto had heard the stories of this extraordinary meeting, and they piqued his curiosity, both about the visitors and the world beyond Patuxet.

The foreign boats floating in the bay off Patuxet dropped their anchors, and the smaller of the two ships, the *Discoverer*, launched a shallop, a small vessel for a shore landing. Six men rowed the shallop toward shore while many more palefaces watched from the decks of the boats. The men in the small boat carried muskets but kept them low. They moved slowly and inconspicuously. As they stepped on shore, the men began to hand out gifts: hats, beads, and apparel. They were Englishmen.

The Englishmen waded onto the beach and into the company of the Patuxet people. The Patuxet men appeared intimidating, built tall and strong. They wore next to nothing except a waist covering and the occasional breastplate of brass. They held black and yellow painted bows, nearly six feet long, each with a quiver of finely crafted arrows.

Four of the Englishmen began walking toward the woods, leaving two to guard the shallop. They searched intently for something among the shrubbery, closely examining the ground and combing the edge of the forest. Their quest puzzled the Patuxet people. Finally one of the Englishmen raised a bush to show the others: sassafras.

Sassafras had become a wonder drug in Europe. In the mid-1500s, Spanish explorers had observed Native Americans using it medicinally and had experimented themselves. When the Spanish explorers brought it back across the Atlantic, apothecaries hailed it as a cure-all. Europeans consumed it voraciously and merchants spied a fortune. Demand in England alone encouraged colonizing expeditions to North America to abandon their plans. Instead, they filled their ships with sassafras and returned to England.

By 1603, a band of merchants had planned a transatlantic voyage solely to harvest sassafras. Under the command of twenty-three-year-old Martin Pring, the *Speedwell* and *Discoverer* had set sail from Milford Haven, England, in April. The expedition had arrived at Maine in early June and made its way down the coast to Patuxet, naming it "Whitson Bay" in honor of John Whitson, the mayor of Bristol.

At Patuxet, the explorers indeed found sassafras—and significant amounts of it. Once word of the discovery reached their ships at anchor, Pring began preparing to move men ashore. He beached the *Discoverer* to rapidly deploy his men and quickly fortify themselves.

Within a few days the Englishmen had erected a fifteen-foot-square stockade close to the woods and above the high tide line. The stockade door opened to the beach, and in its corners they built platforms, seven feet off the ground, to aim down on an attacker.

Four men remained on constant guard at the stockade with another four constantly securing the anchored *Speedwell*. The remaining nearly forty men worked tirelessly in the woods cutting and uprooting sassafras.

Like the residents of Patuxet, Indians from nearby villages took an intense interest in the Englishmen. People would approach the English by the dozens—once even in a group as large as 120. Most simply wanted to catch a glimpse of the unusual sight, but many also had trade in mind.

For Pring and his men, this was their first encounter with the inhabitants of North America. They had seen the remnants of fires and human activity along the coast but had witnessed no life until Patuxet. They found the interaction equally spectacular and curious. Pring wrote of the Patuxet:

> They wear their hair braided in four parts, trussed up about their heads with a small knot behind. They stick many feathers and toys in their hair for bravery and pleasure. They cover their privates only with a piece of leather drawn between their legs and fastened to their girdles behind and before, from which they hang their bags of tobacco.
>
> They seem to be somewhat jealous of their women. We saw very few of them. The women wear leather aprons down to their knees in front and a bear skin like an Irish mantle over one shoulder.[4]

In the evenings, the English and the Patuxet mingled. They dined together on the beach—the English ate peas while the Patuxet preferred fish. After dinner, one of the Englishmen would break out his gittern, an old-fashioned guitar, and delight the Patuxet with his music. The Patuxet would form a ring of twenty to dance and chant, "Lo, la, lo, la, la, lo," with big, theatric gestures.[5] The dancing and singing would continue until one of them broke the ring—he would then receive the group's ridicule, and the dance would begin all over again.

By the end of July, the English had filled the *Discoverer* with sassafras and sent her back to England. The English then turned their attention toward loading the *Speedwell*.

The summer had proceeded peacefully until one afternoon when seven Patuxet men surrounded the small stockade. They gave no indication of an intent to trade but repeatedly asked the Englishmen to come outside. The Englishmen did not know how to interpret the request and treated it with suspicion. They refused, standing their guard on the high pedestals of the stockade.

Watching from the *Speedwell*, the master of the ship feared the Patuxet might attack not only the stockade, but his nearly unaccompanied vessel. He prepared the *Speedwell* for defense and fired a large cannon, intending to scare the Patuxet and rally his sailors who were harvesting sassafras in the woods. At the sound of the cannon, the men in the woods dropped their work and ran down to the ship.

The English sailors had brought two large mastiffs for protection and found that the Patuxet people trembled at the sight of them. When the men and dogs reached the beach, the seven Patuxet men surrounding the stockade immediately fled.

Pring took the confrontation at the stockade as a warning. He decided it would be wise to sail for England, rather than wait and see if the situation escalated. As the expedition prepared the sails, a wisp of smoke began to rise from the woods adjacent to the beach. Within minutes, a white plume gathered and grew to a raging forest fire. The blaze, nearly a mile wide, stormed toward the English sailors' landing site.

When the Patuxet people saw the ship preparing to leave, the Patuxet began to gather in great numbers along the shore. Many of the men rowed out in their canoes, bidding the English to come back. The sailors refused and pulled anchor.[6]

Squanto had seen the English sailors work in the woods near Patuxet, he mingled with them on the beach, and he now watched as their boat sailed off into the horizon. For him, the departure was, perhaps, bittersweet. These Englishmen had come from somewhere unknown to him or his people, from a place far, far beyond Patuxet. The men looked different, dressed differently, and sailed in on ships scarcely imaginable to him. The visit had reframed his world and proved how little of it he truly knew, confirming that much more existed beyond Patuxet and beyond the few tribes with whom Squanto interacted.

He was an orphan—and an orphan at the bottom of Patuxet's hierarchy. The village and its people offered him little future. His birthright had allotted him few friends, and his masters were a poor substitute for family. He could spend his life in Patuxet, continuously serving his superiors, or he could discover what lay beyond Patuxet's borders, perhaps, even the land from where the Englishmen had come.

In the spring of 1604, Squanto walked out of Patuxet.[7] He turned north, following the coast and in the direction the Englishmen had sailed out of their harbor. Like most young Patuxet men, he could survive on his own by hunting, fishing, and gathering in the forest. And as he wandered north, he regularly came upon Indian villages, which would typically share shelter and food.

By midsummer, Squanto arrived at the Kennebec River in modern-day Maine. The Kennebec people welcomed him but sternly cautioned him: proceed no farther. A few days' travel up the coast, he reached the Tarrantines, bitter enemies of the Kennebecs and hostile toward tribes from the west or south. They were suspicious of him, and he risked his life if he ventured any farther.

With fall arriving soon, Squanto asked if he could stay with the Kennebecs. Maneddo, a Kennebec leader, agreed that Squanto could stay if Squanto would work as his servant. Squanto would be treated well and receive the protection of the Kennebec tribe. For Squanto, the offer afforded him an opportunity to experience life outside Patuxet with a different leadership.

Much like the social hierarchy of England, the native tribes of North America had a social structure. Royal lineages held top honors, followed by nobility. The commoners, or braves, made up most of the tribe, followed lastly by a class of servants. With the Patuxet, Squanto would remain at the bottom. With the

Kennebec, he remained at the bottom but in close association with one of its leaders.

⁓

On March 5, 1605, Captain George Weymouth's *Archangel* sailed out of the Thames River and turned west for the open ocean. Weymouth (sometimes spelled *Waymouth*), only twenty years of age, had already lived a life intertwined with the sea.

Described as a man who knew "most of the Coast of England and most of other Countries (having been experienced by implements in discoveries and travails from his childhood)," Weymouth focused on the ocean from an early age.[8]

Studied in shipbuilding and mathematics, he secured his first major nautical expedition at age sixteen. The newly formed East India Company sought to find the elusive Northwest Passage across North America. This theorized trade route would significantly expand shipping to Asia and provide an alternative for European sailors to the arduous trip around the tip of Africa. Weymouth accepted the challenge and set sail in 1601.

Weymouth's expedition did not have much success. His ships suffered close encounters with icebergs, his men fell ill, and he failed to find a navigable route. Off the coast of Greenland, his men staged a mutiny, forcing their eventual return to England. The East India Company organized a follow-up expedition for Weymouth, but it never materialized.[9]

With no immediate opportunity for a new Northwest Passage expedition, Weymouth found himself positioned for an expedition to the "northern coast of Virginia" (modernly New England). The already financed voyage would survey "the commodities and profits of the countrey, together with the fitnesse of plantation."[10]

On May 6, 1605, only three months and one day after leaving England, the expedition crew spotted the forested coast of North America.

⁂

With strong, fast strokes, Squanto and Maneddo rowed their canoe toward a ship that had anchored in the waters near the mouth of the Kennebec River. The large, foreboding vessel bobbed slowly before them.[11] Flanked by two more canoes, the small Kennebec fleet stopped short of the large vessel, landing instead at a small island from where they could observe the unfamiliar visitors. With several hours of daylight remaining, the men built a fire and positioned themselves at a place on the island where they could assess the situation.

On board the ship, men milled about on its deck. Once they spotted the Kennebec men on the island, they began waving and shouting—beckoning them to the boat.

Maneddo sent over one canoe paddled by three braves. When they neared the foreign vessel, one of the Kennebec braves stood, boldly asking in his native tongue from where the visitors came. With his paddle he motioned about the bay, as if to convey that these waters belonged to Kennebec people, then pointed it toward the sea, indicating that this vessel should leave.

The men in the ship brandished knives, not to threaten the Kennebecs, but as if to offer them as a gift. One of the sailors retrieved a long piece of wood from the deck and brought it to the rail. He began to shave a knife along the wood, back and forth, until he had whittled the end down into a point. Then he began thrusting the sharp pole forward in the motion of a spear.

With this display of generosity, the Kennebec trio paddled forward, approaching the boat. They agreed to come on board.

Draped in their deer and beaver skins, which hung down to their knees, with their long black hair pulled back into braids, the Kennebec men stood before the sailors. They were a curious sight for the sailors, whom the Kennebec men found equally strange with their extensive layers of clothing, hats, and beards.

One of the men on the ship presented them with the knife. Other sailors brought out bracelets, rings, peacock feathers, and tobacco pipes. Their Kennebec counterparts watched intently from the island. As the gifts began to flow, four Kennebec braves paddled over from the island to join the ceremony.

After the sailors distributed all their gifts, they motioned for the Kennebec braves to return to the island for the night. They could resume trading in the morning.

Early the next morning, the Kennebec braves eagerly returned to the boat. One canoe paddled over, and the sailors invited the braves onto the ship. They fed the Kennebecs pork, fish, bread, and peas and showed them around the *Archangel*. The Kennebec men marveled at the metal pots and coveted their helmets. The guns, however, filled them with fear, and when one sailor fired a demonstration round, the Kennebec all dropped flat to floor.

In lieu of a common language, they resorted to gestures. The sailors signed for the Kennebec braves to bring skins and furs to trade for knives and other trinkets. The Kennebec group had come to investigate, not to trade, so they had nothing at hand to offer. Promising to return, the Kennebec party paddled back to their village.

Two days later, the Kennebec braves returned to the *Archangel* with forty of their best otter and beaver skins. Eager to trade for these, the sailors invited them back on board the ship. Once on deck, they met Captain Weymouth.

Weymouth gathered the Kennebec trading party around

him and then gently drew his sword. He reached calmly for his knife and carefully placed it upon a block of wood. He slowly raised his sword and hovered it over the knife. *Woosh*—the sword plucked the knife up against it with sudden force, surprising his Kennebec audience. Then he separated the knife from the sword and placed it back on a block. Waving his sword over the knife, it began to rotate. Finally, he performed the same trick with a needle. His magic astounded them.

"This we did to cause them to imagine some great power in us," admitted James Rosier, chronicler of Weymouth's voyage,[12] "and for that to love and fear us."[13]

Weymouth had magnetized the sword, a trick to instill both admiration and terror in the Kennebecs, as if he possessed force beyond their control. After the charade, he dismissed his Kennebec visitors, telling them to go back to the mainland. They could trade again, but Weymouth and his men would come to them.

The *Archangel* launched a rowboat with a shore party fifteen men strong. They rowed toward land alongside the Kennebec canoes. When they could clearly see the flames of the Kennebec fires on shore, Weymouth stopped their progress, including the canoes. Before his men would take a step on land, he required a scout from their party to visit and assure their safety. Not wanting to risk a hostage situation, Weymouth requested that Maneddo remain in the rowboat. Maneddo refused, but offered a young man in his place—Squanto.

When the English scout returned, he shared troubling news. He claimed that the Kennebec tribe had gathered 283 men armed with bows and arrows, as well as domesticated dogs and wolves. Fearing that the Kennebecs intended to draw the rowboat into the river, then attack, Weymouth immediately turned his men back to the ship.

"These things considered," Rosier wrote, "we began to join

them in the rank of other savages, who have been by travellers in most discoveries found very treacherous; never attempting mischief, until by some remissness, fit opportunity afforded them certain ability to execute the same. Wherefore after good advice taken, we determined so soon as we could to take some of them, least (being suspicious we had discovered their plots) they should absent themselves from us."[14]

The next day, six Kennebec men, including Squanto and Maneddo, paddled canoes back to the *Archangel*. When they offered to trade, the sailors invited them back onto the ship. Maneddo acquiesced, taking one of his men along, while Squanto and his companions waited in the canoes.

The sailors worked to entice Squanto and the three Kennebec men on board. They refused. When words failed, they resorted to gifts: first bread, then a can of peas. When the Kennebec men finished eating, Squanto climbed on board the *Archangel* with the empty can to return it.

Squanto soon realized the English sailors did not intend to trade for furs. They wanted him.

Rosier wrote of the conspiracy to capture the Kennebec men and their particular interest in Squanto: "[H]e being young of a ready capacity, and one we most desired to bring with us into England, had received exceeding kind usage at our hands, and was therefore much delighted in our company."[15]

Unaware of what had taken place on board the *Archangel*, three Kennebec men still waited in the canoe below. The sailors wanted to capture them all and sought Weymouth's advice in the matter.

"When our captain was come," Rosier recounted, "we consulted how to catch the other three."

The sailors conceived of a distraction to get the Kennebec men out of their canoes. Eight sailors launched a rowboat with one presenting a box of trinkets and another holding a platter of peas. They began to row toward shore, and the three Kennebec men followed in their canoes. They rowed toward the place where the Kennebec braves had earlier started a fire, and its embers still glowed.

When they reached shore, the sailors presented the men with the plate of peas. One of the Kennebec braves immediately fled into the woods, but the remaining two began to eat.

"[W]hile we were discussing how to catch the third man who was gone," Rosier wrote, "I opened the box and showed them trifles to exchange, thinking thereby to banish fear from the other, and draw him to return. But when we could not, we used little delay."

In unison, six of the sailors lunged for the two unsuspecting Kennebec braves, wrestling them to ground.

"It was as much as five or six of us could do to get them into the light horseman," Rosier wrote. "For they were strong and so naked as our best hold was by their long hair on their heads."

Rosier described the abduction as "a matter of great importance for the full accomplishment of our voyage."

With their captives in hand, the *Archangel* pulled anchor and sailed away from the Kennebec River. For the next twelve days, Weymouth's expedition explored the coast, mapping its inlets and islands. Squanto, Maneddo, and the two other Kennebec men remained on the ship under guard.[16]

Rosier wrote about the captives:

I have thought fit here to add some things worthy to be regarded, which we observed from the Savages since we took them.

First, although at the time when we surprised them, they made their best resistance, not knowing our purpose, nor what we were, nor how we meant to use them; yet after perceiving by their kind usage we intended them no harm they have never since seemed discontented with us, but very tractable, loving and willing by their best means to satisfy us in anything we demand of them, by words or signs for their understanding; neither have they at any time been at the least discord among themselves; insomuch as we have not seen them angry but merry; and so kind, as if you give to one of them, he will distribute part to every one of the rest.[17]

The sailors mingled with their Kennebec captives, learning from them and beginning to teach them the basics of English language and customs.

"We have brought them to understand some English, and we understand much of their language; so as we are able to ask them many things," Rosier wrote.[18]

By late July 1605, they had crossed the Atlantic Ocean. Weymouth piloted the *Archangel* into England's Plymouth Sound on the southwest coast of the island.

Plymouth Sound had a history of notable mariners and naval events. Sir Frances Drake began his around-the-world journey from the Sound in 1577. During the Anglo-Spanish War (1585–1604), it played a strategic role in the Royal Navy's defense of England against a Spanish invasion. By the time of Weymouth's transatlantic voyage, Plymouth Sound's chief administrator was an iconic leader: Sir Ferdinando Gorges.

As a younger man, Gorges had fought the Spanish in Holland and served King Henry IV during the French Wars of Religion. His service in France earned him knighthood from the Earl of Essex in 1591, with many commendations to follow. In 1596, Queen Elizabeth named him commander of England's Plymouth Fort, perched on a high bluff overlooking the sound.

Gorges and the fort had a singular purpose: to protect England from a naval invasion.

Upon Weymouth's return to Plymouth Sound, he turned Squanto and the Kennebec men over to Gorges, who took an immediate and intense interest in the men. He gave them room and board in the captain's house at the fort and began meeting with them regularly.[19]

Neither Weymouth nor Gorges viewed the capture of the Kennebec men as kidnapping, much less slavery. The men made for an acquisition of intelligence. With increasing multinational prospecting in the New World, Gorges predicted a forthcoming free-for-all power struggle among European nations. Kings could make constructive claims to portions of North America, but these amounted to mere pomp and rhetoric. Nation-states needed actual corporal possession of the land. And for such states to be truly recognized as titleholders, their claims would need military backing to defend it.

Spanish, Dutch, and French proprietors all had eyes on North American real estate, yet establishing military occupation on the continent presented immense challenges. Mariners could sail there, survey the coast, and perhaps establish a seasonal outpost, but operating a more permanent establishment was difficult. European explorers did not know anything about North America beyond what they could observe from their boats or the trivial beach landing. They did not know its geography or climate. They did not know where to find freshwater or what could grow in its soils. And perhaps most importantly, they did not know if native tribes would welcome their presence.

If Gorges were to establish a permanent presence in North America, he needed boots-on-the-ground intelligence. It would take years and dozens of costly expeditions to gather the kind of details he needed—unless he gained unprecedented access to local expertise. With Squanto and his compatriots at Plymouth Fort, Gorges intended to draw extensively on his captives' knowledge of the rivers, lands, and tribes of North America.

"I made them able to set me down what great rivers ran up into the land," Gorges wrote of their regular meetings, "what men of note were seated on them; what power they were of; how allied; what enemies they had and the like."[20]

The meetings boosted what would become Gorges's lifelong interest: establishing English settlements in the New World. Gorges wrote:

> And so it pleased our great God that there happened to come into the harbor of Plymouth (where I commanded) one Captain Weymouth, that had been employed . . . for the discovery of the Northwest Passage.
>
> But falling short of his course, happened into a river on the coast of America, called Pemaquid from whence he brought five of the natives, three of whose names were Manida, Skettwarroes, and Tasquantum, whom I seized upon; they were all of one nation, but of several parts, and several families. This accident must be acknowledged the means under God of putting on foot and giving life to all our plantations [in the New World].[21]

Gorges took the Kennebec men under his wing, assigning David Thomson, a thirteen-year-old boy, to act as their guide. Gorges had employed Thomson's parents in London for many years. After Thomson's father died in the plague, Thomson and his mother came to Plymouth Sound to work as servants for Gorges. His new duty to the Kennebec men had the primary function of interpreter and the unusual demand of learning to bridge the language gap. His early service to Gorges as a linguist would act much like an apprenticeship, preparing him for future opportunities with Gorges's affairs in the New World.

About once a week, the Kennebec men would meet with Gorges in the captain's house at Plymouth Fort. With a scribe at the ready, Gorges would query them about geography—he first intended to map the area under control of the Kennebec tribe. In later meetings, he began inquiring about other tribes, their sizes, their leaders, and their customs. More broadly, Gorges wanted to create a crude dictionary of basic words in the Kennebec language, including animals, geographic terms, and food. Squanto, now about sixteen, and Thomson had the ambition and interest to lead the translation work.

The presence of the Kennebec men in England inspired Gorges. They opened his eyes to a world of untapped opportunity and resources, rousing him to advocate for the establishment of permanent English colonies there. Although he would never travel there himself, he saw colonization of the New World as an endeavor that England must pursue, but also as a personal investment.

Gorges became associated with a group of fellow organizers, calling themselves the Virginia Company. Like many "companies" of the day, the Virginia Company was comprised of aristocrats and wealthy merchants who spied great financial gain in the New World. These investors chose the company model because the cost of such expeditions rose beyond the means of what any one individual could fund. With men like Gorges among its fellowship, the Virginia Company wielded considerable influence. Indeed, on April 10, 1606, fewer than nine months after the arrival of the Kennebec captives on Plymouth Sound, King James granted the Virginia Company a charter that included the rights to settle at least two colonies in the New World.

The 1606 charter formally founded the Virginia Company as a joint-stock company organized to plan and outfit expeditions. The sale of stock raised the expedition's capital and promised its investors profit from the New World's exploited resources. In the meantime, the investors would appoint a council to manage the activities of the company.

The Virginia Company had two branches, one at London and the other at Plymouth Sound. Gorges associated himself with the latter, given his proximity. Each branch had a distinct geographical area of the New World to fall under its purview: northern and southern seaboards. The Plymouth Company received authorization to settle in the northern region, between 38 to 45 degrees latitude (modern-day Maryland and Massachusetts, or what is generally known today as New England). Farther south, the charter authorized the London Company to settle between 34 to 41 degrees latitude (between modern-day Virginia and South Carolina). The plan allotted for a three-degree overlap where either company could settle, but restricted them from settling within one hundred miles of each other.

Gorges had learned enough from the Kennebec men about their region of North America to offer a suggestion: settle near the Kennebec River. He further recommended establishing a colony on the "maine" land, as they spelled it in Old English, distinguishing it from an island or geographically disconnected piece of land. The name would stick, eventually and formally becoming an area known as Maine. Gorges prepared to dispatch a ship in August to survey the coast in preparation for establishing the colony. Maneddo and Squanto would join the voyage as guides and interpreters.

The *Richard of Plymouth* set sail on August 12, 1606, from Plymouth Sound. The small, fifty-ton vessel carried twenty-nine Englishmen along with Maneddo and Squanto. Although their formal orders called for a simple survey of the coast, if they found conditions suitable for a settlement, they had instructions to leave as many men in the New World as they could spare.

By the end of August, the *Richard of Plymouth* passed through the Canary Islands off the coast of West Africa, then turned west. A strong southerly wind blew the ship far off course with a loss of six weeks of sailing before they reached the Antilles Islands.[22] After sixty-eight days at sea and more than forty-five hundred nautical miles, they docked at that island of Saint Lucia on October 19 to replenish their food and water.

The Caribbean port left the *Richard of Plymouth* crew on edge. As canoes filled with native residents lined up along its hull, the sailors looked on with increasing trepidation. The sailors shared rumors of murder, deceit, and treachery among the tribes of the Caribbean. The pilot of the ship, for instance, claimed that only one year earlier a Caribbean tribe had massacred more than forty Englishmen. The crew grew more and more anxious to pull anchor, and after three days the *Richard of Plymouth* set a course northward.

Passing the island of Dominica, the sailors spotted a white flag on shore. Reckoning that it might be a shipwrecked European sailor, they decided to make a closer inspection. As they turned the ship, a canoe launched from the beach, paddling toward them. They waited for the canoe to come close enough to clearly see its occupant: a Catholic friar.

"I beseech, as you are Christians," he shouted in Latin from the canoe, "for Christ his sake to shew some mercy and compassion on mee. I am a Preacher of the Word of God, a Friar of the order of Franiscus of Sivill, by name of Friar Blasias."[23]

The sailors lowered their ropes and pulled the friar on board the *Richard of Plymouth*. Naturally they wondered immediately about the friar's circumstances. He explained that a Caribbean tribe had enslaved him and two companions sixteen months before. They had murdered his companions, sparing the friar's life only because they had a task for him. This tribe had recovered sailcloth from the wreckage of three Spanish ships on the island of Guadeloupe. They coveted the European's ability to sail and had kept him alive solely because he promised to teach them how to rig their canoes with sails.

The friar had come to the New World at the order of the king of Spain, who annually sent "great monastery Friars, into the remote parts of the Indies, both to seeke to convert the Savages, as also to seeke out what benefits of commodities might be had in those parts."[24] With the friar on the ship, the *Richard of Plymouth* sailed for Puerto Rico. Arriving on October 29, they left the friar in the hands of two herdsmen willing to help him.

The *Richard of Plymouth* continued cruising north and, a few days into November, sailed into a severe storm. The storm tossed the boat for fifty-six hours until the tempest died and left them in a dense fog at night. As the sun began to rise and the fog lifted, they suddenly found themselves in the company of eight ships, all within cannon shot.[25]

The windward vessels bore down toward the *Richard of Plymouth*, one firing a cannon shot across the bow. As the boats closed in, the sailors could make out their flag: Spanish.

The Spanish ships surrounded them, and the *Richard of Plymouth* could not escape. Sailing to within earshot, the Spaniards demanded to know the ship's nationality and to conference with the captain—a surprising request, considering that since the signing of the Treaty of London in August 1604, Spain and England were no longer at war.

As a show of resistance, the English captain raised the flag and pointed the *Richard of Plymouth* toward the leading vessel of the Spanish squadron. Once the British flag rose, the Spanish ships began to fire their cannons at the British masts, dropping its sails to the deck.

With the *Richard of Plymouth* immobilized, the Spanish admiral docked and boarded. Following him came twenty-two Spanish sailors, who ambushed the English vessel with swords and spears.[26] The English put their hands in the air and surrendered peacefully.

The Spanish mariners exchanged no further words with the English. For no reason, they proceeded to beat them all, including the captain, and to stab two of the sailors in the head. Squanto received the worst of their punishment. They tortured him, mutilating his body and thrusting a sword through his arm.

"King James, King James, King James his ship, King James his ship," Squanto cried as they stabbed him.

Corralling all the English sailors below deck, the Spanish beat them again. Once the English had suffered to the point where they could not fight back, the Spanish sailors marched them up and onto the Spanish ship. The Spanish refused to speak a word to them, nor listen to their pleas for mercy. Despite their attempt to present the captain's written commission allowing passage in these waters, the Spanish paid them no attention.

With the English crew captured and subdued, the Spanish fleet dispersed. Three of the Spanish ships sailed away, while those remaining looted the *Richard of Plymouth* of her supplies and items of value. Among the remaining ships, the Spanish divvied up twenty-eight English sailors, as well as Squanto and Maneddo.

The squadron set sail for Spain.

❧

For the Spanish fleet, the voyage back across the Atlantic proved long and arduous. Although the ships started together on the same heading and bound for the same destination, they slowly drifted apart. Once separated, they struggled chiefly with navigation. One ship arrived in Spain, but another missed the Iberian Peninsula altogether, accidentally landing on the French coast. On board yet another ship, the captured English navigator had to intervene to assist the Spanish in setting the course. Squanto's ship, on the other hand, remained at sea, and on course.

The first ship in the Spanish fleet docked at Sanlucar, Spain, a month before the boat carrying Squanto and Maneddo arrived. The English captives on the first ship received a hearing before the duke of Medina, a man who oversaw southwest Spain and served as Admiral of the Oceans. At the hearing, the duke declared the capture of the *Richard of Plymouth* illegal and ordered the release of the English sailors, much to the dismay of Spanish sailors.

Under the duke of Medina, Spain had suffered two decades of grim naval losses, including the humiliating defeat of the Spanish Armada. This track record left the duke vulnerable to a growing undercurrent of distrust. Discontent with the decision to free the English captives, the Spanish sailors defied him and moved their prisoners fifty miles upriver to Seville.

Seville functioned as the maritime hub of Spain and a gateway to the Mediterranean. Seville's Casa de Contratacion (or "House of Trade") controlled the empire's exploration, colonization, and commerce. All Spanish maritime efforts, private or official, required the authorization of the Casa de Contratacion. The agency also carefully accounted for the flow of goods into Spain, levying taxes where possible. Because of the Casa de Contratacion, Seville had become one of the greatest ports of the world, with all trade between Spain and America flowing through it. The Casa de Contratacion locked horns with Britain militarily and philosophically over which nation would control trade with the New World.

In addition to its regulatory functions, the Casa de Contratacion provided an important service to the world: map-making. Over the years, it amassed teams of the world's greatest cartographers, aggregating information brought back by Spanish sailors the world over. Among the more prominent figures to take office there was Amerigo Vespucci (1454–1512), the famed Spanish explorer credited with revealing to Europe that America formed a separate, unknown landmass from Asia.

The Spanish sailors brought their captives before the president of Seville at the Casa de Contratacion. Under the president's authority, the English captives received a far different treatment. He declared that the English had invaded Spanish waters, then ordered them to jail.

By the time Squanto's ship arrived in Sanlucar, a month behind schedule, the first set of English captives had already transferred to Seville. He and his colleagues faced a similar scenario: exoneration in Medina followed by a separate judgment in Seville. Squanto and Maneddo soon joined the other English prisoners.

England knew nothing of the fate of the men of *The Richard of Plymouth*, nor did the nation have a reason to suspect anything sinister. And, perhaps, they would never have known anything, presuming *The Richard of Plymouth* lost at sea when it did not return. But when the Spanish ship that had sailed off course arrived on French shores, French officials approached the vessel and questioned its purpose. They learned of the circumstances, set the English captives free, and brought the matter immediately to the attention of Ferdinando Gorges.

Gorges responded immediately. He believed the *Richard of Plymouth* had been captured unlawfully, and he suspected the other Englishmen to be held in Spain. He made a diplomatic attempt to secure their release but made little headway.

The unfolding circumstances boiled to a crisis when two of the English sailors escaped from their Seville prison in February 1607. They covertly made their way to England, arriving in March and carrying letters to Gorges from the captain of *The Richard of Plymouth.*

Gorges wrote back to the captain, telling him to demand a "court of admiralty" and mandate the immediate release of his sailors and the Kennebec Indians. Gorges added that the captain should leave Spain with compensation from the Spanish government for the injustice and expect no less than five thousand pounds.

For the English sailors in Seville's prison, life was hard. One of the English sailors fell ill and suffered for three months before his illness finally claimed his life. Upon his passing, the Spanish jailors paraded the man's naked body through the halls of the jail, dragging him on his heels, and crying "Behold the Lutheran," echoing tension between Catholic Spain and Protestant England. They finished the procession with a public dismemberment. Despite their pleas, the Englishmen could not persuade the Spanish jailers to provide a proper burial.

Spain's animosity toward England became ever more apparent upon the murder of one of the English sailors. After an imprisoned Spanish slave stabbed him to death, the other prisoners petitioned the president of Seville for justice.

"He demanded what we would have of the slave," one of the English sailors explained. "And we requested, that as he had slaine an honest an worthy man of ours causelesse, that he might die for it according to the law."

"No," the president replied. "But if [you] would have him condemned for two or three yeares more to the Gallies, [I] would. The King of Spaine will not gave the life of the worst slave that he hath, for the best Subject that the King of England hath."[27]

The Spanish had ulterior motives for their English captives beyond simply harboring prisoners of war. The Spanish aspired to control all of North America, but they had explored very little of it. They could spend the next decade launching transatlantic expeditions to chart it, or they could seize years of maritime experience by absorbing the English captain and crew. The English sailors had already demonstrated their nautical superiority, as they proved by out-navigating their Spanish counterparts on the disorienting Atlantic crossing. The Spanish coveted their ability and sought to employ it.

Perhaps recognizing the risk of giving a prisoner the responsibility to direct their fleet, they made the pilot of *The Richard of Plymouth* an offer: pledge his service to Spain in exchange for freedom. To sweeten the deal, they included a significant salary. The captain refused, preferring prison to the service of an enemy. Instead, the Spanish tried persuading him to make maps of the ports and coasts of Virginia. Again, he declined.

As refusals persisted, the Spanish grew increasingly suspicious of the English prisoners. Perhaps, their Spanish captors concluded, they had seized not simply mariners, but English strategists for the New World. The company of Squanto and Maneddo added fuel to the theory: it smacked of a New World alliance to the exclusion of Spain.

Eventually, the Spanish captors gave up on cooperation and turned to torture. When the pilot of *The Richard of Plymouth* received a tip about the plan to torture him, he bribed the prison guards to grant him leave for the afternoon. Along with two of his companions, they fled Seville, leaving behind the captain and sixteen others in prison. By November, the men had arrived in England and reported directly to Gorges.

Squanto, Maneddo, and the other Englishmen remained in prison for the better part of two years. After their sentence expired, the officials in Seville remanded them to slavery in galleys—the lower level of oar-powered tugboats. Every day, they rowed massive, multi-oared boats up and down the Guadalquivir River, supplying the manpower to transport government officials or bring arriving ships to port.

It seemed as though Spain may be their final destination.

Chapter Three

Dissenters

1606

SCROOBY VILLAGE, NOTTINGHAMSHIRE, ENGLAND

A cool breeze blew through Scrooby village, sweeping across its vast green fields and gently rolling hills. Few people had reason to visit Scrooby. Occasionally, travelers journeying along the Great North Road, linking London to Scotland, would stop for a rest.[1] Most simply passed by Scrooby, saving their breaks for larger towns.

The sleepy rural hamlet was little more than a collection of half-timber houses. Their characteristic architecture of brown beams and white clay stood in sharp contrast to the stone Gothic cathedral in the center of town. The tall, medieval spire of St. Wilfrid's Church rose prominently above the village. It was the town's beacon and constant reminder of the residents' civic duty to attend.

Scrooby looked like any other agrarian village dotting the English countryside. But the village was different. Despite its unassuming nature, Scrooby hid an illicit secret.

Not far from St. Wilfrid's stood an old stone manor house. Sprawling across six acres, it boasted thirty-nine rooms and a history of prominent tenants. Its owner, the archbishop of York, regularly turned down offers from royalty to buy it. The archbishop had appointed William Brewster Sr. as an administrator, which included the title of postmaster. The appointment came with room at the manor house for Brewster and his family. When Brewster passed away, his son, William, succeeded to his post.

Every Sunday night, William Brewster, Jr., concealed in the manor house a clandestine worship gathering for Separatists. The group bonded not only over the shared belief that the Church of England was not a true church of Christ, but also over the forbidden nature of their meeting. Their need for secrecy had only increased in recent years.

Three years earlier, in 1603, Queen Elizabeth had passed away, and a change in leadership renewed hope for freedom of religion. As King James ascended to the throne, he immediately faced tremendous pressure to maintain the integrity of the Church of England. His religious advisers identified the unvanquished legacy of Barrow and Greenwood as one of their greatest threats. James quickly placed the Separatists in his crosshairs.

Speaking to a gathering of religious leaders at his palace, the king declared his intention to rid England of Separatism: "I shall make them conform themselves or I shall harry them out of the land!"[2]

Despite the voices lobbying James for leniency, the king began his reign by enacting stricter religious requirements. No longer could religious meetings be held privately, and the use of prayer books was mandatory in every service. He took aim at the Puritans, clashing frequently with their leaders, and within a year, removed three hundred Puritan ministers from the pulpit.

One Sunday evening in Scrooby, sixteen-year-old William Bradford attended his regular meeting of the Separatist congregation at Brewster's house. He had attended for four years, regaling weekly in the sermons of Pastors John Robinson and Richard Clyfton.

The pastors often railed against the theatrics of the Church of England. They denounced the austere architecture, exquisite paintings, and even its organ music. They called kneeling "popish" and hated the hierarchical church structure and tradition. Robinson and Clyfton, instead, encouraged private prayer and personal faith. The simplicity of Separatism resonated with young Bradford, as did its quest to model the early church. He became a member.

Bradford had grown up in Austerfield, a small farming town in northern England only slightly larger than Scrooby. In a day when peasant farmers eked out a meager, subsistence living, his family had prospered in agriculture, buoyed by a lineage allegedly traceable to English nobility.

Bradford held incredible promise for a boy in his day but suffered continuous loss and family disarray. His father had died when Bradford was only one year old. His mother remarried shortly after but then sent him away to live with his grandfather. Two years later, tragedy struck again when his grandfather died. This loss forced young Bradford's return to his mother. Almost four years later, his mother died, too, followed soon thereafter by his sister. At age seven, he could call himself an orphan. Bradford and his older sister went to live with their next of kin, two uncles.

Bradford, too, endured his own physical trials. An unidentified "long sickness" prevented him from joining the ranks of farmers and laborers[3] but also sheltered him from many temptations in youth.

Since Bradford could not work in the fields, he read voraciously. With a childhood confined largely to the mind, he quickly developed an intellectual curiosity about the world that many of his peers could not themselves appreciate. He dove into the classics of philosophy and religious writings. The Geneva Bible became a constant companion.[4] He devoured church history, including Eusebius's *Ecclesiastical History* and John Foxe's *Book of Martyrs*.

Bradford had worshipped with his relatives at St. Helena's, a small, stone church in Austerfield, but even at a young age, he did not feel comfortable there. He found his reading of the Bible did not reflect the teachings of the Church of England. He struggled to understand the divergence.

A friend invited Bradford, age twelve, to listen to a preacher in the nearby village of Babworth: the Reverend Richard Clyfton. Clyfton served as rector at the Church of All Saints but had gained notoriety for preaching a religiously divergent theology from the Church of England. He conducted services using material not contained in the *Book of Common Prayer*, refused to wear vestments, and did not use the sign of the cross at baptisms. His unorthodox teaching struck a chord in the region, drawing an audience from surrounding towns and villages.

Bradford lived ten miles from Babworth—a significant walk—and his uncle objected to his going to hear Clyfton, perhaps because of distance more than content. Despite the opposition, Bradford went. He found Clyfton's sermon moving—the reverend's indifference to the Church of England gripped young Bradford.

He was "a grave and reverend Preacher," according to Bradford, "who, by his pains and diligence had done much good; and, under GOD, had been the means of the conversion of many."[5]

Bradford began attending Clyfton's services regularly. Three miles into his journey, he passed through the village of Scrooby, walking by the home of William Brewster. Brewster, too, made the journey to listen to Clyfton's sermons, and so the pair began walking together. Brewster became a mentor to the adolescent Bradford on their Sunday strolls and further encouraged him to explore Separatist ideas.

Clyfton's unorthodox methods eventually stoked the ire of England's religious authorities. The Chancery Court summoned him and accused him of being a "nonconformist and nonsubscriber."[6] The inquiry led to his removal from his church at Babworth in 1605.

This brought a short end to "his faithful and painful Ministry," as Bradford described it.[7]

Removing Clyfton did little to halt his flock or his theological ideas. William Brewster offered his home, and the congregation followed Clyfton to their new secret location in Scrooby. The manor house served the growing assembly well, and the following year, they decided to officially call themselves a Separatist congregation. Like similar Separatist congregations, they nominated leaders. Clyfton would serve as pastor, and Brewster as elder. John Robinson would also join them as a teacher.

In 1607, the bishop of Yorkshire learned of the secret Scrooby meeting and began pursuing them under England's religious nonconformity laws. Many members had their houses watched day and night, while the bishop had some jailed in horrendous conditions.

Authorities allowed them "neither meat, drink, fire or lodging," Bradford noted of the jailed Separatists. Nor would they allow "any whose hearts the Lord would stir up for their relief, to have any access to them."[8]

Eventually English authorities issued a warrant for Brewster, arresting him and several other attendees. The men paid hefty fines—twenty pounds—and they forced Brewster to resign his duties as postmaster.[9]

The Separatists decided they could no longer live peacefully in England. Their harassment had increased until, as Bradford wrote, they "were hunted and persecuted on every side."[10]

The Scrooby congregation was not the only Separatist community in the region. In nearby Gainsborough, a similar Separatist congregation had established itself and come under comparable persecution. Although the Scrooby and Gainsborough leaders sparred over finer points of theology, they agreed on a broad ideology and united over their common threat. They knew their congregations would need to do something dramatic, and they would be stronger if they worked together. Bradford wrote:

> So many therefore of these [preachers] saw the evil of these things, in these parts; and whose hearts the LORD had touched with heavenly zeal for his truth: they shook off the yoke of antichristian bondage. And, as the LORD's free people, joined themselves, by a Covenant of the LORD, into a Church estate, in the fellowship of the Gospel, to walk in all his ways made known, or to be made known, unto them, according to their best endeavours; whatsoever it should cost them, the LORD assisting them. And that it cost them something, this ensuing History will declare.[11]

Joined by the Gainsborough group, the Scrooby congregation carefully considered the growing persecution against them, coupled with the king's warning to eradicate them from England. The congregations deliberated over whether they should voluntarily flee England for a place where they could worship freely or stay and work for broad social change.

The proposition to move triggered an unusual contradiction: although King James threatened to remove their congregations from England, they needed governmental permission to leave the country. Officially emigrating would seem like a simple, mutually agreeable option, but the English government, paradoxically, refused such permission to nonconforming religious groups, particularly Separatists.

"Most were fain to fly and leave their houses and habitations, and the means of their livelihood," as Bradford put it.[12] Mostly farmers and craftsmen, few of the Separatists had traveled beyond their region of rural England.

"Yet seeing themselves thus molested," he continued, "and that there was no hope of their continuance there [as a Church]: by a joint consent, they resolved to go into the Low Countries, where they heard was Freedom of Religion for all men; as also how sundry, from London and other parts of the land [of England], had been exiled and persecuted for the same Cause, and were gone thither, and lived at Amsterdam and in other places of the land [of Holland]."[13]

Bradford, now seventeen, faced the dilemma of fleeing with the Scrooby Separatists or remaining in his comfortable life in England. His relatives objected to the Scrooby option, wishing him to stay in England. Bradford, however, had developed immunity to change and loss. Bouncing between relatives as he lost close family members bred an independent spirit in him. His sickly childhood spent studying the classics instilled an intellectual curiosity, a desire to know things beyond Scrooby.

Yet he had much to sacrifice, enjoying a comfortable inheritance left by his parents and with a bright future ahead of him in England. Leaving would mean forsaking wealth for poverty, navigating new lands and languages, and abandoning all family and friends.

Bradford deliberated, then chose to follow the Scrooby congregation.

The race for the New World had already begun.

On April 26, 1607, three ships made landfall at Chesapeake Bay on North America's eastern coast. The London Company, one of two branches authorized to settle in the New World, had underwritten the journey with visions of spirited commerce and untapped resources. The voyage had been unexpectedly long, taking the merchants south as far as Puerto Rico. When they reached Chesapeake Bay, they quickly deemed the area too vulnerable for a settlement, but found a large, navigable river with potential. They named it "James River" and set a course to sail into it.

Forty miles up the river, they found a large peninsula that appeared suitable for a settlement and proper defenses. The peninsula created a bend in the river with a strategic line of sight, ideal for a fort. While they worried about French or Spanish attacks, regional Indian tribes presented more imminent security concerns. Fortuitously, it seemed these tribes had overlooked this strategic location. It had promise, and eager to establish a colony, the London Company settlers dedicated little effort to vetting other potential sites. They named the site "Jamestown."

Once they had committed themselves to the location, it became apparent that the site would not meet expectations. In actuality, the beautiful peninsula consisted of swampy wetlands unsuitable for agriculture, much less construction. In addition to incompatible land, they desperately needed clean, potable water, but could only find undrinkable brackish water. More importantly, they had fallen far behind schedule. Because of their delays, the prime growing season had passed. By the time they could begin to work the land, the window for planting would escape them altogether—even if the poor soil could be cropped.

As conditions rapidly deteriorated, the Jamestown residents starved. Within a few months, 51 of the 144 settlers had perished.

Supply ships were set to arrive in 1608, along with craftsmen from Poland, Germany, and Slovakia who could make tools and establish an industry in the New World. Those who survived the "starving time" knew they could not hold out another year until their arrival. Many began considering desertion, seeking refuge with native tribes as the only plausible chance for survival.

By the time the resupply ships arrived in 1608, two-thirds of the Jamestown settlers had died. The unsuspecting immigrants stepped into a more hopeless desperation than those who had come before them. Almost immediately, many of the newcomers defected to the Indian tribes too.

The Jamestown colony teetered on the brink of utter failure. Although it had been an experiment, none imagined such a dismal beginning. Still, Jamestown was neither the first European settlement in North America, nor the first to fail on the continent. Two decades earlier, in 1585, English settlers established Roanoke Colony, on an island off modern-day North Carolina. One hundred and seven men arrived that year. By the time the next expedition passed through in 1587, all had disappeared without a trace. The expedition left another 115 men, women, and children to reestablish Roanoke Colony.

When a subsequent expedition arrived in 1589, the Roanoke colonists had once again mysteriously vanished. They left no conclusive evidence as to what caused their demise, except for "CROATOAN" ominously scrolled into a fence post—suggesting they had perhaps relocated to Croatoan Island. They were never found.

Popham Colony in Maine had a more successful run, but challenging conditions ultimately forced its abandonment. It had started the same year as Jamestown, and a late arrival prevented a spring planting, and thus yielded no fall harvest. A cold and difficult winter made the season excruciating, yet only one colonist died. Popham Colony had a principal purpose: build ships in North America. With vast, untapped virgin forests and a burgeoning fishing trade, the colony's purpose seemed strategic. They built a thirty-ton pinnace—*Virginia*—and almost exactly one year after their arrival, the colonists sailed it back to Europe permanently.

The Jamestown catastrophe frustrated the London Company. They intended the settlement chiefly as an investment, not an expedition. As such, the London Company had funded the venture in exchange for the right to resources and exports. Certainly, they had speculated on the investment, but with bounty like the earlier sassafras harvestings, they anticipated a sturdy reward. Yet after one year, Jamestown had nothing to show.

In 1608, the London Company dispatched a second resupply ship bound for Jamestown. Along with its precious cargo came a letter of demands. First and foremost, Jamestown colonists must return exports proportional to the cost of the voyage. Additionally, the London Company stipulated three specific demands: the Jamestown colonists must send a lump of gold—assurance of North America's rumored vast gold reserves; they must provide proof they had found the South Sea (passage to the Pacific Ocean); and they must send one surviving member of the Roanoke Colony.

The colonists could fulfill none of these demands.

⸻⟡⸻

In Scrooby, the Separatists began preparations for their flight to mainland Europe. Their escape would need to happen in secret to circumvent England's severe restrictions—and avoid the undoubtedly painful retribution. First, they needed a destination.

The Separatists chose Holland. The Dutch Republic offered

freedom of conscience where religion could be openly practiced. Holland not only spoke of defending religious freedom but had a record of doing so. It had become home to other religious exiles in recent years, including the Huguenots, French Protestants driven out by the Catholic Church. They trusted Holland.

On England's east coast, in the town of Boston, the Separatists found an English captain willing to ferry them across the two-hundred-mile stretch of the North Sea to Holland. It was a daring proposition for the captain, who risked his own liberty by assisting them. They agreed upon a location, day, and fee—and he demanded an exorbitant rate for the risky service. With no other options, they obliged. As the ship's lone cargo, the Separatist group would make a nighttime rendezvous in October 1607. They would gather at the designated meeting point and depart immediately.

When the long-awaited night arrived, a large company of Scrooby Separatists assembled in Boston, England, to join the voyage. Many breathed a sigh of relief at the sight of the vessel dropping anchor. The Separatists swiftly loaded their belongings on the boat and gathered on deck.

As the captain prepared to cast off, government officers arrived at the dock. They came prepared to conduct a search of the vessel, to which the captain showed no surprise or alarm and gave no protest.

He had betrayed them.

The officers corralled the Separatists into open boats, giving them no opportunity to flee or hide. "[A]nd there rifled and ransacked them," Bradford described the scene, "searching them to their shirts for money; yea, even the women further than became modesty."[14] The officials confiscated not only their money, but their books and belongings.

The officers proceeded to usher them back to Boston.

There, they paraded the Scrooby Separatists through town, making them "a spectacle and wonder to the multitude; which came flocking on all sides to behold them."[15]

The officers turned the Separatists over to Boston's local magistrate judges. Messengers were sent to inform the Privy Council, which administered the country on behalf of the Crown, and in the meantime, the magistrates committed the Separatists to jail. After a month of imprisonment, the council allowed the magistrates to dismiss a majority of the Separatists, but not everyone. Seven of the church's leaders received extended prison sentences, including Bradford.[16]

After the final seven returned to Scrooby, the church gathered again to discuss its future. The ordeal in Boston had only hardened their resolve and sense of persecution. The congregation continued to see no alternative other than fleeing England. Despite the risks, they would try again.

In planning their second attempt, they judged the risk of betrayal by an English captain as too great. After some searching, they found a Dutch captain sympathetic to their cause. Despite residual uneasiness after their previous encounter, they trusted the Dutch captain, and he assured them to "have no fear."[17] They would meet on the bank of the Humber River, northeast of Scrooby, near the town of Grimsby.

To avoid attracting attention, the Separatists traveled to the rendezvous location in two groups. The men went together over land. The women and children sailed out the river in a bark—a three-masted boat—along with their luggage.

The journey downriver was swift, but rough. The bark arrived a day before the intended rendezvous with the Dutch captain, but seasickness had afflicted many of the women and children. The sailors beached the bark in a creek to let their passengers rest and wait until morning. When the sun rose, they found themselves aground and unable to proceed. The tide had receded overnight and left them stranded. Finally, around noon, they broke the bark free of the mud and continued toward the meeting spot.

The Dutch vessel arrived at the rendezvous point as planned, but the bark carrying women and children was delayed. While the Dutch captain sent his small landing boat to begin ferrying the men from shore, the bark carrying the women and children arrived. They landed on shore to facilitate the transfer of passengers and luggage. After the first boat, filled only with men, unloaded at the main ship, the Dutch captain spotted unusual activity off in the distance: "a large body of horse and foot, armed with bills and guns and other weapons—for the country side had turned out to capture them."[18]

At the sight of English officials, the Dutch captain swore his country's oath and weighed anchor.[19] With a good wind, he hoisted a sail and set a course for the sea. Although the Separatists still had many people and belongings to transfer, he would not jeopardize himself or his ship.

"The Poor men already aboard were in great distress," Bradford wrote, "for their wives and children, left thus to be captured, and destitute of help—and for themselves, too, without any clothes but what they had on their backs, and scarcely a penny about them, all their possessions being aboard the bark, now seized. It drew tears from their eyes, and they would have given anything to be ashore again. But all in vain, there was no remedy; they must thus sadly part."[20]

The contingent onshore divided themselves. Those physically able fled the scene, and a small group of men stayed with the women and children who could not escape capture.

"What weeping and crying on every side: some for their husbands carried away in the ship; others not knowing what would become of them and their little ones; others again melted in tears, seeing their poor little ones hanging about them, crying for fear and quaking with cold!"[21]

The apprehension of so many women and children confounded local officials. Public sentiment of the day would cry foul should they imprison women and children for simply following their husbands. Yet the officials could not release them to go home—most no longer had homes; they had sold them.

This unusual ordeal caught the attention not only of authorities, but of commoners, too, who wondered why English-born citizens would go to such great lengths to leave the country. That they would defy the Church of England made it even more interesting. "[T]heir cause became famous, and led many to inquire into it," Bradford wrote of arrests that catapulted the Separatists, and their faith, to a national platform.[22]

Those on board the Dutch vessel uneventfully began their short voyage across the North Sea. Not long into the journey, a massive storm bore down upon them, battering the boat. For seven days they could not see the sun, moon, or stars as they tossed and turned over the ocean. Even the sea-hardened sailors had not endured such an incredible tempest, often wailing in despair. The storm took such a toll that the boat began to list. "We sink! We sink!" the sailors cried out as waves broke over the deck inundating everyone on board.[23]

Members of the Separatist congregation gathered together. They began to pray aloud: "Yet LORD, thou canst save; yet LORD, thou canst save!"[24]

"But when man's hope and help wholly failed," Bradford wrote, "the Lord's power and mercy appeared in their recovery; for the ship rose again, and gave the crew courage to manage her."[25]

Almost immediately upon their prayers, the storm began to dissipate. When the storm subsided enough to regain navigation, they learned that the gale had blown them four hundred miles to the north, near the coast of Norway.

When they finally limped into the port in Holland, people came flocking, "astonished at their deliverance." Their arrival was long overdue, and most assumed that the Dutch vessel had been lost at sea. Their survival was a remarkable sight.

For the Separatists now in Holland, they had arrived. While many would wait for loved ones, this offered the chance to start the life and freedom they imagined for many years. They could begin to worship freely, but also build their sacred community. For the foreseeable future, they would call Amsterdam home, and the men would take jobs in this port city's growing global economy.

The Separatists unable to board the Dutch ship spent the next tumultuous months passing among English authorities. No authority wanted to deal with them or take responsibility. Eventually all the members received their release.

"Some few shrank from these first conflicts and sharp beginnings, as it was no marvel," Bradford admitted, "yet many more came on with fresh courage, and greatly animated others."[26]

The ordeal had battered the Separatist church, but not broken it.

"In the end, not withstanding all these storms of opposition, they all got over . . . some from one place, some in another; and met together again . . . with no small rejoicing."[27]

Chapter Four

Return to Slavery

1614

NEWFOUNDLAND, NORTH AMERICA

The cool, spring wind blew through Squanto's hair. He stood on the deck of *Susan Constant* watching the horizon.[1] The icy waters of the Atlantic broke under the ship's piercing hull. With England to his back, he looked out on the watery expanse toward the west—he was going home.

Squanto had survived his detention in Spain—two years in Seville's prison and two more years of slave labor in the galleys. The Spanish had finally relented to Britain's diplomatic pressure, and in 1611, they released the remaining captives from *The Richard of Plymouth*, Squanto included.

Squanto had traveled to England with the returning sailors. In London, a merchant by the name of John Slany gave Squanto room and board. A shipbuilder by trade, Slany had an intense interest in the development of North America and, in 1610, helped charter the Newfoundland Company. After its incorporation, he served as the treasurer of the Newfoundland Company with the goal of colonizing Cuper's Cove on the island's southern peninsula.

Squanto lived with Slany for three years, and Slany welcomed his guest with both humanitarian and commercial intent. Slany worked with Squanto on his English fluency and exploited his knowledge of North America. Slany also enjoyed flaunting his guest as a curiosity to Londoners.

Squanto wanted to return to North America, and in time, Slany helped make arrangements. Slany found an opportunity for his passage with the storied explorer Captain John Smith, who had gained notoriety as an unbridled and controversial member of the Jamestown expedition.[2] He survived Jamestown's most dire seasons; then, after two and a half years, injuries from a gunpowder accident forced his return to England. He desperately wanted to continue his work in the New World and had plans for an expedition to North America in 1614. If Squanto served as interpreter, Smith would provide him passage.

In the spring of that year, a two-ship expedition led by Smith had set sail from the coast of England. Smith took the helm of the *Susan Constant*, and the *Godspeed*, mastered by Thomas Hunt, trailed along with the smaller pinnace *Discovery*.[3] The expedition had been charged with finding "whales and gold mines." If neither goal could be accomplished, then "fish and furres" would suffice.[4]

For Smith, the New World had become an obsession. Back in London in 1609 after his failure at Jamestown, he had turned his attention to northern Virginia, the prospecting grounds of the Plymouth Company. His personal agenda had also evolved. He no longer wanted to merely collect commodities; he wanted to expand the field of cartography. He intended to create the first detailed map of northern Virginia. He had already mapped southern Virginia, and this cartological achievement would complete a significant body of work.

In April 1614, Squanto and Smith arrived at Monhegan Island, off present-day Maine. After an extensive search, they found no gold mines, and whaling proved unproductive. The expedition turned to its backup plan—fishing. With the crew at work trying to haul in fish, Smith turned his full attention to exploring and mapping the Virginia coast. He took eight men and Squanto as the interpreter.

Smith worked south along the coast of Maine. Soon, they reached the Kennebec River, Squanto's adopted home. At this place, nine years ago, Weymouth's expedition had kidnapped him. Squanto introduced Smith to Tahanedo,[5] one of the Kennebec men who had been kidnapped by Weymouth, then returned to America on a recent expedition. Tahanedo agreed to help Smith with the geography of the parts of Maine familiar to the Kennebec peoples.

Smith's expedition continued farther south, eventually to Cape Cod and Patuxet. He named the region stretching from Newfoundland to Long Island Sound "New England."[6]

At this point, Smith relieved Squanto of his duties as interpreter so he could rejoin his birth tribe, the Patuxet. From there, Smith's mapping expedition sailed north to rendezvous with the fishing contingent. The fishing had been plentiful in the early spring but slowed significantly throughout the summer. Their weak haul would not justify the cost of the expedition.

Smith returned to England on the *Susan Constant* with their meager cargo of fish.[7] He ordered Thomas Hunt, master of the *Godspeed*, to finish loading his ship, then sail it to the Mediterranean for the Spanish seafood market.

Hunt pulled in his nets in September 1614, leaving Monhegan Island with a course set for Spain. The route took them south along the coast of North America before they turned east to cross the Atlantic. This course allowed them to make one more stop for provisions, including water, food, and wood, before the long voyage for Spain.

Hunt sailed into Cape Cod and stopped near the Patuxet area. Squanto paddled out, along with several canoes filled with Nauset and Patuxet Indians, to greet the ship and offer to trade. Hunt signaled his willingness and invited all two dozen men on board. Hunt offered to show his visitors the boat, including the cargo hold below deck. When all the Indians had climbed down the stairs, Hunt's men slammed the hatches shut and locked them. Immediately, they set sail, taking the Indians captive. For Squanto, the journey would mark his third crossing of the Atlantic Ocean.

In Malaga, Spain, Hunt sold the fish on behalf of the Newfoundland Company. He then turned his attention to his American Indian captives, putting the men up for sale as slaves for his own personal gain.

News of Hunt's decision to take captives reverberated throughout England. Explorers and merchants, in particular, expressed much disapproval. They condemned him less for his trade in slaves, and more due to the political ramifications this would cause among the Indian tribes. At a minimum, the Indians would be much less willing to engage with Europeans, but more importantly future expeditions to North America would undoubtedly be in greater danger of attack—and justifiably so. For Ferdinando Gorges and the investors banking on the New World, diplomacy with the North American tribes would take a giant step backward.

In Spain, the Indian men proved more difficult to sell than Hunt had anticipated. His captives aroused unexpected sympathy, so no one came forward to buy them. Eventually, a group of Spanish monks adopted Squanto and his companions, hoping to convert them to Christianity in the process.

Hunt's decision not only cost him the captives, but also his career. No expedition wanted to risk employing him, and many maritime leaders publicly rebuked him.

Gorges would call Hunt "a worthless fellow of our nation."[8] Smith, too, would later chastise him: "The vilde act kept [Hunt] ever after from any more employment in those parts."[9]

Sadly, the scorn for Hunt and outcry against his actions did not deter everyone. Hunt's deed soon led imitators to conduct similar kidnappings all along the North American coastline. Among them was an English captain who began systematically capturing natives with the intention of selling them into slavery. With twenty-nine men of various tribes on board his ship, he sailed for England with plans to sell them at a market for Spanish buyers. The buyers, however, found the Indians too "unapt for their uses," leaving the American Indian men in London.[10]

Among those kidnapped by Hunt was an Indian man named Epenow. When Hunt could not sell Epenow as a slave in London, he turned him into a public spectacle. English promoters constantly placed him on display as a public wonder and curiosity, likely inspiring Shakespeare to write about the "strange Indian" in *Henry VIII*.[11] Gorges, who still housed Accumset, one of the Kennebecs captured by Captain Weymouth, eventually took in Epenow.

Under Gorges's roof, Epenow crafted a shrewd plan to secure his freedom and return to his home at Capawock (today's Martha's Vineyard). He convinced Gorges of the existence of a gold quarry near Capawock and offered to guide him there. Gorges pounced at the proposal, quickly authorizing an expedition with the primary purpose of finding this gold mine.

When the expedition reached Capawock in 1614, crowded canoes of Nauset Indians, including Epenow's relatives, rowed out to investigate the ship. Epenow, purposefully detained below deck, had secretly planned to flee upon his arrival. Fearing he might lose his chance to return home, he put up a fight. He managed to break free of his guards and scrambled onto the deck.

With a giant leap, he dove into the ocean. From their canoes, the Nauset Indians opened fire, sending a barrage of arrows onto the crowded deck of stunned English sailors. Unprepared for a battle, the English took a severe hit. The captain and many of the sailors received injuries, forcing them to immediately set sail for England. They returned home with nothing to show.

When Gorges learned of the incident, it dawned on him that Epenow had orchestrated the events. Hunt had kidnapped Squanto and he "contracted such an hatred against our whole nation, [that he] immediately studied how to be revenged."[12]

Epenow's plot dampened Gorge's once rosy outlook on the New World. "They brought home nothing but the news . . . of a war now new began between the inhabitants of those parts, and us," Gorges recounted.[13]

⚜

Squanto had passed three long years in Spain. He spent most of this time in the company of the Catholic monks who gave the Indians shelter and taught them about Christianity. He had not intended to remain in Spain for so long, but very few ships sailed between Malaga, Spain, and Northern Virginia—or between Malaga and anywhere in North America, for that matter. Finally, in 1618, Squanto found passage on a trading ship bound for the Cuper's Cove trading post in Newfoundland. He joined the ship and its cargo of wine, which the captain planned to exchange for fish.

Squanto, now twenty-seven, arrived at Cuper's Cove and coincidentally recognized a face from the expedition with Smith. Captain Thomas Dermer had sailed to New England with Smith and Squanto in 1614 and returned to Cuper's Cove on assignment from Gorges to explore the Newfoundland region. He had sailed

back to England before Hunt kidnapped Squanto, but the shared
expedition gave him an intimate knowledge of Hunt's misdeeds.
Squanto's presence on Newfoundland now gave Dermer the
opportunity to right some of the wrongs committed in the name
of England.

Dermer listened to Squanto's story and agreed to help him
return to Patuxet. Dermer, unfortunately, could not help immediately. Regular shipping proceeded back and forth between
Cuper's Cove and England, but not up and down the North
American coast. Until an expedition sailed through, Squanto
would have to wait indefinitely.[14]

In the three years since Hunt had abducted Squanto, relations between European settlers and North America's tribes had
degenerated considerably. On the heels of Hunt's kidnapping,
other European captains committed equal or more heinous
crimes. One English captain invited a group of natives on board
his ship and then, with no provocation, proceeded to slaughter
them indiscriminately.

Along with these incidents came mounting anger and mis-
trust. Previously friendly relations between Europeans and
Indians quickly dissolved, and trading missions no longer found
themselves welcome along the Cape Cod shoreline. The increasingly tense situation culminated with Nauset warriors seizing a
French ship. They killed, or enslaved, the unsuspecting crew,
and burned the vessel on the beach.

Dermer noted the rapidly changing posture of North
America's tribes toward the Europeans, saying they "bear an
inveterate malignity to the English."[15]

Dermer immediately identified Squanto as an opportunity to
establish peace. If he could help Squanto get to Patuxet, Dermer
imagined that Squanto could diplomatically begin to thaw relations with the tribes around Cape Cod.

Dermer sent a letter to Gorges in England asking him to authorize the peace mission. In addition, Dermer needed supplies and personnel for such an expedition. If Gorges approved, Dermer and Squanto would proceed to Monhegan Island off the "Maine" land, then tour native settlements down the coast until finally reaching Patuxet.

After many months of waiting with no ship to be found, Dermer decided that he and Squanto must sail to England for a face-to-face meeting with Ferdinando Gorges. From England, they could more effectively organize the peace mission, then sail directly to Monhegan Island.

Dermer found a fishing vessel bound for England in 1619. It would sail for Plymouth Harbor, where Dermer knew he would find Gorges. Squanto joined him for yet another transatlantic voyage.

Part Two ——————————————————————

FREEDOM

Chapter Five

A New World Awaits

1619

LEIDEN, HOLLAND

Freedom abounded in Holland. The nation welcomed religious diversity, and the Scrooby congregation had enjoyed a decade free from persecution.

In the 1570s, only a few decades before the arrival of the Scrooby congregation, Calvinist uprisings across northern Europe united Holland against a formidable force: the Holy Roman Empire and, along with it, Spanish authorities. Hollanders fought not merely for the Dutch Republic, but for the principle of freedom of religion. Accordingly, they granted freedom of conscience to everyone in Holland.

"[E]very citizen should remain free in his religion," declared Dutch law in 1579, "and no man be molested or questioned on the subject of divine worship."[1]

As the handmaiden of freedom of conscience, Holland consequently recognized freedom of the press. While England burned nonconforming religious books and tracts, in Holland they could be printed without fear. The Congregationalists, including Barrow and Greenwood, had already exploited this freedom, using Dutch printers to publish their writings and then ship them to England.

By the time the entire Scrooby congregation had arrived on Dutch shores in 1609, it appeared that Holland's course would not change. A Twelve Years' Truce on April 9, 1609, with Spain ensured that Holland would remain free from the imposition of the Catholic Church. But now, the truce would soon draw to a close, and the Scrooby congregation no longer felt certain about the future.

Holland, despite all its freedoms, was evolving. The Scrooby congregation had arrived at a tipping point in Dutch history, the beginning of an era in which the nation would rise to great power in Europe. While most European nations had focused on military aggression as their means for international muscle, the Dutch had quietly built an empire upon their seamanship and trading prowess. Holland now held an important strategic position. Religious toleration had served Holland economically as well, attracting refugees from across Europe and, with them, great wealth. Jews driven out of Portugal brought the diamond industry. Flemings from Antwerp brought financial institutions.

The Scrooby congregation had settled quickly, enjoying the opportunity to worship freely, publicly, and without fear. Work abounded, too—the Dutch Republic had booming international industries hungry for help. But the Separatists felt the downside of rapid industrialization. The labor was hard and largely factory based, a far cry from their quiet rural life in the English countryside. Economic progress left those who came to Holland without the backing of an industry, like the Scrooby congregation, with the most backbreaking and menial of jobs.

Despite their great enjoyment of Holland's freedoms, the

bustling metropolis of Amsterdam had not made for an easy transition. At the very least, the Scrooby congregation encountered extreme culture shock.

"They saw many goodly and fortified cities," Bradford wrote, "walled and guarded by troops of armed men."[2]

Many of these English expatriates likely had not ventured very far beyond the limits of Scrooby. Many had, perhaps, never seen London. The sight of Amsterdam filled them with awe and fear. They struggled not merely with its size and scope but with its culture.

"Strange and uncouth," they called the Dutch language, one of the many differences they immediately noted. Manners, customs, and even Dutch attire left them so out of place that Bradford felt they had "come into a new world."[3]

While they struggled to adapt to Dutch life, the Separatists soon had a more pressing problem: their livelihoods. This was, as Bradford put it, "another kind of war to wage."

"For though they saw fair and beautiful cities," Bradford wrote, "flowing with abundance of all sorts of wealth and riches, yet it was not long before they saw the grim and grisly face of poverty coming upon them like an armed man, with whom they must prepare for action, and from whom they could not flee."[4]

In England, the congregation had unified in opposition to the Church of England and rallied around the shared dream of freedom. Their fight against dogma overwhelmed any desire to quarrel about religious minutiae. In Holland, they had freedom of worship when they wanted, where they wanted, and how they wanted. With such unchecked freedom came bitter divides over doctrine, such as the place of infant baptism in their churches. To make matters worse, the seeds of dissension sowed in England between Scrooby and other Separatist congregations began to germinate.

Between a fracturing church and their difficulties assimilating to life in Amsterdam, the church's teacher, John Robinson, led a charge to move the Scrooby congregation out of Amsterdam. They had only lasted one year in the sprawling metropolis, but he feared that if they waited any longer the church would not survive. Robinson chose neighboring Leiden, still a bustling city of forty thousand, but smaller and more comfortable than Amsterdam, for a new home.

By the time they made the move in May 1609, their contentious debates in Amsterdam had already split the original Scrooby congregation. Richard Clyfton, the Anglican priest turned Separatist who originally brought together the Scrooby congregation, parted ways with his flock to remain at a church in Amsterdam. Clyfton landed in the minority, however, as the Scrooby congregation's move added to their number by attracting members from other congregations.

In Clyfton's void, John Robinson's influence grew, and he took on greater responsibility and leadership. To give their congregation a better home in Leiden, Robinson bought a house with a large, walled yard to serve as the hub for the church. In the yard, he designated space for members of the congregation who could not yet afford their own houses. Before long, the congregation had transformed his yard into a small village of houses.

From the outset, Leiden provided a better environment for the Scrooby congregation. Its slower pace and lessened focus on commerce gave them a respite from the chaos of Amsterdam. At about one-third of Amsterdam's population, Leiden dwelled in the shadow of its larger sister's growing position as a global hub for commerce and sea trade. Leiden concerned itself more with academics than business. The quiet town was "made famous," in Bradford's words, "by its university, in which recently there had been so many learned men."[5]

Leiden also retained a sense of tranquility and connected the Scrooby refugees to their agricultural roots. The Old Rhine slowly rolled around Leiden's towering walls acting as its moat, then flowed through the town, flooding its network of canals and streams. Outside the city walls, the land opened up into a patchwork of gardens, farms, and orchards. The countryside reminded them of Scrooby.

"[A] fair and beautiful city, of a sweet situation," Bradford wrote of Leiden. The Scrooby congregation found contentedness here, "valuing peace and their spiritual comfort above and other riches whatsoever," he wrote. "And at length they came to raise a competent and comfortable living but with hard and continued labor."[6]

For Bradford, the Leiden years offered a time of maturation. He voyaged across the North Sea as little more than a boy. While the experience had aged him and hardened his resolve, in Holland he found himself thrown into a wonderful and strange world. He received a daily education in diplomacy as he helped his fellow Congregationalists navigate their new life. He tried his hand at commerce, made mistakes, and learned from them. But in Leiden he was more at peace. Perhaps with his love of books, he felt at home in the academic atmosphere created by Leiden's prominent university, or perhaps he simply enjoyed its more quiet surroundings.

Not only did the Scrooby congregation like Leiden, but they found themselves well liked by the Dutch. Despite their poverty, the Scrooby transplants always kept their word and worked hard. Dutch merchants and business owners quickly recognized this and often trusted them in business dealings, even when they had no money.

As Leiden prospered, so did its industry. The city had specialized in the cloth trade. Fabric houses bustled with clacking looms and the banter of textile merchants. They served not only Holland's domestic market, but a growing international demand for their craft—even England sent cloth to Leiden for its expert finishing.

The increasingly energetic pace of life in Leiden began to catch up with the English peasants—and change them. Unfortunately for the Scrooby group, they had few skills to grant them access to the guilds and trade unions of Leiden. Uneducated and unqualified, many from the congregation landed on the fringe of the wool trade with tedious and painstaking work. Bradford, for one, found employment at a corduroy factory.

Men, women, and children all went to work to earn a living wage for their families. From dawn to dusk, they labored six days a week in the factories. A bell in the yarn market rang to announce the beginning and end of the workday. The unrelenting pace began to erode the values and culture they worked so hard to preserve.

Not everyone toiled in Leiden's textile mills. William Brewster, the former postmaster turned church elder, started a publishing house to print religious materials.[7] He focused his efforts on printing Congregational materials for distribution in England. He hired a young man from the church to assist him, twenty-two-year-old Edward Winslow. Brewster's publishing house would typeset religious tracts, then print them at a Dutch printing house to defer some responsibility.[8]

Brewster's publications, which may have numbered as many as fifteen, rustled up serious controversy. *Perth Assembly*, in particular, made a blistering attack on King James. Prior to its publication in 1619, Brewster's efforts had attracted little attention from English authorities. Indeed, the Scrooby congregation's departure had largely gone unnoticed. *Perth Assembly* changed that. The book made weighty accusations against the king, alleging that he forced Scottish Presbyterians to accept the authority of the English bishops.

Brewster had arranged for someone to smuggle the book into England and Scotland, where it eventually found its way into the hands of the king.

Irate, James went looking for the culprit. Immediately, he arrested a printer in Scotland, though he would not be able to link the printer to the incident. Then, England's ambassador to Holland informed him that the seditious materials likely originated in Leiden.

"I sent your honour a book entitled *Perth Assembly*," the ambassador wrote to the king's secretary of state, "of which finding many copies dispersed at Leiden, and from there some sent into England, I had reason to suspect it was printed in that town . . . [by] is one William Brewster, a Brownist, who hath been for some years an inhabitant and printer at Leiden."[9]

King James declared Brewster guilty of sedition, an offense carrying a hefty penalty: a combination of unpayable fines, cutting off a nose or ear, and life imprisonment in Fleet Prison. James did not merely want to prosecute Brewster; he wanted to destroy his printing house.

In a departure from Holland's respect for religious freedom, the Dutch authorities answered England's call for Brewster's arrest. Holland mobilized the States General, deputies in charge of controlling Holland's provinces. The States General assisted English authorities by searching door-to-door in Leiden.

England's secretary of state, Robert Nauton, wrote the English ambassador Dudley Carleton in Holland:

[The Dutch government] will not take it for an unreasonable request, since he is his own native subject; they having formerly remanded some of their own hither upon His Majesty's like motion.

. . . you are required to move the States [General] to

take some strict order, through all their Provinces, for the preventing of like abuses and licentiousness in publishing printing and venting underhand such scandalous and libelous pamphlets.[10]

The manhunt for Brewster extended beyond the city limits of Leiden, and rumors of his whereabouts surfaced across the Dutch countryside. Brewster, however, could not be found. His role in the printing operation further confounded Dutch authorities. They eventually concluded that he served merely as the agent between the author and the printer, explaining his absence as a clandestine trip to London.

"[Brewster is] three weeks removed from there, and gone back to dwell in London," the English ambassador wrote to the secretary of state, "where he may be found out and examined; . . . if he was not the printer himself, he assuredly knows both the printer and author for, as I am informed, he hath had, whilst he remained here, his hand in all such books as have been sent over into England and Scotland. . . ."[11]

While they had underestimated Brewster's role, they had correctly guessed at his trip to London. By the time Dutch authorities realized Brewster had indeed left Holland, and his letters to England had exchanged hands, it was too late.[12] He quickly disappeared into hiding among Congregationalist churches in London.

For the Congregationalists in Leiden, the matter felt ominously similar to the persecution they fled in England. And now, their elder who had led and stewarded the congregation from Scrooby would forever remain a fugitive in hiding. The ordeal confirmed they could no longer truly exercise their faith in Holland with full freedom and enjoyment.

The congregation began to discuss its future.

In England, plans for Dermer's and Squanto's 1619 peace mission to New England began to unfold.

Squanto appeared to be the model peace ambassador. To England's benefit, he had mastered the language and could speak fluently in several Native American dialects. He knew two tribes intimately: the Patuxet and the Kennebecs. And perhaps most importantly, Squanto was a survivor. He had been the victim of at least two crimes against the people of North America, so if anyone could defuse and reframe the problem, he could.

Squanto's strength, however, also presented a significant risk. Epenow had feigned loyalty until reaching the North American coastline. His epic betrayal deflated Europe's enthusiasm for trade with the Indians and drove a wedge of distrust more deeply between the continents. Squanto had as much, if not more, reason than Epenow to flee Dermer at his first opportunity.

Squanto had developed a rapport with Gorges, Smith, and other English leaders who could authorize the mission. Despite the Epenow matter, they believed Squanto would remain loyal to both sides—he had truly become a friend of England. Gorges and Smith further believed that Squanto could distinguish between "good" and "evil" white men—the majority of Englishmen, the "good" ones, abhorred the crimes committed against the Indians and wanted peace. Hopefully, these leaders reasoned, Squanto could explain this to the tribes who had been devastated by the actions of Weymouth, Hunt, and the Spanish expeditions that left heartache and brokenness in their wake.

At England's Plymouth Harbor, Gorges received Dermer and his proposal for the peace mission with enthusiasm.

"Notwithstanding these disasters," Gorges wrote, "it pleased God so to work for our encouragement again, as he sent into our hands Tasquantum [Squanto], one of those savages that formerly had been betrayed by this unworthy Hunt . . . by whose means there was hope conceived to work a peace between us, and his friends, they being the principal inhabitant of that coast. . . ."[13]

For Squanto, the return to Plymouth Harbor was a homecoming of sorts. He reunited with his young friend David Thomson, who had guided Squanto around the harbor in 1605. Thomson had since received a promotion to serve as Gorges's assistant. But their stay in Plymouth Harbor would be short. Gorges wanted the peace mission to commence as soon as possible, and he searched earnestly for a voyage to which they could attach this endeavor.

With the impending arrival of the spring fishing season, a two-hundred-ton ship, *Abraham*, was being equipped to sail for Monhegan Island. Gorges negotiated with *Abraham*'s owner for the ship to transport Dermer and Squanto to Maine. Since Gorges wanted to monitor the progress of the effort, he ordered Thomson to sail with them, then return on board the *Abraham* at the end of the fishing season.

In late March of 1619, the *Abraham* sailed out of Plymouth Harbor. Dermer had three objectives for the goodwill mission: (1) implement procedures for avoiding race conflicts in New England, (2) trade with the Indians for furs, and (3) evaluate potential settlement locations.

Gorges and Smith shared a long-term vision of establishing settlements, so a mutual understanding of this between the Europeans and Indians would be critical to peace. Dermer specifically hoped to propose that when English settlers arrived, they would make peaceful contact with their tribal neighbors. From that point of contact, they would establish a mutual-defense compact, with each party guaranteeing not to harm the other. Gorges acknowledged that unfortunate violations would occur, so he included a resolution plan. If a race-related incident should occur, the injured party should notify the other and send the wrongdoer to them for punishment. They entrusted Squanto and Dermer to deliver this message.

By May 19, 1619, Dermer, Squanto, and Thomson had arrived at Monhegan Island and readied a smaller, five-ton boat for their goodwill mission. Along with three additional English sailors, they sailed to Pemaquid Point near the mouth of the Kennebec River.

As the men cruised down the coast, they spied the remnants of deserted villages. This once densely populated area had become "now utterly void."[14] They called it "the Plague," which they recognized by the sores of the few survivors they spotted.

At Pemaquid, they reached the Kennebec tribe and found Tahanedo, who had been captured by Weymouth in 1605 but returned to his homeland on a voyage with Martin Pring in 1606. He happily provided Squanto with counsel on which tribes to visit and where to find them. Upon Tahanedo's advice, they would first sail south for Cape Cod. There they would find a Sagamore named Massasoit, who wielded much power in the region, and they would also find Patuxet, Squanto's home village. From there, they would sail farther south, around the Cape to Capawock, the home of the Nauset tribe.

After some time at Pemaquid, the peace mission began its slow progression down the coast. By June, they sailed into Cape Cod and identified a natural harbor. On his earlier mapping expedition, Smith had coined the large, protected harbor "Plymouth," but Squanto knew the area as Patuxet. The roaring waves and beaches formed a natural channel into the harbor, set against a backdrop of forests. It all seemed familiar to Squanto, yet curiously quiet. Absent were the trappings of summer around

Patuxet's harbor: canoes skirting the shoreline, men fishing along the streams, and children playing on the beach.

As they approached the Patuxet village, Squanto and Dermer scanned the shore for the flicker of fires. They could spot none. They watched for canoes that would inevitably glide out to meet them, offering to trade. No one appeared to acknowledge their presence. Patuxet remained eerily silent.

They beached the small sailboat near Patuxet. Still, no one came to greet them. Upon further inspection, the village had been abandoned—not as if the people had fled in fear of their arrival, but as if the people had simply disappeared.

In fact, they had. The men determined that a plague had annihilated Squanto's Patuxet home and its inhabitants. With nothing to offer at Patuxet, they prepared for the next visit: Massasoit.

Massasoit was a man to be revered. He commanded respect and power throughout the region as a sachem, or chief. His name translated to "great sachem," a title he had earned through courageous action and wise leadership. Massasoit had forged a sturdy alliance with many of the region's tribes, forming a confederacy of otherwise politically unruly clans. Yet Massasoit was their rock—a steady hand, slow to speak, and tactful. Should Dermer's diplomatic envoy meet any leader in the Cape Cod Bay, they should meet Massasoit.

Tahanedo told them to find Massasoit at Namasket,[15] a fourteen-mile overland journey from Patuxet. Squanto led the way. After the destruction at Patuxet, the men had no idea what they might find.

At Namasket, they saw signs of life, but barely. The plague had devastated the village, but unlike at Patuxet, it left survivors. The village was sparse and lethargic, but alive. They could not, however, find Massasoit. They confirmed that he had survived the plague and remained in power, but he had left Namasket temporarily. Squanto dispatched one of the villagers to deliver a message to the chief requesting a meeting.

Soon, fifty guards armed with bows began filing into Namasket village. Following the long train of guards were two chiefs: Massasoit and his brother Quadaquina.[16]

The meeting opened with hostility. Massasoit did not trust the men—Dermer, in particular—and he showed little interest in them. The sachem knew well the accounts of Weymouth and Hunt, which had left Massasoit suspicious of Dermer's motives. The sachem, in fact, was of the mind that it would be easier to kill Dermer now than risk the peril he might bring upon them.

The intensity quickly escalated, and Massasoit appeared ready to take Dermer's life at any moment. Squanto put himself between the sachem and Dermer, pleading for his European companion's life. The daring effort spared Dermer. "[T]hey would have killed me . . . had not he entreated hard for me," Dermer later acknowledged.[17]

Although tempers waned, Massasoit remained suspicious of the men. He tentatively allowed them to stay with him, although he would keep them under close watch.

Massasoit's cooling off gave the men a chance to understand and appreciate the sachem. After a decade of misdeeds, the relationship between North America's tribes and European emissaries would need healing, justifying their peace process.

Casting off from Patuxet, they sailed out around the arm of the Cape and proceeded to Capawock, home of the Nauset tribe. Although the Nausets were unrelated by blood to Massasoit's Wampanoag, Massasoit had power and control over the lands they occupied, thus including them in the Wampanoag confederacy. This structure occasionally left Nauset leaders at odds with Massasoit.

Arriving at Capawock, Dermer was shocked to find Epenow

there and alive. Dermer had believed him to be dead. The story of Epenow's dramatic escape from the English ship had failed to be told in England. In fact, Dermer had heard quite the opposite. The sailors had reported Epenow dead, along with many other Nauset Indians, in their own victorious battle.

Although Epenow had deceived the English before, he agreed to meet peacefully with Dermer and Squanto. The Nauset chief recounted for them his daring escape from the English vessel and laughed as he described how he fooled them, leaving their ship to limp home.[18] Dermer and Squanto had a long visit with him, and Epenow treated them well. Feeling as though they had made diplomatic progress with Epenow, and with promising winds for their voyage, Dermer and Squanto pushed back out to sea.

From Capawock, the peace mission met with several other tribes in the region, redeeming a second shipwrecked Frenchman before sailing back to Maine. On June 23, they arrived at Monhegan Island where they found the *Abraham* loaded with fish and ready to depart.

Dermer decided to stay in North America, preferring to winter at Jamestown.[19] With Patuxet decimated, Squanto chose to stay in Maine. The *Abraham* would leave without them.

Chapter Six

Escape

The Scrooby congregation began to feel very uneasy in Leiden. Europe had become gripped by a political power struggle, cloaked in the religious vestments of the Catholic and Protestant churches. In central and eastern Europe, a series of what would become four consecutive wars between the churches had begun—collectively, the Thirty Years' War.

In Holland specifically, the Twelve Years' Truce, which had ended Spanish control in 1609, would soon expire in 1621. With only two years remaining in the truce, the Scrooby congregation knew the possibility of war, and Catholic control would not fare well for them.

The congregation's leaders took note of the changing political landscape. After nearly twelve years in Leiden, their governors and elders gathered "to apprehend present dangers and to scan the future and think of a timely remedy."[1]

They had few options. The Separatists could not return to England, especially now that Brewster's books had raised their profile. They would surely be jailed. The congregation could not

flee to another nation. No other European country offered sufficient religious freedom, and most would not purposely welcome
an enemy of King James.

They could stay in Holland. While they had felt comfortable
there initially, the country grew more inhospitable by the day.
The threat of religious oppression intersected with a threat to
their lifestyle, so the country would no longer serve them as they
intended. They wanted a place where the congregation could
live freely and replicate the Scrooby experience.

The matter grew to a great debate among the congregation
and weighed heavily on their consciences. Slowly, the deliberation
began to shift toward the notion of leaving Holland. Eventually,
"they began at length to incline to the idea of removal to some
other place," Bradford wrote, "not out of any newfangledness or
other such giddy humor, which often influences people to their
detriment and danger, but for many important reasons."[2]

More immediate than the possibility that Spain could retake
Holland was their destitution. The people had few means, and
their church had almost no money. In fact, the church had barely
grown. They had not received the surge of followers they expected
from England—in eleven years only three hundred had made the
journey. These numbers dwindled after the reports of job prospects
in Holland. They attracted another two hundred Hollanders, presumably mostly Dutch, who grew the congregation to almost five
hundred.[3] They had not sparked a religious revival.

Chief among the congregation's deterrents for staying in
Holland included its low socioeconomic status. Many of their
flock still clung to the bottom rungs of society. Even after a decade in the country, they had not risen out of the menial factory
labor that economics forced them to accept when they arrived.

They also wanted to grow their congregation. Many had
friends and family remaining in England, but the challenging

conditions in Holland dissuaded them from crossing the North Sea. The hard labor turned away the most people, and many would rather accept the Church of England as an inconvenience than resign themselves to Dutch factories.

"Some even preferred prisons in England to this liberty in Holland, with such hardships," Bradford admitted.[4]

A decade of hard work and toil had not only taken a collective emotional toll on them, it had taken a physical toll. "Old age began to steal on many of them," Bradford wrote. Holland's toilsome work wore on their bodies with both age and injury. Even the children had to labor in the factories, often becoming "decrepit in their early youth."[5]

Hard labor was not their only cause for concern. They worried about the future of the congregation because the next generation was turning away from them.

"But still more lamentable," Bradford grieved, "and of all sorrows most heavy to be borne, was that many of their children . . . were led by evil example into dangerous courses, getting the reins off their necks and leaving their parents."[6]

Some of their children became soldiers, mercenaries fighting a foreign battle. Perhaps more disturbing, others answered the call of the ocean, joining Holland's merchant vessels notorious for long voyages and hard living. Still others, Bradford alluded, followed even worse courses to the danger of their souls.

Much to the dismay of their parents and elders, the Scrooby children were becoming Dutch. The vision of a religiously free mirror image of their life in England had been corrupted by the trappings of modern Holland as their children rejected the old way of life. If anything, perhaps, this concern held the greatest burden on their hearts. They had sacrificed a great deal to flee England to save their faith and lifestyle, and they would not see it squandered now by the rising generation.

"According to the divine proverb," Bradford wrote, "a wise man seeth the plague when it cometh, and hideth himself." And so the elders wondered if they could hide their community somewhere else where they would not be "surrounded by their enemies." As long as they continued living in Holland, the Dutch influence would deter their old way of life and impede their future. "Within a few years more," Bradford admitted, "they would be in danger to scatter."[7]

The elders vowed to begin a search. If they could find an easier, less distracting place to live, it might secure their future. Still, uprooting the congregation and moving it out of Holland posed a significant decision. They could accomplish their first two goals of improving their labor prospects and protecting the children. But the Scrooby congregation had altruistic reasons for a move too: it fulfilled the biblical call to spread the gospel.

They imagined their plan "for the propagation and advance of the gospel of the kingdom of Christ in those remote parts of the world." This vision stoked "great hope and inward zeal" among the congregation and galvanized their decision to leave Holland. "The place they fixed their thoughts upon was somewhere in those vast and unpeopled countries of America," Bradford recounted, "which were fruitful and fit for habitation, though devoid of all civilized inhabitants and given over to savages, who range up and down, differing little from the wild beasts of themselves."[8]

North America, uncharted and unregulated, shone as a beacon of hope. Despite their initial enthusiasm, the notion of uprooting to the New World had, from the outset, many detractors. Some presented well-founded reasons, citing known dangers and acknowledging many still inconceivable perils. Others turned to fearmongering, attempting to divert the undertaking.

Indeed, the congregation had many reasons to proceed

cautiously. As with any sea travel of the day, they expected casualties at sea. Not everyone would endure the arduous voyage, and those who did would find new miseries in wait. "They would be liable to famine, nakedness, and the want," Bradford noted. "The change of air, diet, and water would infect them with sickness and disease."[9] They would need to expect casualties upon arrival as well.

If they did survive the challenges of seventeenth-century travel, they would find themselves at risk of "the savage people." Bradford and the congregation had heard the stories of North America's native peoples. They would pose, perhaps, the greatest risk to their plan. Bradford detailed what he knew of them:

> . . . cruel, barbarous and most treacherous, being most furious in their rage and merciless where they overcome; not being content only to kill and take away life, but delight to torment men in the most bloody manner that may be; flaying some alive with the shells of fishes, cutting off the members and joints of others by piecemeal and broiling on the coals, eat the collops of their flesh in their sight whilst they live, with other cruelties horrible to be related.[10]

The mystery, rumors, and stories of North America, and its inhabitants, terrified the Scrooby congregation. Indeed, "the very hearing of these things," Bradford wrote, "could not but move the very bowels of men to grate within them and make the weak to quake and tremble."[11]

Beyond speculation and gossip, the congregation presented some practical reasons not to leave. Most notably, such a voyage would be costly. Not only would they need to furnish a boat and outfit it with several months of supplies, but they would need to hire a restocking voyage to follow. The congregation estimated that such plans could cost more than the combined value of their estates.

Then they recalled the hardship of their recent, short voyage across the North Sea. They had faced great challenges in this small endeavor, from the betrayal of a captain to the logistics of moving. It had not been an easy move, nor had their transition to Dutch life been smooth. They struggled to live in a strange place with unusual customs and unfamiliar languages. Yet Holland was a wealthy, developed neighboring nation. If they had struggled so severely with their European transition, could they really survive transatlantic emigration?

When they most needed comfort and encouragement, they received disheartening news. Another congregation of English Separatists had preceded the Scrooby congregation in its departure from Europe. In 1618, this congregation attempted a move to Virginia, but winds blew their ship far off course and sickness set in on them. The voyage claimed the life of the captain, most of the crew, and 130 of the 180 passengers on board. The tragedy cast a shadow of uncertainty over the Scrooby congregation's budding plans for the New World.

The debate over whether to move split the congregation. Bradford fell among those who held the position that they should leave Europe. They reasoned that, yes, it would be difficult, but all the presented dangers could be overcome. They would need the protection and fortitude of God, and they believed he had divinely anointed their purpose.

"Their condition was not ordinary," Bradford wrote, "their ends were good and honourable, their calling lawful and urgent; and therefore they might expect the blessing of God in their proceeding. Yea, though they should lose their lives in this action, yet might they have comfort in the same and their endeavours would be honourable."[12]

Eventually, the consensus coalesced toward departure. They believed their condition in Holland would not improve, and more likely, it would worsen. With the expiration of the Twelve Years' Truce upon them, they could hear "nothing but the beating of drums and preparing for war."[13] If they came under the dominion of the Spanish Crown, their liberty would surely be further suppressed.

What the Scrooby congregation had heard of North America came in myopic doses of propaganda—chiefly pamphlets and books published by adventurers and explorers. Many of these writers oversold North America, hoping to encourage colonization or justify the great expense of their rather lackluster expeditions. Other writers wanted to glorify themselves, consequently painting the journey in harrowing detail rife with danger and casting the Indians as their stories' compulsory villains.[14]

The Scrooby congregation prayed for guidance. Then, in short order, they came to a consensus: they must leave Holland. The burden in Holland was too great, and the risk of persecution too high. With an agreement as to their general intention, they stumbled into a much more divisive question: Where?

Guiana, in South America, made for an early and popular suggestion. Several of the congregation's leaders had read propaganda for Guiana: "rich, fruitful, and blessed with a perpetual spring, where nature brought forth all things in abundance without any great labour, and that the Spaniards, having much more than they could possess, had not yet settled there, or anywhere very near."[15] The warm climate and fertile soils sounded attractive. Others lobbied for North America's Virginia, primarily because English explorers had started mapping the coastline and occasionally sailed through on trading missions.

Yet for every positive perspective, they uncovered an equally alarming horror story: "grievous diseases, and many noisome impediments which other more temperate places are freer from."[16]

In addition to dangers of a tropical climate, they worried that the Spanish, who exercised great power in South America, could take their colonies at will. The Spanish had done so with the French in Florida, and the Scrooby congregation could do little to fortify against the Spanish navy. Britain certainly would not offer protection.

Virginia also had its shortcomings. The greatest risk they faced there might be from the person they had originally fled: King James. As English settlements increasingly dotted the Virginia coastline, the king would undoubtedly hear of known and notorious religious defectors. His wrath could easily find them.

Perhaps the Scrooby congregation could settle a sufficient distance from these colonies, but it would be hard to prevent a new English settlement from establishing itself close to them. Then, eventually, the convenience of trade would be outweighed by English zeal for control. If they lived, "so near them as to be under their government they should be in as great danger to be troubled and persecuted for the cause of religion as if they live in England and it might be worse."[17]

The Scrooby congregation carefully considered northern Virginia. They paid no attention to the lands that John Smith had deemed "New England," perhaps because of reports from Monhegan Island fishing outposts that winters proved too cold and inhospitable for a settlement. Or perhaps they feared that the name itself—New England—would presumptively subject them to English authority.

Should they choose Virginia, the Scrooby congregation had a practical challenge to overcome. First, the pioneers needed a "patent"—written permission to settle on the land. Originating from the practice of medieval guilds, a patent holder received a royally approved monopoly for an industry in exchange for paying taxes or duties.

The Virginia Company had obtained a "charter" for land along North America's eastern seaboard. The charter effectively gave the Virginia Company the approval to act as the settling agency, but it did not transfer land ownership of these lands to the company. For "ownership," they would need King James's signature on a patent. The leaders of the Virginia Company assured the Scrooby congregation that obtaining the patent would be no trouble.

"At length," Bradford wrote, "the conclusion was reached that they should live as a separate body by themselves under the general government of Virginia; and that through their friends they should sue his majesty to be pleased to allow them freedom of religion. That this might be granted they were led to hope by some prominent persons of rank and influence, who had become their friends."[18]

To secure royal permission, the congregation dispatched two of its elders to England, John Carver and Robert Cushman.[19] Both men had achieved some prominence and wealth in England, which the congregation reasoned might increase their chances of success. They carried a twofold objective: secure a royal patent for the land and negotiate the details of their voyage with the Virginia Company.

The Virginia Company had a grand vision for the colonization of America. Yet England's would-be emigrants to a new and uncharted land reciprocated with little enthusiasm. With only a few willing participants waiting on the fringe, they did not have the numbers to fill a ship. Adding to low demand, the cost of promoting the opportunity had run the company dry.

The Virginia Company had come upon hard times. For its doors to stay open, the company needed a quick influx of cash and the trophy of a successful settlement. Naturally, the company very much wanted to court the Scrooby congregation to North

America under its auspices. And it would willingly tiptoe around their Congregationalist notoriety to get the deal done.

To the Virginia Company's Edwin Sandys in London, John Carver delivered a letter dated December 15, 1617, from Robinson and Brewster outlining their intentions. In part, it read:

> We verily believe and trust that the Lord is with us, unto Whom and Whose service was have given ourselves in many trials; and that He will graciously prosper our endeavors according to the simplicity of our hearts therein. . . .
>
> We are knit together as a body in a most strict and sacred bond and covenant of the Lord, of the violation whereof we make great conscience, and by virtue whereof we hold ourselves straitly tied to all care of each other's good. . . .
>
> Lastly, we are not like some, whom small things discourage, or small discontents cause to wish themselves at home again.[20]

The congregation's ambassadors found their task of securing the patent much harder than the Virginia Company had led them to believe.[21] The patent would require King James's personal approval, but it would not be easy to receive, particularly for those who had already run afoul of him. Brewster's printing press confrontation would make it no easier.

Leveraging many of their old friendship and business contacts, the congregation drew up a patent request that eventually made its way to the desk of the king's chief secretary through a private motion.

The Scrooby Congregationalists presented themselves as "such people (who could not comfortably live under the government of another State) to enjoy their liberty of Conscience under his gracious protection in America, where they would endeavor the advancement of His Majesty's Dominions and the enlargement of the Gospel by all due means."[22]

The motion omitted the connection to Brewster, the persecution suffered in England, and Congregationalism altogether. King James failed to make the association. The religiously motivated appeal resonated with his sense that God favored his church. He also hungered to colonize the New World and knew his nation needed settlers willing to risk their lives.

"This is a good and honest motion," King James told his secretary. "What profit might arise in the part they intend?"[23]

"Fishing," the chief secretary replied.

"So God have my soul 'tis an honest trade," the king replied. "'Twas the Apostles' own calling."

The king's tacit approval came with the condition that they bring the matter to the bishops of Canterbury and London for their blessing. Although new men had taken these high-profile positions since the trial of Barrow and Greenwood, it still presented a formidable hurdle. These bishops would scrutinize the religious underpinnings of their request and likely connect them to the Congregationalist movement. Carver and Cushman thus received advice "not to entangle themselves with the bishops" and "to take what they had of the King's approbation."[24]

Indeed, they knew they could not trust the bishops, who would certainly deny the request and most likely pursue further punishment. They did not know whether they could, ultimately, trust King James either. Perhaps he had sincerely approved their request, but it was also plausible that he appeared to approve it, knowing the bishops would immediately quash it.

Word of their failure to secure a patent drifted back to the congregation in Leiden.[25]

"It provided a harder piece of work than they took it for," Bradford wrote, "for though many means were used to bring it about, yet it could not be effected; for there many of good worth laboured with King to obtain it (amongst whom was one of his Chief Secretaries) but it proved all in vain."[26]

After further deliberation, the congregation decided to avoid the king's approval altogether. They found a speculator willing to cooperate with them on arranging the voyage, including securing the patent in his name.[27] This resolution disappointed the Scrooby congregation since it would not be in the name of any in their party, but they could imagine no other path forward.

"And this matter of the patent is a true emblem of the uncertain things of this world," Bradford wrote, "when men [who] have toiled to acquire them vanish into smoke!"[28]

Cushman conveyed the dispiriting report from London and tried to present it as positively as possible: "I see none here discouraged much," he told them, "but rather desire to learn to beware by other men's harms, and to amend that wherein they have failed."[29]

Following this news, the congregation gathered together for "a solemn meeting and a day of humiliation to seek the Lord's direction."

Pastor Robinson read from 1 Samuel 23:3–4: "And David's men said unto him, see, we be afraid here in Judah; how much more if we come to Keilah against the host of the Philistines? Then David asked counsel of the Lord again. And the Lord answered him, and said, Arise, go down to Keilah for I will deliver the Philistines into thine hands."

"From this text," Bradford recalled of Robinson, "he taught things very aptly and befitting the present occasion—strengthening them against their fears and perplexities, and encouraging them in their resolutions."[30]

Following their day of prayer, the Scrooby congregation leaders emerged determined to go to the New World. The congregation turned to the next task: Who should go and who should stay? Those who would remain in Holland would do so only temporarily, the congregation assured itself. As soon as they had established the colony, they would send for the others.

Although Brewster remained in hiding, they nominated him as their leader for the voyage to the New World. John Robinson, their pastor, would stay with the flock in Leiden until they had established the colony. He would join the others on a later migration.

With Carver and Cushman in England building support, Captain John Smith took an immediate interest in their cause. Unlike most New World promoters, Smith had greater interests than mere financial gain. He wanted to lead them. The Scrooby congregation needed a military adviser to accompany them since no one had the experience to defend a colony. The congregation planned to hire one, and Smith desired to return to Virginia, so he duly proposed himself as their leader.[31]

Smith's proposal turned off Carver and Cushman. The decorated captain seemed too aristocratic and dismissive of their ideas of a self-governed community. More importantly, he distanced himself from their religious motivations. Carver and Cushman declined. This reply surprised Smith, who later dismissed the congregation's rejection by saying, "my books and maps were . . . cheape[r] to teach them, than myself."[32] He later complained of their democratic ideas, lamenting that they wanted to be "Lords and Kings of themselves."[33]

Arrangements with the Virginia Company began to disintegrate, and the congregation grew increasingly skeptical. They felt misled about their prospects for receiving a patent and generally discouraged by their lack of assistance. They began considering other options for arranging the voyage and inquired with several Dutch shipping agencies.

About the same time, Thomas Weston, a London merchant,

came to Leiden. Weston knew many of the Scrooby members and had assisted them in some of the later arrangements for moving the congregation to Holland. When Weston learned of their troubles, he requested a meeting with Robinson and the church leaders. He encouraged them to keep pursuing their journey but not to rely on Dutch shippers or the Virginia Company.

"[F]ear neither want of shipping nor of money," he told them, "what they needed should be provided."[34] He had another option for them.

Weston presented them with an offer. If he and the Scrooby congregation could come to terms, he might persuade his friends in London to fund the venture. They had received a land grant from the king for the northern coastline of New England, and now they needed settlers to colonize it. The offer sounded perfect to the Scrooby congregation, particularly since they had a history of successful arrangements with him. Together with Weston, they drafted an agreement for him to review with his friends in London. Weston assured them he could get the voyage funded.

Trusting Weston's confidence, the members of the Scrooby congregation began preparing furiously for their departure. Many sold their homes and property and pooled together their money. It seemed the congregation had found the perfect partner and a reason to finally dismiss the Virginia Company.

In London, Weston's friends reviewed the contract. Calling themselves the "Merchant Adventurers,"[35] they agreed to fund the voyage, pending significant revisions to the contract, largely in their favor. Still in London, Carver and Cushman met with the Merchant Adventurers to negotiate the modified terms without consulting the Scrooby congregation.

The contract read that the partnership with the Merchant Adventurers would last seven years with profits held in common stock. After seven years, capital and profits, including houses, land, and all goods, would be divided equally between Merchant Adventurers and settlers. After the division, the parties would be free of each other.[36]

The contract did not sit well in Leiden. Carver and Cushman had not consulted the congregation with respect to final terms. In particular, the Merchant Adventurers struck the congregation's request to allow the settlers to work for themselves two days each week. Under the modified provision, the Merchant Adventurers owned the rights to all their labors and work product—all week. Also, the congregation had originally intended that at the end of the seven-year partnership, their property, including land, homes, and personal goods, would remain the property of the congregation. Not so under the new contract, which required them to split it with the Merchant Adventurers.

As the dispute progressed, several members of the congregation backed out of the voyage. Many of those who had the most to lose under the contract left first, and along with them went their money. The retractions left the congregation far short of the money the Merchant Adventurers required to underwrite the voyage.

"There is fallen already amongst us a flat schism," Cushman said, "and we are readier to go to dispute than to set forward a voyage."[37]

Weston had organized seventy investors. With a significant amount of money on the line, as well as his reputation, he remained determined to find a way to make up the financial shortfall. He immediately began soliciting interested candidates in London to join the voyage.

The Merchant Adventurers readily found willing participants to fill their ship. Much to the chagrin of the Scrooby congregation, the Merchant Adventurers cared little about the religious convictions of the new volunteers. Most of the new applicants would not be Separatists, and the Scrooby congregation would give them the sobriquet of "Strangers." Many of the Strangers called them-selves Puritans, which the Separatists regarded as pragmatically equivalent to the Church of England.[38] Others claimed to be non-religious or agnostic, but to the Separatists, all were undesirable and polluted their religious ambitions for the voyage.

Despite fading hope in the voyage, the congregation had proceeded too far to completely back out. The majority still believed that their faith risked more by idling in Holland than journeying to the New World accompanied by a theologically incorrect minority. Then suddenly, their plans lurched forward. "At length after much travail and these debates of all things were got ready and provided. A small ship was bought,"[39] Bradford wrote.

At only sixty tons, the *Speedwell* would journey with them to the New World, then remain there in their care for exploration and fishing. The vessel, different from the one of the same name on Martin Pring's expedition, had its own illustrious history, participating in the sea battle that defeated the Spanish Armada and making various international expeditions. Yet time had taken its toll on the vessel, and the *Speedwell* arrived in a poor, leaking condition.

With the passenger list ballooning to accommodate the Merchant Adventurers' contingent, the expedition would require a second vessel. The Scrooby congregation had purchased the *Speedwell*, but they would only charter the second boat, which had been arranged for them. They would rendezvous with the second ship, the much larger *Mayflower*, in London.

At 100 feet in length and 25 feet wide, the *Mayflower* made an excellent cargo ship for transport across Europe.[40] During the previous decade, the vessel had made many such trips across the English Channel, to Scandinavia, and throughout the Mediterranean. Its design was common for its day, built for long ocean voyages and sizable storage. For the convenience of its captain and crew, the *Mayflower*'s main deck had "castles" aft and fore—boxy rooms providing protection from the wind and waves. Towering over its deck stood three masts with square-rigged sails. The *Mayflower* would loom over the *Speedwell*.

By the time Weston arranged its charter, the *Mayflower* had passed its prime. It was now an old ship nearing the end of its useful life—a standard of approximately fifteen years for its day. Master Christopher Jones had captained the *Mayflower* for eleven years, principally ferrying wine to England from France.[41] The proposed journey to North America would account for its most arduous voyage thus far.

Instead of Captain Smith, the Scrooby congregation appointed the role of military adviser to a man named Miles Standish.[42] Despite being a man of small stature, Standish embodied a large persona. His quick temper and bellicose personality let him excel on the battlefield but often got the better of him on the home front. Standish carried the weight of disappointment. He alleged a rightful stake in a large family estate, but his inheritance had somehow been revoked. This incident, in part, had led him to join England's armed forces.

Standish arrived in Holland in the care of the English military. Prior to the Twelve Years' Truce, England had sided with the Dutch to oppose Spanish occupation near their shores. Standish served as an officer among the English troops sent to Holland.[43] After Holland and Spain signed the truce, Standish and his wife, Rose, decided to stay in Holland and settle in Leiden. There he came into the orbit of Pastor John Robinson, and although he did not join Robinson's church, he became quite close to the pastor. When Robinson's flock went looking for a military adviser, Robinson recommended Standish.

By July 1620, the congregation had two boats arranged, thirty-five Separatists committed, and a military adviser hired.

The reality of the voyage finally began to set in upon them. Friends and family knew they would soon be saying good-byes. The Leiden contingent planned to cast off the mooring lines in only twenty-two days.

". . . the rest of the time was spent pouring out prayers to the Lord with great fervency, mixed with abundance of tears," Bradford wrote.[44]

⚬⚬⚬⚬

As spring arrived in North America, Thomas Dermer departed Jamestown to sail for Maine. There he would rendezvous with Squanto to continue their work for peace. After Jamestown, he eagerly anticipated his return to the fishing outpost on Monhegan Island, where he could once again send and receive messages on English vessels.

From Monhegan Island, Dermer and Squanto continued their mission throughout the summer. They also sent a message back to Gorges with specific recommendations: "I would [advise]," Dermer wrote to Gorges, "that the first plantation might here be seated if there come to the number of fifty persons or upward."[45]

After sending their letters, the peace mission set sail back down the coast for Virginia with Squanto, Dermer, and several English sailors. Eventually they reached Capawock, where they had met with Epenow the previous summer. Dermer expected a cold but courteous welcome from Epenow. He knew Epenow had deceived the 1614 English expedition that returned him to North America, but Dermer believed his peace mission had made progress. Their risky, but peaceful meeting last year, in Dermer's view, had significantly promoted diplomacy. Their return visit would only build upon that foundation.

Dermer and Squanto sailed into Capawock. They landed

on the beach with intentions of trading and meeting with Epenow.[46] A crowd surrounded them. Suddenly Epenow's warriors scattered among the gathering and rushed at Dermer and Squanto, attempting to capture them.[47] Dermer fought back and, wrestling his arm free of his attackers, drew his sword.[48] Dermer managed to reach the boat and climbed on board. Behind him, all his men had fallen. Only the boatman, who had waited on board their vessel, survived. Even Squanto had been captured. Epenow had suffered a loss, too, with several of his warriors among the dead.

As they hurriedly sailed away from shore, Dermer directed his boatman to set a course for Virginia. Lying on the floor of the boat, Dermer bled profusely. He could count fourteen wounds.[49]

Epenow retained Squanto under guard on Capawock. As likely a gesture of allegiance, Epenow sent word of Squanto's capture to Massasoit, who might better assess Squanto's loyalty and navigate the political implications of his European ties and his claimed Patuxet roots. Since the Patuxet tribe fell under the dominion of the sachem's confederacy, Squanto might be one of the last, if not the last, of a people pledged in allegiance to the sachem. Indeed, Massasoit wanted the captive and arranged with Epenow for his transfer.

Dermer was not as fortunate as Squanto. His ship made it to Virginia, but he succumbed to his injuries there.

❧

In Leiden, the Scrooby congregation bustled with preparations for an imminent departure. Not everyone would go. Families would divide and promises would be made to come on the next trip. For those leaving, these would be their final moments in Leiden.

"[T]hey knew they were pilgrims," Bradford famously wrote,

"and looked not much on these things, but lifted up their eyes to the heavens, their dearest country, and quieted their spirits."[50]

They would convene together as a congregation one final time at the docks. "[T]hey were accompanied with most of their brethren out of the city, unto a town sundry miles off called Delfshaven, where the ship lay ready to receive them," Bradford noted, ". . . so they left that good and pleasant city, which had been their resting place near twelve years."[51]

On July 21, 1620, the day before their departure, the Pilgrims gathered together in Delfshaven with their friends and families. Pastor Robinson had prepared a farewell sermon. He began with a reading from Ezra 8:21: "And there at the river, by Ahava, I proclaimed a fast, that we might humble ourselves before our God, and seek of him a right way for us, and for our children, and for all our substance" (GENEVA BIBLE).

Robinson would not join the Pilgrims, although he very much wanted to do so. With his congregation divided, he felt compelled to remain with the members in Holland. They needed his cohesion more than the Pilgrims unified by a common goal. He promised to join them in the New World on an upcoming voyage.

Then he began his sermon:

> We are now ere long to part asunder, and the Lord knoweth whether ever he should live to see our faces again. But whether the Lord had appointed it or not, he charged us before God and his blessed angels, to follow him no further than he followed Christ; and if God should reveal any thing to us by any other instrument of his, to be as ready to receive it as ever we were to receive any truth by his ministry.[52]

Robinson had put a great deal of thought into the Pilgrims' departure and had practical advice to offer them. He saw the

New World as an opportunity for a fresh start and new identity. They could distance themselves from the stigmatizing labels of Brownist, Barrowist, and Separatist, "a mere nickname and brand to make religion odious," he said.

Robinson further recognized that the Pilgrims might tread into English territory in the New World, and for many, the wounds of Scrooby had not yet healed. Robinson advised "rather to study union than division." At the very least, they should mitigate their estrangement.

The pastor worried about the Pilgrims' spiritual journey in his absence. He feared they would become self-righteous in their quest—appointing themselves as a chosen people called out by God for this noble mission. As such, he worried that the Pilgrims might expect intense revelations from God, or scorn his abandonment in hard times. Robinson would not be there to guide them through. "It is not possible the Christian world should come so lately out of such thick antichristian darkness, and that full perfection of knowledge should break forth at once," he warned them.

For the Pilgrims, this July evening grew to a long and emotional night. They all knew the morning would radically change them. Friends and families would be divided. Husbands and wives would be separated. Bradford would take his wife but leave behind his son. The Brewsters would take their two youngest children but leave behind their two oldest children.

"That night was spent with little sleep by most," Bradford recollected, "but with friendly entertainment and Christian discourse and other real expressions of true Christian love."[53]

On July 22, 1620, the Pilgrims and their families began gathering at Delfshaven's wharf along the old, wooden seawall. Above them, tall, narrow houses crowded the canal banks and compressed the emotional turnout.[54] Among the intricate series of canals lined with ships sat the *Speedwell*, readied for their departure. Bradford wrote:

> [T]he wind being fair they went aboard and their friends with them, where truly doleful was the sight of that sad and mournful parting, to see what sighs and sobs and prayers did sound amongst them, what tears did gush from every eye, and pithy speeches pierced each heart. . . . Yet comfortable and sweet it was to see such lively and true expressions of dear and unfeigned love.[55]

On the dock, a group of Dutch had amassed at the sight. As they watched, they, too, could not refrain from tears.

"But the tide, which stays for no man, calling them away that were thus loath to depart," Bradford wrote. They gathered, fittingly, in front of Oude of Pelgrimvaderskerk, an old church near the docks.[56] With his congregation around him, Pastor Robinson fell to his knees with tears streaming down his face. All those surrounding him soon joined him. Robinson broke into the "most fervent prayers to the Lord" asking for his blessing on the voyage and on the congregation staying in Leiden. "And then," said Bradford, "with mutual embraces and many tears they took their leaves one of another, which proved to be the last leave to many of them."[57]

The *Speedwell* cast off its bowlines. With the Union Jack flying high on the mast above them, they fired a volley of musket shot and three rounds of ordnance as they drifted out of the harbor. The Leiden congregation watched as the *Speedwell* disappeared over the horizon.

Chapter Seven

Storms on the Ocean

NORTH SEA

JULY 1620

T he *Speedwell* set a quick tempo under a "prosperous wind" as it darted its way toward England.[1] The Pilgrims would dock at Southampton on England's southern coast to rendezvous with the *Mayflower*. From there, the two ships would voyage into the unknown.

In Southampton, the Leiden contingent would finally meet the Strangers—the settlers recruited by the Merchant Adventurers to make up the funding shortfall. The two parties did not mix well. Hard-line religious affiliations aside, they had members with strong personalities and a different sense of duty.

Their first clash involved port fees: Southampton demanded one hundred English pounds to clear port.[2] The Leiden group had invested everything in the voyage, even more so as their subscription declined. When Strangers refused to contribute toward the fee, the Leiden passengers were forced to take drastic action.

"So they were forced to sell off some of their provisions to stop this gap,"[3] Bradford explained. They had packed light, not imagining they would need goods to barter with in England, and thus had little they could spare. Only butter had a ready market and a manageable risk of loss. They sold it all.[4] The butter—concentrated fat—was their insurance policy for surviving a harsh winter. Its extensive supply, in emergency, would have provided a ration of approximately forty pounds of butter per passenger.

Such extreme measures drove the Leiden leaders to pen a letter to the Merchant Adventurers: "We are in such a strait at present, as we are forced to sell away sixty pounds' worth of our provisions to clear the haven and withal to put ourselves upon great extremities, scarce having any butter, no oil, not a sole to mend a shoe, nor every man a sword to his side." Wrote another passenger, "We are willing to expose ourselves to such eminent dangers as are like to ensue, and trust to the good providence of God."[5]

Still docked at Southampton, mariners discovered technical problems: the *Speedwell* had sprung a leak. The leak forced them to retrim the boat, an effort that would put the Pilgrims another week behind. In addition to complications with their vessel, the Pilgrims had not yet agreed to the final contract with Weston. Neither party would compromise on the terms, and on the day they prepared for departure, the Pilgrims categorically rejected it.

Finally, after much labor, the captain deemed the *Speedwell* seaworthy. On August 5, 1620, the *Speedwell* weighed anchor and, notwithstanding adverse winds, set sail for the New World alongside the *Mayflower*.

Despite their best repair efforts in port and a promising start, the *Speedwell* began leaking again at sea—without ceasing. The captain of the *Speedwell* signaled to the *Mayflower*, and the ships rendezvoused to discuss the dilemma. This was no minor leak: the crew could not pump the water out fast enough to keep up.

After a thorough inspection, the crew discovered a loose

plank, two feet long, where water flowed in as freely "as a mole hole," in the words of the *Speedwell* captain.[6] Cushman pronounced the vessel "as open and leaky as a sieve."[7]

After only six days of sailing, the *Speedwell's* captain scrubbed the mission. He tacked the ship, turning the *Speedwell* back toward the English coast with plans to dock at Dartmouth for repairs. The repairs would consume nine grueling days of labor, made even more painful as passengers watched favorable winds pass. The days lost to repairs would have put them significantly close to halfway across the Atlantic.

"She was here thoroughly searched from stem to stern," Bradford said. "Some leaks were found and mended, and now it was conceived by the workmen and all, that she was sufficient, and they might proceed without either fear or danger."[8]

The tension between the Leiden group and the Strangers grew severer as delays jeopardized the journey. One Stranger became intolerable. Christopher Martin had amassed sizable wealth as a merchant, but his vocal Puritan beliefs embroiled him in a public conflict with the Anglican Church. The New World had long interested him, and he possessed the means for the voyage. Leaving England would help him avoid further consequences for his beliefs. Martin wanted to see matters resolved as he directed and would meddle as he saw fit. His continual intrusions frustrated the captain and crew to the extent that they began to plot against him and he found himself continually at odds with the other passengers. As exasperation with Martin reached its peak, the passengers learned that the *Speedwell* was seaworthy.

Once again, the *Speedwell* and the *Mayflower* set sail together, departing from Dartmouth on August 23.[9] No farther than three hundred miles from land, the hull of the *Speedwell* began to fill with water yet again. Although they pumped what water they could, it began to fill at a dangerous pace and they could not keep up.

The master of the *Speedwell* gave them two choices: return to England or sink at sea. The *Speedwell*'s inevitable return, unfortunately, would jeopardize the entire plan. It carried passengers and cargo critical to the group's settlement, and its return would force the *Mayflower* to turn around as well. Together, the *Mayflower* and *Speedwell* sailed into England's Plymouth Harbor where the *Speedwell* underwent an immediate inspection.

"[N]o special leak could be found," Bradford explained, "but it was judged to be the general weakness of the ship, and that she would not prove sufficient for the voyage. Upon which it was resolved to dismiss her and part of the company, and proceed with the other ship."[10]

Many of the Pilgrims remained unwilling to blame the delay on structural problems.[11] Instead, they suspected a conspiracy led by the *Speedwell*'s captain.[12] "[B]y the cunning and deceit of the master and his company, who were hired to stay a whole year in the country and now fearing want of [food provisions], they plotted this stratagem to free themselves."[13]

Conspiracy or not, the emergency stop in Plymouth Harbor would not be a short one. Down to one boat, it would now be impossible for everyone to make the journey. They would remain in the harbor until a new plan could be put in place.

Plymouth Harbor played host to voluminous maritime traffic, particularly as a departure point for North America. The harbor's fishing fleet, dedicated to the summer season off the coast of Maine, had grown to more than fifty vessels. And from Plymouth's docks departed many of the expeditions and trading missions to the New World.

Captain John Smith made his home at Plymouth Harbor, and several Pilgrims met with him. Smith remained a strong proponent of New England. In addition to providing the Pilgrims with important firsthand information on the coastline, much of which he had documented in his maps and his book, *A Description of New England*, Smith made a final pitch to join them, offering to lead and advise the Pilgrims. He ominously warned them to expect conditions much harsher than they imagined. The Pilgrims declined again.

The Pilgrims spent fourteen days in Plymouth Harbor, putting their voyage now, in total, nearly seven weeks behind schedule. To make matters worse, Christopher Martin used the opportunity to widen the rift among the voyagers. A growing contingent no longer wanted to proceed, "either out of some discontent or fear they conceived of the ill success of the voyage seeing so many crosses befall and the year time so far spent."[14]

Counting the passengers who changed their minds and those who had to stay behind due to limited available space on the *Mayflower*, twenty of the voyagers returned to London on board the *Speedwell*. The most notable among them included Robert Cushman. Although Cushman, a respected elder who had negotiated the voyage, could have had priority space on the *Mayflower*, he had become seriously ill to the point where he could not proceed. He and his entire family bid farewell to their friends. Eleven remaining passengers from the *Speedwell* packed into the already crowded *Mayflower*, lifting the total head count to 102.

"Wednesday the sixth of September, the wind coming east-north-west, a fine small gale, we loosed the Plymouth," noted Edward Winslow.[15]

At approximately one hundred feet in length, the *Mayflower* granted each passenger only a few square feet of personal space.[16] The voyagers spread out as much as they could, sleeping not only in the *Mayflower*'s hull, but also on its deck, in its longboat, and in the "shallop," an open boat with oars and sail that they would assemble upon arrival.

The *Mayflower*'s three decks offered little respite from its crowded discomforts. In good weather, passengers might spend time on the main deck, milling around the *Mayflower*'s three masts in the space between the fore and aft castles. The floor below—the gun deck—contained the shared living space. The cannons that might regularly be positioned along the edges of the gun deck had been locked up in the rear to create more open space. For bathroom facilities, a simple bucket offered their only toilet. The lowest deck—the cargo hold—held their belongings and food stores.

The years and months since the Pilgrims decided to leave England had significantly transformed them. They now looked very little like the congregation in Scrooby, inspired by a flight for religious refuge. Although the *Mayflower* now boasted a crowded 102 passengers, they had retained only 35 Pilgrims from the Leiden church. By contrast, the demography included nearly 40 English Puritans, 18 servants, and 5 hired men.

Only six members of the original Scrooby congregation were among the *Mayflower* passengers.[17] Some, like Bradford, had married and started families in Leiden, but overall very few shared the history rooted in Scrooby. Nonetheless, the Pilgrims had retained the heart and soul of Scrooby: Bradford and Brewster.[18]

Of the servants, eleven men were contractually indentured, a practice common in English colonies. These men had agreed to work exclusively for their master for a period of time—typically seven years—in exchange for room, board, and passage on board the *Mayflower*. Those who agreed to indenturement often came from a life of grinding poverty and found servitude a means of rising into a new class, and even a form of apprenticeship.

The most serious loss from the delay at Plymouth Harbor

was that they had missed the best summer wind patterns. The sailing had started out fine, but halfway across the Atlantic, the *Mayflower* cruised into an autumn gale. The winds fought against the ship, bringing its progress to a near standstill as it slowly tacked upwind in a zigzag fashion. For the passengers, seemingly unending rough waters led to widespread seasickness.

Despite the chaos and continual setbacks, the Pilgrims accounted for God's providence in even grisly incidents:

> There was a proud and very profane young man, one of the seamen, of a lusty, able body, which made him the more haughty; he would always be contemning the poor people in their [sea]sickness, and cursing them daily with grievous execrations, and did not let to tell them, that he hoped to help cast half of them overboard before they came to their journey's end, and to make merry with what they had; and if he were by any gently reproved, he would curse and swear most bitterly.
>
> But it pleased God before they came half seas over, to smite this young man with a grievous disease, of which he died in a desperate manner, and so was himself the first that was thrown overboard. Thus his curses light on his own head; and it was an astonishment to all his fellows, for they noted it to be the just hand of God upon him.[19]

The Pilgrims' hubris in such moments galvanized their aspirations to continue the voyage in spite of the tumultuous circumstances. During one of the fiercest storms they encountered, the main deck beam cracked. Such extensive damage led to discussion of turning back for England again. They decided, instead, to attempt a repair at sea.

The Pilgrims had brought an iron screw jack for building homes. They placed a post under the beam and raised it back into position. The precarious operation sealed the crack and reinforced the beam. It worked.

The storms kept coming. At times, the winds grew so strong that it forced the *Mayflower* to furl its sails and drift in the waves, occasionally for days at a time. Such periods adrift set them back farther and left North America feeling unreachable.

During one of these storms, John Howland, a young man accompanying the Leiden group, ventured above deck. Howland had grown up in rural England and, now in his early twenties, joined the voyage as servant to John Carver. Howland quickly learned that the deck of the ship during a storm could become a dangerous place.

Between the waves breaking across the deck and sudden shifts of the boat, Howland tripped and fell over the railing. Drowning in the dark, frigid water, his hands astonishingly found a rope. He held on tightly to the line dragging from the ship's highest sail. Waves broke over him, and between swells the rope pulled him down ten feet.

From the deck of the *Mayflower*, the crew spotted Howland amid the waves and started to pull him toward the boat. Once they had pulled him to within a few feet, they reached down with a boat hook to snag him and pull him on board.

Between the coincidental death of the profane sailor, the surprising repair of the broken beam, and the miraculous rescue of Howland, the Pilgrims found proof that God had anointed their voyage.

Despite the perilous trip and dangerous North Atlantic storms, the Pilgrims lost only one of its number—a young man who had been ill for most of the voyage. Their community also grew by one member, a baby boy born at sea and fittingly named Oceanus Hopkins.

Tempering the pain of losing a member of the party, only

three days later they caught their first glimpse of North America. It appeared, at first, as a simple line on the horizon, but soon a vast, unsettled coastline spread out before them. They had finally found the Atlantic shoreline of Cape Cod. It was a joyous sight.

With land now mere yards from their ship, it seemed farther away than ever. Although Captain Jones and the Pilgrims desperately wanted to anchor the *Mayflower* and go ashore, they would have to wait. They could see no place to safely land. The tumultuous Atlantic violently tossed itself upon a rocky shoreline in boat-crushing, unforgiving waves. A shore landing, even in the nimbler long boat, would be impossible. They turned the *Mayflower* south to sail parallel with the coast and set their bearings.

The Pilgrims deliberated with Jones on where they should attempt a landing. They agreed to continue south and make their settlement near the mouth of the Hudson River, an area at the northern border of the Virginia Company's patent.

With promising winds and seas, they set a course to sail south down the Atlantic shore of Cape Cod. After half a day, conditions grew precarious. The wind rose and seas grew rough. Before they could change course, the *Mayflower* sailed into dangerous shoals, roaring surf, and boiling seas. Terrified, many of the passengers huddled together anticipating the ship to run aground or capsize. Jones reacted swiftly, sailing them back into safer waters.

After their near disaster, Jones changed course, refusing to continue south toward the Hudson River. He decided to return to Cape Cod, tacking the *Mayflower* and sailing northeast for the open Atlantic Ocean. The Pilgrims objected—they had chosen the Hudson River, not Cape Cod. Jones would not comply, leading the conspiracy theorists to speculate that Dutch prospectors had bribed Jones to make the change. Perhaps, they wondered, this redirection would allow the Dutch to settle the Hudson River for themselves.[20]

The next morning, Jones caught up to the arm of Cape Cod, tacking along its shore until he could anchor in the wind shadow behind its hook.

"Being thus arrived in a good harbor and brought safe to land, they fell upon their knees and blessed the God of heaven, who had brought them over the vast and furious ocean, and delivered them from all the perils and miseries thereof, again to set their feet on the firm and stable earth, their proper element," Bradford wrote.[21]

With a vast area of land before them, they could finally venture out to find "a place for habitation."[22]

Bradford wrote of their joy:

What, then, could now sustain them but the spirit of God, and His grace? Ought not the children of their fathers rightly to say: Our fathers were Englishmen who came over the great ocean, and were ready to perish in this wilderness; but they cried unto the Lord, and He heard their voice, and looked on their adversity . . . let them therefore praise the Lord because He is good, and His mercies endure forever. Yea, let them that have been redeemed of the Lord, how He hath delivered them from the hand of the oppressor. When they wandered forth into the desert-wilderness, out of the way, and found no city to dwell in, both hungry and thirsty, their soul was overwhelmed in them. Let them confess before the Lord His loving kindness, and His wonderful works before the sons of men!"[23]

Part Three ———————————————

THANKS

Chapter Eight

The New World

NOVEMBER 1620

CAPE COD

Twenty-three thousand years before the *Mayflower* voyage, glaciers had formed Cape Cod's curious landscape—a desolate and foreboding stretch of sand arcing more than fifty miles out into the Atlantic.[1] The Cape resembled the shape of a bent arm adorned with a handlike hook at its tip. The hook formed a natural harbor where the *Mayflower* could anchor in much calmer waters.

By the time the *Mayflower* set its anchor in mid-November 1620, winter had nearly set in upon them.[2] Time was now of the essence. From the deck of the *Mayflower*, they gazed upon the cape—an inhospitable stretch of vast, barren sand dunes. As unwelcoming as it may be, and as undesirable a place as it appeared to settle, the Cape was at hand.

The Pilgrims knew almost nothing of the mainland except what they had read in Captain Smith's books. They heard rumors of miles upon miles of virgin forest. They expected oaks, pines, and junipers that grew down to the water's edge, holding back rich, black earth. They read about cedars and maples covering the hills, while swampy marshes made their homes in the valleys. The Cape looked nothing like what they had imagined.

The late season and precarious weather made them decidedly less fastidious about the land they would settle—they needed immediate emergency refuge. Perhaps the promises of Smith's books existed somewhere in the New World, but not here on the Cape. The real-life vision of the New World before them felt as far away as Europe, but they had run out of time to search. The Pilgrims needed to go ashore.

On the deck of the *Mayflower*, the voyagers gathered in the cold November breeze. They assembled, not to celebrate their landing, but to settle long-churning disputes before anyone stepped off the boat. With "discontented and mutinous" speeches, men came forward to air grievances that had started while they tossed and turned on the Atlantic. The divide between the Separatists of Leiden and the Strangers of England had grown deeper. If this enterprise continued, they would need to reconcile.

A technical dilemma exacerbated the situation: the patent gave them settlement rights in Virginia to the south, not New England—their current location. If they settled in Virginia, as they had planned, then the Virginia Company patent controlled, establishing a prearranged government structure with ultimate authority resting in King James. Settling in New England, as appeared imminent, would leave them unbound by a patent and without an overriding government structure. Once they stepped off the *Mayflower*, their small band of voyagers became a rogue nation.

The Strangers flexed their muscles around this interpretation, threatening that once on shore, "they would use their own liberty, as none had power to command them."[3]

Through the diplomacy of John Carver, they deliberated over their differences. All agreed that very little of the fall season remained and that they might expect difficulties over the winter. They had overheard the sailors saying that if the voyagers did not disembark soon, the captain might force them ashore so the *Mayflower* could return to England before winter.

In short order, they agreed to find a path to work together. In the absence of lawfully binding government authority, they determined to first establish an authority of their own creation. With many well-read leaders, they departed from contemporary European thinking. Unlike Europe, they would have no king, pope, or state church. They would have a government operating by the consent of the people.

They agreed, at least on paper, to pledge the colony's allegiance to King James. For the safety of the colony, and particularly for the Puritans on board, they needed to appear as though they had not staged a rebellion against the Crown. Practically, as well, they all recognized their reliance, at least in principle, on the king's patent.

Still on board the *Mayflower*, the Separatists and Strangers agreed to commit this new model of government to writing. On November 11, led by John Carver, they scrawled out a document: the Mayflower Compact.

IN THE NAME OF GOD, AMEN. We, whose names are underwritten, the Loyal Subjects of our dread Sovereign Lord King *James*, by the Grace of God, of *Great Britain*, *France*, and *Ireland*, King, *Defender of the Faith*, &c.

Having undertaken for the Glory of God, and Advancement of the Christian Faith, and the Honour of our King and Country, a Voyage to plant the first Colony in the northern Parts of *Virginia*; Do by these Presents, solemnly and mutually, in the Presence of God and one another, covenant and combine ourselves together into a civil Body

Politick, for our better Ordering and Preservation, and Furtherance of the Ends aforesaid: And by Virtue hereof do enact, constitute, and frame, such just and equal Laws, Ordinances, Acts, Constitutions, and Officers, from time to time, as shall be thought most meet and convenient for the general Good of the Colony; unto which we promise all due Submission and Obedience. IN WITNESS whereof we have hereunto subscribed our names at *Cape-Cod* the eleventh of November, in the Reign of our Sovereign Lord King *James*, of *England*, *France*, and *Ireland*, the eighteenth, and of *Scotland* the fifty-fourth, *Anno Domini*; 1620.[4]

The Mayflower Compact was an experiment—born out of necessity, but an experiment no less. They needed a local government, and they needed to maintain the whole of their enterprise. For this experiment, they had no template—a government formed contractually by the consent of the governed was revolutionary. For much of the world, and England in particular, monarchy and feudalism reigned as the practiced form of rule. The Separatists and the Strangers had never seen, nor experienced, an official democratic process. Yet Carver and Brewster had studied the classics of literature and philosophy. The opportunity to thoughtfully craft a new approach for the New World excited them.

The drafters intended that the Mayflower Compact be signed before anyone stepped ashore. One by one, every adult male passenger who intended to permanently settle in North America inked his name at the bottom of the compact. From the Separatist contingent, their most respected leaders put their names on the document, including Carver, Brewster, Bradford, Standish, and Winslow. The Strangers agreed to it as well, including the contentious Christopher Martin. In total, forty-one men ratified the agreement.

After all had signed it, they convened again in the captain's room. They had one final question to resolve before they could go ashore. Who would act as governor to administer the colony?

While several men from the Strangers may have wished for this authority, a Stranger as governor would not sit well with the Separatists. They had organized the voyage, and the Strangers had accepted their empty seats. The leader would be a Separatist.

William Brewster's seniority and influence naturally positioned him for the colony's chief leader. Brewster's résumé, however, had one condemning title: clergy. The Separatists and Strangers had suffered long enough under the combined authority of church and state. Although they believed their faith to be true, they refused to make the same fatal error again. A clergyman would not serve as governor.

John Carver, on the other hand, was not clergy. He not only had the confidence of his Separatist colleagues, he appeased the Strangers. He had served as lay leader of the church in Leiden, but never as a minister. Administratively, he led efforts to negotiate their passage to the New World and acted informally as governor on board the *Mayflower*. He wrote the Mayflower Compact and offered his signature to it first.

They chose John Carver, and his election set a tone for the separation of church and state.

With a consensus on government, the Pilgrims could now go ashore. Sixteen men volunteered to make an initial survey of Cape Cod. They lowered the ship's longboat and began rowing toward the sandy beach. The men remaining on the *Mayflower* turned their attention to assembling the shallop, which would stay with the Pilgrims when the *Mayflower* returned and would accommodate a larger shore party.

That evening, the longboat returned. Reconnaissance from

the investigators returned little information of value. They recovered some juniper for firewood but saw no signs of people and found no freshwater.

On Monday, the longboat began shuttling passengers from the *Mayflower* to the beach. This retreat from the *Mayflower* offered the first chance in many months for the Pilgrims to stretch their legs. They posted guards along the beach while the children played in the sand and anyone physically able searched for shellfish—their first fresh food in more than two months.

That day, the men moved the shallop off the deck of the *Mayflower* and floated it to shore. Once fully assembled, they would use it to explore more of the coastline in search of a proper settlement site. After the treacherous Atlantic crossing, the shallop needed more repair than anticipated. It would require several days of work to be seaworthy.

The Pilgrims had hired Captain Miles Standish to head their security and military strategy. On board the *Mayflower*, all military authority had rested in Captain Jones as master of the ship. On shore, Standish's command began. He was eager to employ his talents and too impatient to rely on the shallop repairs.

Standish organized a group of men to proceed on foot to patrol the area and investigate beyond the beach. The Pilgrims desperately needed freshwater, and they craved more fresh food. But based on the reports they had heard in Europe, they feared an Indian attack could come at any moment. Standish's reconnaissance would help gauge their risk.

With Standish in the lead, the patrol plodded along the sand dunes, armed with matchlock muskets, swords, and corselets. No more than a mile along the beach, they spied a small group of Indians in the distance—walking in their direction.

Suddenly the Indians turned and ran into the woods. Standish and his men gave chase, following their tracks in the sand. They wanted to ward off any ambush, but Standish also hoped to make peaceful contact.

The tracks continued at length, and before they could find their makers, dusk set in upon them. Standish and his men made camp for the night on the dunes and found freshwater. The next morning, they rose early and began following the tracks again. In short order, the tracks disappeared.

The Pilgrim party hiked four more miles, then trudged over to a bay where they spied an area undoubtedly cleared by human hands. The clearing encircled several unnatural mounds. Curious, Standish and his men dug into a mound. From it, they unearthed a bow and arrows. The discovery brought them to an abrupt halt—a warrior's grave, they presumed. Superstition led them to promptly rebury the items, restore the mound, and leave the area.

Hiking beyond the clearing, they came upon a river. Standish and his men followed the river to a meadow, filled with more unusual mounds. The size suggested these were not graves—smaller, recently made, and most certainly constructed by humans. Once again, they began to dig into a mound.

Under the dirt, they found bulky baskets filled with maize— large, colorful ears of corn. The Pilgrims had never seen such a food before, but they recognized it as an edible grain and imagined they could use these ears for planting. Also in the mound, they found an old iron kettle of European origin—likely acquired in trade or recovered from a shipwreck. The Pilgrims filled the kettle with maize, promising themselves they would repay the owners. After all of this, they returned to the *Mayflower.*

For the next ten days, the Pilgrims lived onboard the moored *Mayflower* and rowed to the beach to continue repairs on the shallop. Once they deemed the shallop sufficiently seaworthy, they set out along the inner coast of Cape Cod. Standish wanted to return to the river where they found the corn, and Jones volunteered to sail the shallop.

As they sailed south in the shallop, the weather began deteriorating. A cold wind arose, followed by heavy snow. Jones recommended that they return to the *Mayflower* rather than try to land. The Pilgrims on board the shallop insisted on going ashore, and Jones eventually conceded. They continued ahead into the storm.

As the shallop neared the beach, its hull began to drag on the shallow, sandy bottom until they came to a halt several yards from shore. The Pilgrims began clambering over its rails and into the icy water. Cold and sopping wet, they hunkered down on the beach to wait out the storm. With strong winds, blowing snow, and freezing temperatures, the decision would prove costly.

"Many took the origin of their death here," wrote Bradford.[5]

When they rose in the morning, the Pilgrims found six inches of snow had fallen, and the ground had frozen. Still cold and wet, they broke camp and began exploring the area. They returned to the place where they had uncovered the corn in the mounds. Standish's party had not dug up all the mounds, so they now had more to inspect. With their swords, the men began to scrape and dig. From under the dirt, they recovered ten bushels of corn as well as beans.

"And here it is to be noticed a special providence of God, and a great mercy to this poor people," Bradford said, "that they got seed to plant them corn the next year or else they might have starved, for they had none, nor any likelihood to get any till the season had been past. . . . But the Lord is never wanting unto His in their greatest needs: let His holy name have all the praise."[6]

Back on board the *Mayflower*, the Pilgrims' attention returned to the question of establishing a permanent settlement on dry land. Some of the Pilgrims suggested that the group act quickly, suggesting the place where they found the baskets of corn. Others argued against it, contending that it lacked sufficient freshwater to sustain them longer.

One of the *Mayflower* voyagers had traveled to New England on a previous sailing expedition. He remembered a notable place with a safe haven for their ships: "[A] navigable river and good harbor almost right over against Cape Cod," pointing to a place directly across the bay.[7]

The prospective location sounded intriguing—no one else had a credible recommendation—so they readied the shallop to see it firsthand. Led by Standish, more than ten men set off across the bay on a bitterly cold day, Bradford among them. As the shallop broke through the waves, the sea spray rebounded onto them and froze to their coats like an icy glaze.

When the Pilgrims neared land across the bay, they saw a party of Indians on the beach hovering over a large black object. As they landed the shallop about a mile away, the people on the beach fled into the woods, leaving the black object behind. The Pilgrims stepped onto shore, built a fire, and concocted a barricade from driftwood.

The following morning, the Pilgrims broke into two parties. The first party returned to the shallop to patrol the coast, both for security and in search of rivers. The other party marched up the beach to identify the unusual black object—a fifteen-foot orca whale washed up on shore.

By the end of the day, they had not spotted any additional signs of human life, nor a suitable place to make their settlement. The men retired to the barricade and huddled around the warm fire. Several men stayed awake to keep guard, while the rest slowly drifted off to sleep.

"Awooooo!"

A shrieking "hideous and great cry"[8] broke the stillness

THEY CAME FOR FREEDOM

of the night—a piercing sound unlike anything they had ever heard.

"Arm, arm!" called out one of the guards.

The men jumped to their feet and took up their matchlock muskets. They took aim at anything and nothing in the night. In tense anticipation, they waited—watching for moving shadows in the woods or flying arrows. Nothing stirred.

One of the *Mayflower* mariners calmed them. He had heard wolves on a voyage to Newfoundland and suggested that this must be a howling wolf—not a human. The explanation provided some relief, but everyone remained on edge. Eventually the Pilgrims returned to their beds and managed to fall asleep.

The next morning, the men prepared breakfast and began to pack up camp. Standish told them to keep their muskets close at hand. Nonetheless, some of the men wrapped them in their coats and set them near the water's edge a short distance from camp.

"Awooooo!"

A new "great and strange cry" suddenly shrieked from the woods. Wolves again, many thought. But now they heard many voices with varied notes and pitches.

"They are men! Indians! Indians!" one of their men shouted as he came running into the campsite.

Woosh! Woosh!

A barrage of arrows followed him. Then the Pilgrims saw Indian men coming out of the woods, making their way toward the guns on the water's edge. The Pilgrim men, many of whom still had their armor and knives, dashed for their weapons.

Only Standish and one other Pilgrim had retained their guns. They fired and reloaded as quickly as possible, providing cover and buying the men time to reach their matchlocks.

With loaded matchlocks, the Pilgrims began to fire, driving the Indians back into the woods.

"Yet there was a lusty man," Bradford recalled of one Indian, "and no less valiant stood behind a tree within half a musket shot of us, and there let his arrows fly. He stood three shots of a musket. At length one took . . . and after which he gave extraordinary cry and away they all went."[9]

Unwilling to end the skirmish on the defensive, Standish ordered the Pilgrims to pursue, with each man firing a round or two. Once it appeared that they had driven the Indians back, the Pilgrims regrouped on the beach near the shallop. None were injured, and "after we had given God thanks for our deliverance, we took our shallop and went on our journey, and called this place, The First Encounter."[10] Then they worked quickly to put the shallop back in the water and get under sail.

The Pilgrims turned north to follow the coast and continue their survey of Cape Cod. They had not yet seen the natural harbor promised by one of the men. Snow and rain began to fall after they had sailed the shallop for several hours. By midafternoon, the wind increased and the seas grew heavy.

As the storm grew more violent, one of the thrashing swells suddenly broke the rudder. With the shallop rocking at the mercy of the wind and waves, two men grabbed oars to improvise a makeshift tiller. With all their muscle, they struggled to keep the boat on an intentional course and managed to hold their direction.

In the distance, the pilot of the shallop spotted a faint sliver of land and then what looked like a safe harbor. He yelled for the men to hold tight. The shallop still had some distance to sail, and the storm continued to grow in fury. With darkness drawing down upon them, every second counted. The Pilgrims bore down on the sail, hoping to drive the shallop harder and reach shore with enough sunlight to navigate into the harbor. The harder they pushed, the more the mast bowed and the boat creaked under the power of the storm.

Suddenly the mast shattered. It broke into three large pieces, with part of the beam falling directly onto the deck. The sail and upper mast fell into the thrashing sea.

Fear and hopelessness overcame the men as if they had been cast away. For now, the Pilgrims could only drift helplessly. When the waves pushed them close enough to land to make out its features, they could see that the shore did not offer a safe harbor at all. Instead, the cove before them gave way to large, breaking waves. The shallop would soon drift into violent surf that would surely tear the boat apart.

One of the mariners spotted a nearby inlet and took command from the pilot. Grabbing an oar himself, he steered and directed the other men to row vigorously. As darkness settled upon them, they rowed furiously toward the inlet in the driving rain. With their tremendous effort, the shallop cleared the rocky cove and reached the inlet. Through the channel, they found a wind shadow behind an outcropping of land—whether an island or peninsula, they did not know—but it provided a refuge to anchor for the night.

Although the men had survived the storm, they still felt vulnerable. They did not know where, or on what, they had landed. More importantly, they did know who else might be out in the darkness. The group argued over whether to spend the night on the boat or on land. Many lobbied to stay on the boat for fear of another attack, while others went on land, preferring the warmth of a fire to the cold dampness of the boat.

The long, cold, and rainy night gave way to a day of warm sunshine. The outcropping of land behind which they took refuge happened to be an island. They felt safe on the island—it would help prevent another surprise attack—and they felt uneasy about returning to the open ocean after two days of storms. Battered and exhausted, and this day being the Sabbath, they chose to rest on the island.

On Monday, the men sounded the harbor and explored the mainland. The harbor had an ideal design. The channel divided two thin strips of beach that held back the waves and protected the harbor. Once inside, the harbor opened up into three large bays. The bay to the north held the island where they camped. They named it Clarke's Island after the *Mayflower*'s first mate.[11]

The south bay appeared most interesting for a settlement site. Well-sheltered and deep enough for the draft of ocean-faring vessels, it would make a fine harbor for the *Mayflower* and many ships to come. Most importantly, it could be well secured with two large hills overlooking the harbor and surrounding land.

Captain John Smith had named the area "New Plymouth" on his map. The Pilgrims found the name appropriate, particularly since their departure had originated at Plymouth Harbor, England. They declared the site fit for habitation.

Rowing the thirty-mile stretch across Cape Cod Bay, the battered shallop limped back to the *Mayflower* with promising news to share. Bradford and the men grew more enthusiastic as they neared the *Mayflower*. Friends and family gathered on the deck to greet them, but not Dorothy May Bradford. Solemn faces, instead, greeted Bradford. William Brewster needed to talk to him.[12]

Dorothy May, Bradford's wife of seven years, had fallen overboard and drowned. Whether her death was a frigid consequence of a misstep or a permanent escape from their depressing condition, Bradford's pen fell silent about her.[13]

Chapter Nine

A Long and Difficult Winter

DECEMBER 1620
CAPE COD

The *Mayflower* tacked back and forth across Cape Cod Bay. Fighting a stinging mid-December headwind, the Pilgrims wanted to make a quick passage to the natural harbor they called New Plymouth. November had passed, leaving them well behind schedule and in need of immediate winter preparation on shore. Not only did they feel pressure from the changing seasons but also from the crew. Their mounting delays left Captain Jones increasingly eager to sail the *Mayflower* back to England.

Jones anchored the *Mayflower* in the New Plymouth channel, and Standish sent a well-armed party to explore the area. Humans had clearly occupied the area in recent years—but not any longer. Everywhere they looked, they saw signs of habitation: remnants of houses, fields left fallow, and large areas cleared of brush; but no people. This was a ghost town.

The Pilgrims could not understand why anyone would desert the area. The land had natural advantages beyond the harbor.

The settlement site had a freshwater stream, clearings for fields, and promising soil. While the unusual vanishing gave them pause, urgency trumped investigation.

Most agreed that this place would suffice for their settlement, but they had lived on the *Mayflower* long enough that few objected to any opportunity to take up permanent residence on land. Those who protested raised concerns that the adjacent forest could camouflage Indian attacks, like their skirmish on the beach. The naysayers, however, could not suggest a better location, so the decision to settle New Plymouth came rapidly.

The Pilgrims chose a spot north of the stream that sloped up a hill to where they could build a lookout and defense post. From there they could overlook the harbor and village they planned to build below. They had brought a cannon on board the *Mayflower* for strategic defense.

Under Governor Carver's command, the Pilgrims quickly developed a plan for New Plymouth. They would begin by building a common house, twenty feet by twenty feet square, which they would use for meetings, defense, and communal living the first winter. Next they would fashion a street running from the stream up to the cannon platform. Adjacent to the street, they would carve out skinny plots of residential land, approximately eight feet wide by fifty feet deep.

Then they developed a plan to allocate the land. Family units but not single men would be eligible to receive land. Single men would be assigned to join a family. Family units would receive one skinny tract for each man, woman, or child in their household. Thus, large families would receive the number of tracts proportionate to the size of their household. In total, they planned for New Plymouth to eventually host nineteen homes.

The Pilgrims had endured their first month well. They had developed a plan and started their construction projects.

They anticipated some casualties but had sustained few. By late December, however, the weather turned on them. The weather grew colder, and their food rations dwindled. They still had not found a regular source of fresh food and continued to survive on the dried salted food they had brought from Europe.

As December wore on, their health decreased rapidly through a lethal combination of malnourishment and disease. By the end of the month, six of the Pilgrims had perished, and another eight died before the end of January. The sick began to outnumber the healthy. When they finished the common house, it became the infirmary—then the mortuary.

Since their November "first encounter" on Cape Cod, the Pilgrims had no contact with the native tribes, nor any sightings. With the sick and dying increasing among their number, they felt more and more alone. The abandoned settlement upon which they made their home added to a sense of desolation on the verge of failure. Crossing a local tribe, even under hostile circumstances, would have at least lifted their confidence that humans could survive here.

Then, suddenly, two men went missing. The men had gone out to gather reeds for their thatched-roof huts but did not return that evening. The Pilgrims feared that Indians had killed or captured them. Perhaps, they wondered, this was the first wave of attacks, or perhaps the Indians would start to pick off the Pilgrims as they left New Plymouth.

The next day, the Pilgrims assembled a search party and fanned out through the woods. They could find no trace of the two men or the dogs that had accompanied them. Night settled upon New Plymouth with no answers.

Late that night, the men stumbled back into the village, starved and chilled. Nearly two days earlier, their dogs picked up the scent of a deer, which the men hoped to follow and kill.

As they tracked the deer, they got lost. Unable to find their way back to the village, they paced all night to keep warm in the snow in constant terror of howling wolves.

By the time they arrived at New Plymouth, they had frostbitten feet and hypothermia, harbingers of death under the Pilgrims' circumstances. Indeed, one of the men would not recover. There would be many more to follow.

"In two or three months half of [our] company died,"[1] Bradford lamented. January and February hit them particularly hard, dwindling the more than one hundred arrivals down to barely fifty.

Bradford wrote:

> And of these in the time of the distress, there were but six or seven sound persons who to their great commendation be it spoken spared no pains night nor day but with abundance of toil and hazard of their own health, fetched them wood, made them fires, dressed them meat made their beds, was their loathsome cloths, clothed and unclothed them; in a word did all the homely and necessary offices of them which dainty and queasy stomachs cannot endure to hear named, and all this willingly and cheerfully without and grudging in the least.[2]

Brewster and Standish were among the few apparently immune to disease and the harsh New England winter. Bradford had remained generally healthy but suddenly collapsed one day while working outside. He recovered, but many others would not, suffering from pneumonia, tuberculosis, and scurvy—the latter resulting from the lack of vitamin C in their diets.

Death erased entire families. Eighteen wives set sail from England, and by March only five had survived. Ten of the fifteen single men had perished. Sickness even overcame the crew of the *Mayflower*, who had been eager to return to Europe but were now forced by health to wait out the winter anchored in the harbor. The crew lost half their number.

In addition to their poor health, the Pilgrims lived in constant fear of Indians. They imagined their every move under constant watch from the shadows. They feared that the Indians were tallying Pilgrims' deaths as an offensive strategy, waiting them out as they weakened in strength and number. Consequently, the Pilgrims concealed their burials under the cover of nightfall, unceremoniously hiding corpses in inconspicuous, unmarked graves.

As their dead increased in number, the Pilgrims began seeing more signs of human life in the woods. Jones spotted two Indians on a nearby island. Not long after that sighting, one of the Pilgrims on a hunting expedition saw a band of warriors walking in the direction of New Plymouth. The Pilgrim fled his hunting post and ran for the village. As he neared New Plymouth, he found a group of Pilgrims clearing brush in the woods. At his alarm, they dropped their tools and ran with him to the village to retrieve their muskets.

With muskets armed and at the ready, the Pilgrims waited. Silence. Nothing happened—not a sound, no rustling of leaves. When the warriors did not appear near the village, the men returned cautiously to their work in the woods. The tools that they had dropped were missing—stolen by the band of Indians.

The ordeal did not sit well with Standish and Carver. The panicked flight for their muskets and the preventable loss of their tools gave rise to a new plan for defense preparedness. The following day, Carver called a meeting to develop a formalized chain of command: they would elect a defense officer. Standish joined the *Mayflower* voyage as the Separatists' military adviser, but the Mayflower Compact had superseded their prearrival chain of command and established a theoretically democratic foundation. They would put military authority to a vote, too, rather than appointment.

Carver naturally recommended Standish as "Captain-General," and a majority confirmed him. Standish's authority arrived on the heels of their new military plan, and only moments before New Plymouth would face its first defensive challenge.

On the hill across the creek from New Plymouth, two Indians appeared in the clearing. When the Pilgrims spotted the men, they immediately alerted Standish. Once the Indians had Standish's attention, they motioned with their hands for the Pilgrims to come to the hilltop. Standish returned their invitation, gesturing instead for them to come to New Plymouth. The two Indians did not move and displayed no intention of coming to the village. Neither party would budge in the negotiation.

Eventually Standish decided the Pilgrims would end the stalemate—he would go to the Indians. Standish, accompanied by another Pilgrim, walked slowly and assuredly out of the village. Several yards away from the Indian men, the Pilgrims ceremoniously laid their muskets on the ground and motioned that they had no arms. Suddenly, the Indian men fled from the hill, disappearing into the woods. Moments later, a great noise of shrieking and shouting arose from the forest. These two men had not come alone.

Standish retreated back to New Plymouth and began barking orders. The Pilgrims would prioritize defense and deterrence. They had brought artillery on the *Mayflower* but had not installed it at the settlement—their cannon remained on the ship. The Pilgrims retrieved it and hauled the cannon up to the hilltop platform Standish had built.

Standish knew the cannon would be impractical as a weapon.

Its accuracy would do little good against an attacking force scattered throughout the surrounding forest. But it could intimidate. Its sounds and repercussions might provide deterrence, as if the Pilgrims could control thunder.

With their cannon situated on the platform and a new defense strategy in place, the Pilgrims put themselves at the ready. They watched the hill across the creek, but no one appeared. They waited. No attack came. For the next several weeks, the woods were silent—not a sound or sight of anyone.

On March 16, a tall young man strode confidently out of the woods and across the land cleared between New Plymouth and the trees. His long, jet-black hair shimmered in the sun, draping down his uncovered shoulders to his nearly naked body. He wore only a small, leather apron and carried a bow and two arrows.

The Pilgrims looked on in shock as he walked through the New Plymouth gates and onto the village street. Men fumbled with their muskets; other villagers froze in disbelief.

"Welcome," he said in English, approaching a group of stunned Pilgrim men.[3] He spoke freely, with broken but comprehensible English. And he came in peace.

The native man went by the name Samoset, and like the Pilgrims, he, too, lived in a foreign land. He had been raised near Monhegan Island and belonged to the tribes of the Northeast coast. There he learned English from fishermen who summered on the island. To validate his story, he listed the names of captains, commanders, and masters who commonly came to Monhegan Island.

Samoset answered many of the Pilgrims' lingering questions. Why had this village been abandoned? New Plymouth had not been intentionally abandoned—this was Patuxet[4] land, and all but one had died in the plague three years before. This survivor, who had been away from Patuxet at the time of the plague, also spoke English—and better English than Samoset.

Samoset told them how the Patuxet people, like the other tribes of the region, including the Nauset, fell under the authority of the sachem Massasoit of the Wampanoag. Samoset warned the Pilgrims to be wary of the Nauset tribe because they hated anyone they could brand as Captain Hunt's people. As evidence, Samoset could offer the example of Captain Dermer.

The Pilgrims had many questions to ask Samoset, and the day grew late. Since it would be a long walk back to his village, he asked to stay the night. It made the Pilgrims nervous to have him staying in New Plymouth, so they agreed if he slept on the *Mayflower*. The weather, however, prevented them from launching the shallop, even for the short ride to the *Mayflower* at anchor. Samoset, instead, stayed in the village under guard.

The next morning, the Pilgrims saw Samoset out of the village. In exchange for the promise to organize trade, they gave him gifts, including a knife, bracelet, and ring.

The following day, a Sunday, Samoset eagerly returned to New Plymouth accompanied by five Indian men. They carried beaver furs and deerskins, as well as the tools stolen only weeks before. Although the Pilgrims enthusiastically welcomed an opportunity to trade, they would have to decline due to the Sabbath. Even when Samoset and his company finished a dance in honor of the Pilgrims, they would not applaud. The Pilgrims held a strict interpretation of the Sabbath as a day of rest and inactivity, disallowing them from working or conducting any business.

The Pilgrims asked Samoset and the five men to come back on Wednesday to trade. All departed New Plymouth, except

Samoset. He had enjoyed the Pilgrims' accommodations the previous night and took a liking to the new flavors of butter and cheese. He wanted to feast again.

On Wednesday, the Indian men did not return as they had planned, so the Pilgrims sent Samoset to find them. The situation made the residents feel uneasy, and they wondered if the party had come to survey them. The encounter had felt hospitable, yet the Pilgrims remained suspicious. The atmosphere grew even more tenuous when two Indians appeared on the hill opposite the village and signaled gestures of battle.

Then Samoset emerged from the forest accompanied by another man they had not yet met. Samoset's companion introduced himself in English as Squanto.

Squanto and Samoset had not come to trade but to deliver an important message. Massasoit, the great sachem of the Wampanoag confederacy ruling the tribes in the region, wanted to visit New Plymouth. The Pilgrims, however, would not have time to prepare. Massasoit would arrive soon.

Before long, Massasoit appeared on the hill opposite New Plymouth. He looked confident, imposing, and dignified. Surrounding him stood sixty armed warriors, bolstering his impression as a hallowed leader.

Massasoit had come to them. Standing stoically on top of the hill, he would not take another step toward New Plymouth. He waited for the Pilgrims to make a move.

Commotion unfolded in the village as the Pilgrims frantically considered what to do. They decided someone from the Pilgrim party would need to go to Massasoit, but who? First contact would need to proceed diplomatically. Sending Standish might be both abrasive and unpredictable. Governor Carver needed to appear at the very least as Massasoit's equal, if not his superior. He would stay in New Plymouth and force Massasoit to come to him. Brewster, as well, might project too high an authority to send and cause confusion over whether leadership lay in Carver's or Brewster's hands. Eventually they settled on young Edward Winslow, an intelligent, confident young man who would fit the role of a messenger, yet conduct himself diplomatically.

Donning armor and securing a sword at his side, Winslow stepped out of New Plymouth, accompanied by Squanto and Samoset. The three men crossed the creek and started walking slowly up the hill toward the mass of men.

Winslow soon found himself face-to-face with the imposing chief: a man strong, poised, and proper.[5] These were "his best years," as Winslow described him, noting the sachem to be of "able body, grave countenance, and spare of speech."[6]

Nearly naked, Massasoit stood before Winslow. He wore a massive, imposing chain of white bone beads draped from his neck and a deerskin tobacco pouch on his back. A long knife, hanging from a string, shielded his sternum, and a beaded belt covered his waist. Oil and red paint concealed his face, applied so heavily that it gave him a greasy complexion. .

The warriors behind him had commanded a similar presence. "[T]heir faces, in part or in whole painted, some black, some red, some yellow, and some white, some with crosses, and other antic works; some had skins on them, and some naked, all strong, tall, all men of appearance."[7]

Winslow approached the chief. In his hands, he held several gifts for Massasoit: a pair of knives, a copper chain with a jewel, biscuits, butter, and brandy. When he reached the top of the hill, one by one he handed the tokens to Massasoit.

The goodwill offering pleased Massasoit, who willingly accepted.

"King James salutes you with words of Love and Peace," Winslow told him, "and accepts you as his Friend and Ally, and that our Governor desires to see you and to talk with you, and to confirm Peace with you, and our next neighbor."[8]

Massasoit listened intently as Squanto and Samoset interpreted Winslow's words. He agreed to meet Governor Carver. Then Winslow buttered the biscuits and poured the brandy to ceremoniously commence the covenant.

After they had broken bread and drunk brandy together, Massasoit pointed to Winslow's sword and armor. He wanted them, too, offering to buy them immediately. Winslow refused.

Massasoit decided that he would proceed to New Plymouth with twenty of his men. For the settlers' safety, Winslow would stay on the hill with Massasoit's brother and the remaining forty warriors.

The Wampanoag men set down their bows and arrows, then trotted down the hill to the brook. Standish and Brewster waited for them at the water's edge, accompanied by six Pilgrim men bearing muskets. The Plymouth company saluted Massasoit, who returned the gesture.

At the entrance to New Plymouth, Massasoit left six of his men under guard as an exchange for Winslow. From there, Standish and Brewster flanked Massasoit as they escorted him to Bradford's house, which had only recently been built. Inside, they unfurled a green rug and spread out several cushions. Massasoit sat down on the cushions, puffing on his tobacco pipe. With Massasoit seated, Governor Carver entered.

Carver gave Massasoit a dignitary's welcome, calling for brandy and fresh meat. Massasoit embraced the offering, indulging himself and drinking his brandy in one sip. Carver and the others pretended to ignore as Massasoit sweated profusely. The Pilgrims brought in their trumpets to play for him, and Massasoit marveled at the instruments. His men tried to play them—but with little success.

The events in Bradford's house transpired beyond a simple greeting as they began negotiating the terms of a treaty. With the Pilgrims' fear of an Indian attack, any ally would make a great asset, and Massasoit appeared to wield the region's power. They asked him to pledge to come to New Plymouth's defense if they were unjustly attacked. In exchange, they would come to Massasoit's aid if his people suffered the same. Massasoit, too, liked the alignment. He preferred their friendship rather than having the Pilgrims align with an enemy. He agreed.

Massasoit had other goals for the treaty beyond mutual defense. He craved European goods, but not just beads and trinkets. He coveted the power of their guns. European firepower would give him stronger control of the confederacy and the region. He recognized that the treaty would give the Wampanoag confederacy direct access to a European market, and a military alliance would increase their chances of acquiring firearms. They would no longer rely on the randomness of European trading vessels.

After the peace treaty was signed, Massasoit left the village and returned to Sowams,[9] his home forty miles southwest of New Plymouth. Squanto, however, chose to remain at New Plymouth, taking on the role of the Pilgrims' guide and interpreter.

Squanto was a treasure. He could explain the confederacy and the role of the tribes. He knew the geography and weather patterns. And he could teach them practical skills. He directed the Pilgrims how and where to plant corn, as well as where to fish. The Pilgrims called him "a special instrument sent of God for their good beyond their expectation."[10] They had attributed many occurrences to God's providence, and here, too, they could imagine no other explanation for Squanto's care and attention.

For Squanto, the Pilgrims' chosen place of settlement held a special meaning. The Pilgrims had settled upon his ancestral land, building New Plymouth on the ground of the derelict Patuxet village—the remnants of which the Pilgrims had observed.

Squanto might be the last living member of the Patuxet tribe. His kidnapping to Europe, coinciding with the worst outbreak of smallpox in the New World, had likely saved his life. Upon his return to the empty village, survival forced him to follow the surrogate leadership of Epenow and Massasoit.

Being the last living Patuxet left Squanto at a disadvantage. Whatever influence the Patuxet had in the Wampanoag confederacy died along with the village. Squanto could not be the chief of one, thus leaving him in a position of inferiority.

For his entire life, Squanto had been a servant or a slave. But he had seen a world beyond the Wampanoag confederacy. Not only had he served Patuxet, Kennebec, and Wampanoag chiefs, but he had been apprenticed by London businessmen and taken under the wing of English leaders such as Ferdinando Gorges. He had submitted to the authority of King James and the House of Habsburg in Spain.

With the arrival of the Pilgrims, Squanto saw an opportunity to employ something he possessed that Massasoit would never have: command of the English language. Squanto had become the gatekeeper to the greatest imbalance of power North America had ever seen, standing squarely in the gap between each side's deepest fears. From his years as a captive at the hands of deceitful English sailors, he understood Massasoit's distrust of them. His time in the company of men like Gorges and Smith taught him about the Europeans' overwhelming fear of "the savages," which they desperately wanted to keep hidden.

Squanto knew everyone's secrets, but none knew his. As interpreter, he could control the conversation—neither the Pilgrims nor Massasoit could tell otherwise. Suddenly the slave had become the master, and no one possessed more power than he.

Squanto knew he could forever live in the shadow of Massasoit or he could dramatically change the direction of his life. He had nothing to lose.

❦

By late March 1621, the *Mayflower* still had not yet departed from the harbor at New Plymouth. Captain Jones had wanted to leave much sooner, and most certainly the Merchant Adventurers in England eagerly anticipated a fruitful return. Yet sickness and death had left his sails furled. Due to the dire condition of his own sailors, Jones could not leave.

"[M]any of the ablest of them dead," Bradford noted of Jones's sailors, "and the rest many lay sick and weak . . . the master dare not put to sea till he saw his men beginning to recover and heart of the winter over."[11]

On April 5, Jones finally felt comfortable preparing to set sail. As spring arrived, the sailors regained strength enough to make the month-long Atlantic crossing. The residents of New Plymouth, too, felt their odds for survival increase as the casualty rate among the Pilgrims began to stabilize. The warm weather renewed the outlook of New Plymouth, and despite the opportunity to flee with Captain Jones, not one Pilgrim boarded the *Mayflower* to return to England.

The *Mayflower* departed with its mariners but not its cargo. The Merchant Adventurers had expected goods—timber, fish, sassafras—anything of market value. But the *Mayflower* had nothing to carry home. The Pilgrims had arrived too late in the fall and grew too weak to outfit the *Mayflower*. When the ship departed, they were still scraping together their own rudimentary shelters and laboring to gather enough food to survive. They had no surplus to offer.[12]

Although spring had buoyed their outlook, the Pilgrims remained on the brink of peril. Disease had not left them, and the work had not become lighter. Until they could reap a harvest, times would remain tough. Indeed, as death would strike during the promise of spring, it would leave a particularly devastating void.

Governor Carver, now fifty-four, came in from the fields one afternoon complaining of a headache. He quickly slipped into a coma and died of an aneurism. The loss of Carver dealt New Plymouth a painful blow. On the *Mayflower* voyage, as dissension rose between the Separatists and the Strangers, Carver had unified them around their singular purpose in the New World. He had negotiated the Mayflower Compact, then the peace treaty with Massasoit. He had gained the respect of a divided community, and the task of finding an agreeable replacement would be difficult.

The residents of New Plymouth gathered to pay their respects to Carver and to discuss leadership. They needed a strong, stable leader immediately. And so, once again, they returned to the Mayflower Compact. Repeating the process performed on board the *Mayflower* less than six months before, they would elect a governor and accept the outcome obediently. As before, they would not pick clergy, intending to maintain their long-fought battle for separation of church and state. Necessity would call for a younger man who might weather sickness, famine, and hard work better than New Plymouth's elders. With Carver gone, Brewster preferred to step aside from political leadership and focus on building the church.

New Plymouth chose William Bradford. He not only possessed the dedication and education, but he made for a symbolic choice. New Plymouth would put its trust in a younger generation of leaders. At the helm of New Plymouth, shaping the colony's future, were Governor Bradford, age thirty-one, Standish, age thirty-six, and Winslow, age twenty-five.

As New Plymouth entered its first April, the villagers turned their attention to the prospects of planting. Acting as agriculture adviser, Squanto offered sage advice on the day to plant: "when the leaves of the white oak were as large as the mouse's ear."[13]

They watched the leaves, and when they grew to the proper size, the Pilgrims began their work in the dirt. By hand, with only mattock and hoe, they diligently turned over twenty acres of farmland. Under Squanto's direction, they scraped together small mounds of fresh, black dirt three feet apart—in the end, more than ninety-six thousand individual mounds. Squanto told them that if they expected a harvest in the fall, their work was not yet done, and they could not yet plant a single seed.

Squanto next directed the Pilgrims to their fish traps and explained that they would need to understand the tides if they wanted to catch fish. At high tide they placed fish traps in the streams near New Plymouth. When the tides receded, they found tens of thousands of captured herring.

As hungry as the Pilgrims might be, the herring were not for their consumption. Instead, Squanto directed them to carry baskets of herring—more than forty tons—to the field. In each of the ninety-six thousand dirt mounds, they placed three herring in a spoke-like pattern, then covered the fish with dirt. Finally, they planted seeds over the buried herrings.

Although the Pilgrims had hoped they could turn their attention to expanding New Plymouth, the fieldwork did not end with planting. Squanto required them to keep the field under constant guard, day and night. Around the clock, patrols would watch for crows scavenging for the seeds and frighten away the wolves lying in wait for the buried herring. As the plants began to grow, the Pilgrims thinned down each mound to the strongest plant and kept the ground well tilled. The work never ceased.

Despite all this effort, the Pilgrims still had nothing on their empty plates. Their diet consisted primarily of bread, butter, and cheese—remaining rations brought from Europe. The native foods of the area—wild game, seafood, and berries—were not only foreign, but disliked. While their palates would need to adapt, they had good reason to be wary. The mussels at Cape Cod had sickened enough of them to frighten them away from shellfish. They worried that wild berries and plants could hold a similar fate. They also lacked the tools and techniques, having brought with them fishnets and large hooks that failed miserably in the nearby streams.

In addition, their visitors consumed their rations. After Massasoit's visit, members of his tribe began coming with growing frequency to New Plymouth. Keeping with custom, members of the Wampanoag confederacy traveled freely throughout the region and enjoyed reciprocal communal hospitality, including a share of the food. The Pilgrims' new and delicious foods, particularly the butter, became the chief attraction for a stay at New Plymouth. The visits quickly became a nuisance to the Pilgrims.

The matter, they decided, could only be addressed by speaking to Massasoit. Once again, they tapped Winslow as ambassador. He enjoyed the duty and had earned Massasoit's respect at their first interaction. With a fellow Pilgrim companion, Winslow and Squanto set out on the forty-mile trek to meet the sachem at Sowams.

Along the way, the trio ate and slept in villages, partaking in communal hospitality and always finding themselves entertained. The Indians in many of the villages had not yet met the Pilgrims, so Winslow left an impression on them. Still

Winslow's musket left the greatest mark. Winslow would often repay their hospitality by showing off his artillery—wowing villagers with the noise—and even sniping a crow from a range of eighty yards.

Sowams, Massasoit's village, had been ravished by plague in recent years. While disease had wreaked considerable havoc, it had not annihilated Sowams as it had Patuxet.[14] Although three years had passed since disease had decimated the region, its tribes had not yet recovered. People had died along the northeast coast so rapidly that burials could not be conducted at the same pace as the dying. For many of the coastal Indian tribes, the disease took the lives of nine out of every ten.[15] Skulls and bones still lay in piles above ground with no one left to bury the dead.

The English assumed smallpox or tuberculosis, but the culprit came by a lesser-known disease: leptospirosis, a bacterium transmitted through rat urine. The skin of the infected would begin to yellow and intense pain and cramping would follow. Finally, the hallmark of the disease would manifest—extensive bleeding from the nose. The rats came to the New World on board the ships of explorers and fishermen and then infected water sources. From there, other animals drinking the water might have spread it farther from the coast. For the Patuxet and other tribes, interacting with the land was their way of life. Perhaps they drank from an infected stream or stepped barefoot into a compromised puddle of water. They lived a life that left them exceedingly vulnerable.

Winslow and Squanto found Massasoit at Sowams. Just as the Pilgrims had entertained the sachem, he reciprocated. Massasoit sat them down and told them stories, and he gave them counsel about the region. Winslow sat patiently until he could finally broach the matter of visits to New Plymouth. Squanto translated in both directions.

"[Massasoit's men] would no more pester us as they had done," Squanto told Winslow.[16]

Winslow countered that the Pilgrims did not want to stop all visits. They welcomed trading and would happily receive anyone who brought beaver skins. Massasoit understood, then affirmed that he considered himself "King James's man," expressing a shared allegiance with the Pilgrims.

With their primary mission complete, Winslow presented Massasoit with several gifts as an expression of gratitude. First he presented a horseman's coat—bright red, tall collar, and trimmed with lace. Massasoit adored it, putting it on immediately and flaunting it to his followers.

After the gifts, Winslow offered an apology. The Pilgrims had "borrowed" corn from several earthen mounds when the *Mayflower* first arrived. Winslow promised to repay Massasoit's people for it.

Winslow and Bradford assumed that, despite their plea, they would continue to see visitors and feared that many visitors would claim to speak on behalf of Massasoit. They had devised a plan to thwart confusion. Winslow presented Massasoit with a copper chain. If the chief intended to send a message to the Pilgrims, this chain would symbolize Massasoit's authority. Anyone carrying this chain would speak as the chief's messenger.

Having accomplished much at Sowams, the Pilgrims and Squanto set off to return to New Plymouth the next day.

"God be praised," said Winslow, "we came safe home that night though wet, weary and [footsore]."[17]

Within a few days, New Plymouth was in crisis. Young John Billington had gone missing.[18]

News of the sixteen-year-old's disappearance shook New Plymouth. John had gone into the woods south of the village but did not return. Despite search teams scouring the woods, several days passed with no sign of John.

John's vanishing came on the heels of Winslow's mission to Massasoit. Based on its proximity to the mission, many of the Pilgrims assumed John had been abducted or murdered by Massasoit's subjects—or enemies. Presumably Winslow's mission had significantly strengthened ties, but an alignment with Massasoit might have created rivalry with his adversaries. Above all, the lack of a plausible explanation for John's disappearance left room to cry conspiracy.

As days passed without any evidence of John, the Pilgrims began to expect the worst. Then word arrived from Massasoit that John had been found alive. After losing his way, John wandered in the woods for five days. He foraged on nuts and wild foods to survive. He covered twenty miles on foot, before stumbling into an Indian village. The village passed John along to the Nausets—the same tribe in whose sandy Cape Cod territory the Pilgrims had first landed and then stolen their corn.

Massasoit was not involved with John but acted as messenger in a show of good faith to the Pilgrims. To retrieve John, the Pilgrims would need to deal directly with the Nausets. They had been warned by Samoset about the Nausets. The Pilgrims knew of their anger toward the English because of Hunt, and while the Pilgrims could say that Hunt was an evil man, the Pilgrims themselves had stolen Nauset corn. Bradford began organizing a team for the precarious diplomatic mission.

The shallop set out for Nauset territory carrying Squanto and ten of New Plymouth's men. As they sailed south toward the Cape, a violent storm came upon them, forcing the shallop to shore. In the morning, they awoke to find the shallop far up on the beach at low tide. They would need to wait for high tide.

Along the beach, they saw men and women collecting shell-fish in the receding waters. Word of the unusual visit spread quickly, and soon a crowd gathered at the scene of the grounded shallop. Among the multitude an elderly woman came forward and demanded to speak to them.

As she laid eyes upon the Englishmen, she began to wail, "weeping and crying excessively."[19] Seven years earlier, she told them, Thomas Hunt had abducted her three sons.

"We told them we were sorry that Englishman should give them that offense," Winslow wrote, "that Hunt was a bad man, and that all the English that heard of it condemned him for the same."[20]

Winslow's diplomacy provided little comfort. He could see how deeply painful Hunt's crime had been to the Indians in the region, and he still had to face the embittered Nausets.

Twenty miles east of their landing location lay the Nauset village. When the tide finally returned, they began the voyage. After several hours of sailing, the Pilgrims landed the shallop near the place of the "first encounter." In November the place had seemed dismally populated, but now, by summer, it was a land teeming with people. The Pilgrims had not expected such an abundance of life but now understood why the Nauset people felt compelled to defend this territory.

Crowds gathered quickly and began approaching the shallop in great numbers. The Pilgrims forced the crowds away and asked that the Nausets approach the shallop in pairs. Among the first to approach was the man whose corn the Pilgrims had stolen. They promised to repay him and asked that he visit New Plymouth to collect.

Around dusk, the sachem of the Cape Cod Nauset arrived, accompanied by more than one hundred warriors. One of the Nauset warriors carried John Billington in his arms. They handed over the teenager, wearing a string of shells about his neck, to the Pilgrims. In return, the Pilgrims gave the chief a knife, and the two parties made a declaration of peace between them.

The satisfaction that they had finally recovered John Billington in good health and recompensed for the stolen corn was short-lived. The Nauset chief had bad news to tell them: Massasoit had been unjustly attacked and captured by the Narragansetts, the most militarily powerful tribe in the region.

If true, then the treaty that they had signed with Massasoit would come into effect. The Pilgrims were now at war.

Chapter Ten

War

JUNE 13, 1621
CAPE COD BAY

The shallop raced toward New Plymouth.

The Pilgrims had more to be concerned about than the simple obligations of their treaty with Massasoit and the Wampanoag: they had left New Plymouth vulnerable to attack. The mission to the Nausets left behind little more than twelve men in the village and no military strategist. Standish had taken some of his most talented troops on the operation to recover Billington. Now he feared the worst. Perhaps the Narragansetts had arranged Billington's recovery, then strategically waited for the Pilgrims to depart on this mission. If indeed the Narragansetts had attacked Massasoit, then the sachem's allies in New Plymouth would surely be next.

The Narragansetts had achieved much of their military might through sheer numbers. Their territory lay farther north than Patuxet and Sowams, providing a geographic barrier from the plague. The Narragansetts had only gained in strength, while other tribes suffered losses and setbacks.

Hours later the Pilgrims on the shallop could see New

Plymouth on the horizon. No plume of smoke arose from the village, nor could they see any suspicious activity. The shallop hurriedly sailed through the channel and into the harbor.

At New Plymouth, Wampanoag contacts corroborated the news that Massasoit had been captured but could not confirm his fate. They believed that a lesser regional sachem had orchestrated his capture to realign power. This sachem, Corbitant, had last been seen at Nemasket, only twenty miles away.

The matter demanded substantiation. Bradford needed a team who could covertly conduct espionage on Corbitant, a sachem of the Pocasset tribe under the Wampanoag confederacy. This would not be a mission for Standish or Winslow. He could send Squanto, but Squanto was not the only Indian who had gained the trust of the Pilgrims. He also had Hobbamock.

Hobbamock was brave, intelligent, and stout. He had been a fierce warrior and gained attention as a *pniese*, an individual with special wisdom. After Massasoit signed the treaty with the Pilgrims, the sachem appointed him as his official emissary to New Plymouth. From there Hobbamock began a close relationship with the Pilgrims, moving his family to a plot of land adjacent to New Plymouth. Whereas Squanto grew close to Bradford, Hobbamock found himself more aligned with Standish's military interests.

Squanto and Hobbamock had made the journey to Nemasket as clandestinely as possible, arriving at night and quietly finding a wigwam in which to stay. They learned that Massasoit was conspicuously absent from Sowams. In the vacuum of the chief's disappearance, Squanto and Hobbamock learned of the new threat posed by Corbitant.

Corbitant had ambitions of regional power and had opposed Massasoit's alliance with the Pilgrims. He saw the Pilgrims as a danger, bringing only plague and peril upon the people of North

America. Massasoit's absence presented Corbitant with an opportunity to seize power and hopefully weaken the Pilgrims.

Corbitant had arranged for another tribe to capture Massasoit, then he began gathering power in the New Plymouth region. He had not come to Nemasket to attack, but to "draw the hearts of Massasoit's subjects from him."[1] This was a Wampanoag confederacy coup.

When Corbitant learned of Squanto's and Hobbamock's presence at Nemasket, he sent his warriors to storm their wigwam and capture them.[2] The warriors brought Squanto and Hobbamock to him. With the men restrained, Corbitant drew his knife and held it to Squanto's chest. He told Squanto and Hobbamock they would die for their alliance with the Pilgrims.

"If *he* were dead," Corbitant pointed to Squanto, "the English had lost their tongue."[3]

Corbitant then turned to Hobbamock and lunged toward him with the knife. Hobbamock dodged the stab with a wild gyration of his body and shook himself free of his captors. He burst out of Corbitant's wigwam and disappeared into the night.

Panting and shouting, Hobbamock burst into the streets of New Plymouth, having run the twenty miles back to the settlement. Gasping for breath, he told the Pilgrims horrific news: Squanto had been murdered.

Bradford rallied his council. Hobbamock explained that he believed Massasoit might be alive but perhaps had lost control of the Wampanoag confederacy. Corbitant had led a hostile coup.

"[Hobbamock] feared they had killed Squanto," Bradford explained to his council, "for no other cause than because they were friends to the English."[4]

The council decided the Pilgrims must act. Not only did this situation invoke their treaty with Massasoit, but "if they should suffer their friends and messenger thus to be wrong . . . next [Corbitant] would fall upon [us]."[5]

Bradford decreed their plan: "[I]t was resolved to send the Captain and fourteen men well armed and to go and fall upon them in the night. And if they found that Squanto was killed, to cut off Corbitant's head, but not to hurt any but those that had a hand in it."[6]

Hobbamock volunteered to guide them to the village and identify Corbitant. Led by Standish, the Pilgrim militia marched out of New Plymouth on the morning of August 15, 1621. The twenty-mile trek took the entire day, and by late evening they arrived outside Massasoit's village and waited in the forest for the village to settle in for the night.

Under the veil of darkness, they quietly moved out of the forest and into the village. Hobbamock pointed them to Corbitant's wigwam. Standish took the lead, signaling for his men to stay back while he moved close to Corbitant's wigwam.

"Corbitant!" Standish yelled, bursting into the wigwam. Hobbamock followed Standish inside, and the wigwam's occupants erupted in frenzied panic. Awakened by the captain's surprise entry, everyone screamed with terror or froze in paralysis.

The dark wigwam offered little light, so Standish could not identify Corbitant among its inhabitants. Hobbamock asked for Corbitant, but no one could locate the chief.

Outside the wigwam, the village spiraled into chaos. Gunshots rang out as the Pilgrims waiting on the outskirts of the village fired volleys to control the crowds and protect Standish. Standish would return to his team empty-handed.

By morning, pieces of the story began falling together. Corbitant had not murdered Squanto, although Squanto's whereabouts remained unknown. Corbitant had indeed been at Nemasket that night but had fled to his home village.

The Pilgrims gathered together the residents of the village to explain the purpose of the military operation. Standish told them:

> [A]lthough Corbitant had now escaped us, yet there was no place should secure him and his from us if he continued his threatening us and provoking others against us . . . [we] never intended evil towards him till now he so justly deserved it. Moreover, if Massasoit did not return in safety from Narragansett, or if hereafter he should make any insurrection against him, or offer violence to Squanto, Hobbamock, or any of Massasoit's subjects, we would revenge it upon him, to the overthrow of him and his. As for those wounded, we were sorry for it, though themselves procured it in not staying in the house at our command; yet if they would return home with us our surgeon should heal them. [7]

The show of force struck much of the village with fear and awe. Men and women came forward with their best provisions as a peace offering. Among them, Squanto reappeared, unscathed, and joined the Pilgrims on their return to New Plymouth.

The Pilgrims' midnight raid would prove profitable in the coming weeks, as word spread of their military fortitude and resolute commitment to the treaty. Massasoit returned safely to his village, and the chiefs of several villages sent complimentary messages to Governor Bradford. More surprisingly, their support for Massasoit won the unexpected admiration of Epenow, the Nauset chief on Capawock who orchestrated the attack on Captain Dermer. Perhaps most significantly, the operation brought Corbitant begging to join the treaty.

On September 13, 1621, nine chiefs representing the Wampanoag confederacy—including Epenow, Corbitant, and

Massasoit's brother—traveled to New Plymouth to sign an official treaty. It read:

> Known all men by these present, that we whose names are underwritten, do acknowledge ourselves to be the royal subjects of king James, king of Great Britain, France, and Ireland, defender of the faith, &c. In witness whereof, and a testimonial of the same, we have subscribed our names, or marks . . . [8]

The formal treaty symbolized far more than mutual defense. The challenge to Massasoit's power had shaken the foundation of the confederacy. The chief's platform had begun to erode, and the Pilgrims and their military prowess filled the void. The assent to foreign rule had begun.

On a morning in early October, a messenger informed Massasoit of an unceasing barrage of gunfire near New Plymouth. Under the terms of their treaty, the Wampanoag had a duty to protect the Pilgrims. Massasoit gathered ninety of his warriors, and they began the journey to New Plymouth.

Prepared to join the Pilgrims in battle, Massasoit found New Plymouth in relative peace and quiet. In fact, he found quite the opposite of the battle—a celebration.[9]

The Pilgrims had started to collect their first harvest and were preparing for winter. Governor Bradford sent four men out hunting for fowl while the residents prepared vegetables from the field. Coinciding with the harvest came the migratory patterns of ducks and geese. This being their first fall in the New World, the Pilgrims had never seen the region so inundated with game birds. They had missed the migration pattern with their late arrival on the *Mayflower*. Now they took advantage of the new opportunity and, as Winslow put it, "we exercised our arms."[10] In only one day they had killed enough fowl and game birds to feed the colony for a week. "And besides waterfowl," Bradford added, "there was great store of wild turkeys."[11]

Indeed, the Pilgrims had regained their health, and the fruits of their labor sprang up in the field. Though much smaller in number, the colony appeared to have largely recovered from its devastating first winter, leaving the residents of New Plymouth with an optimistic outlook. After a year of pain and suffering, Governor Bradford declared that all of New Plymouth should rejoice together.

With no battle to fight, Massasoit directed his men to make camp near New Plymouth for the night. Subsequently he sent several of his warriors out to hunt. Eventually the two groups began to comingle as the Wampanoag gravitated toward the celebration. When Massasoit's men returned, they carried in a kill of five deer and contributed venison to the feast. With Massasoit's company, the harvest celebration swelled New Plymouth to twice its size.

In addition to the venison, they dined on turkeys, quail, pigeons, and partridges. They had gathered gooseberries, strawberries, grapes, walnuts, chestnuts, and plums. They enjoyed their Indian corn, and, of course, they had fish and clams from the sea.

After the Wampanoag broke camp and the Pilgrims wrapped up their festivities, New Plymouth's leaders conducted an inventory of their copious harvest. To their shock, the supposed abundance of food proved far smaller than expected. In their overindulgence, they had consumed so much of the harvest that the crop likely would not last the winter. The realization came as a blow to New Plymouth's leaders. They believed they had surpassed their risk of starvation—a concern they expected never again to relive.

Now it appeared as perhaps they might. Bradford immediately ordered meal rations cut in half.

Chapter Eleven

The Hope of Peace

NOVEMBER 9, 1621
NEW PLYMOUTH

A *ship!*
Word of the sighting chilled Bradford and Standish. Indians farther up the coast had spied the ship anchored near the tip of the cape and passed the message along. New Plymouth had not arranged for or expected a ship.

Perhaps it could be an innocuous fishing expedition, but Bradford and Standish feared the worst: French privateers. A hostile French vessel would undoubtedly be better armed than New Plymouth and hungry for plunder. Bradford ordered Standish to arm his militia and prepare the cannons to fend off an attack.

New Plymouth waited at the ready—and weeks passed.

Before the end of November, the white sails of a fifty-ton ship appeared on the horizon. It slowly lumbered into the waters off New Plymouth and into the channel. The village made defense preparations.

When they could make out its details, they saw that it did not fly a French or Spanish flag, but an English one. Their fears relieved, New Plymouth's residents came out to welcome this "unexpected" gift from Europe as it entered Plymouth Bay.

The *Fortune* arrived at New Plymouth at the behest of the Merchant Adventurers. Chiefly the vessel had orders to deliver the investors' demands to New Plymouth. The Pilgrims had not returned any commodities to England, nor had they renegotiated the contract they had rejected before departure. Since the *Mayflower* had sailed back empty, the *Fortune* had arrived to collect.

Leading the effort to persuade the Pilgrims to fulfill their expectations was the Leiden congregation's former ambassador, Robert Cushman. In addition to Cushman and Merchant Adventurers' list of demands, the *Fortune* carried thirty-five new arrivals—mostly additional Strangers—but a few Separatists from Leiden, including Brewster's son. With only a handful of women and children on board, most of the new arrivals were "lusty young men," as Bradford described them, "and many of them wild enough."[1]

The Pilgrims' hope for an abundant cargo of food stores quickly faded—the *Fortune* had brought no supplies, tools, or rations.

"[T]here was not so much as bisquit bread, or any other victuals for them," Bradford lamented, "neither had they any bedding, nor pot nor pan to dress any meat in, nor over many clothes."[2]

In the Merchant Adventurers' defense, they had good reason to believe abundance flowed at New Plymouth. America's chief salesman, Captain John Smith, wrote glowing accounts of lands teeming with game, fish, and fruits. Perhaps misleadingly, the Pilgrims had corroborated Smith's accounts in letters sent back on the *Mayflower.* They did not want to discourage the rest of their congregation from migrating, nor did they want to represent the colony as a disaster. Everyone, it seemed, had oversold North America.

The flood of thirty-five new residents into the fledgling

colony could hardly have come at a worse time. With New Plymouth already rationing its food, the influx would swell the village by nearly 50 percent. Everyone would need to ration again.

If the *Fortune*'s cargo disappointed the Pilgrims, their disillusionment may have been matched only by the newcomers' depressing reception. They "saw nothing but a naked and barren place," Bradford noted.[3]

November had left the shoreline stark and inhospitable, with the weather growing cold. The colony appeared dilapidated and depressed. The new arrivals had known nothing of the condition of New Plymouth when they had boarded the *Fortune* in England and found themselves vastly underprepared. Most could not imagine how the colony would survive the winter— and then other fears crept upon them.

"They began to think," Bradford said, "what should become of them if the people here were dead or cut off by Indians."[4]

The fear appeared well founded. New Plymouth's winter landscape was nearly as barren as its tables. The Pilgrims had access to water, albeit not particularly safe, as the plagues had proven. In fact, the English had been taught to consider all water unsafe. Several decades before the Pilgrims' departure, English physician Andrew Boorde shaped prevailing thought by saying, "Water is not wholesome solely by itself for an Englishman. . . . If any man do use to drink water with wine, let it be purely strained, and then [boil] it; and after it be cold, let him put it to his wine."[5]

For the Pilgrims, water could only be consumed safely if it was included in the fermentation process of wine. But again, they lacked the fruit to ferment. They possessed no domestic animals, such as cows and goats, leaving them unable to replenish their milk, butter, and cheese.

New Plymouth's prospects looked so bleak that many of the thirty-five new arrivals consulted with the *Fortune*'s captain about reboarding. Ultimately, all were persuaded to stay.[6]

Cushman arrived with an agenda. He faced tremendous pressure from Weston and the Merchant Adventurers to repay the voyage. From Weston's perspective, the Pilgrims had shirked their duties by not yet sending exports to England. But since the Merchant Adventurers had already paid for the voyage and North America had no court system, they had little recourse other than heated words and an appeal to the Pilgrims' pious convictions.

Cushman carried with him a letter from Weston and a new contract with Merchant Adventurers, replacing the contract the Pilgrims had rejected in England.[7] Had the Merchant Adventurers known of the Pilgrims' pallid results, Weston wrote, they never would have funded the voyage.

"That you send no lading back with the [*Mayflower*] is strange," Weston continued, "and very properly resented. I know your weakness was the cause of it; and I believe more weakness of judgment than weakness of hands. A quarter of the time you spent in discoursing, arguing, and consulting would have done much more. . . ."[8]

Cushman, largely coerced by Weston, demanded the Pilgrims immediately sign the new contract. Weston admitted he had not told the Merchant Adventurers that the Pilgrims rejected the first contract before leaving England. This gave Weston what little remaining leverage he might have. The Pilgrims needed the Merchant Adventurers to fund the subsequent voyage, providing passage for the Leiden congregation. If the Pilgrims would sign the new contract, they should anticipate a ship coming with relief supplies and their friends. If they refused, Weston threatened, he would inform the Merchant Adventurers of their delinquency, and preparations for a future voyage would cease.

Weston's threats aside, the Pilgrims had every intention of repaying their debt to the Merchant Adventurers. Despite their precarious condition, the Pilgrims resolved to immediately relieve as much of their obligation as possible. They signed the agreement.

During the next two weeks, the Pilgrims loaded the *Fortune* with oak staves, beaver skins, and otter pelts. At completion, the cargo had an estimated value of five hundred pounds—nearly half of their balance. Cushman would reboard the *Fortune* for the return journey. On the Pilgrims' behalf, he would carry a letter from Governor Bradford to Weston, the Merchant Adventurers' agent in London, and a manuscript recording their first thirteen months in America. The manuscript would become known as *Mourt's Relation*.[9]

On December 13, nearly one year after the Pilgrims first settled on Cape Cod, the *Fortune* sailed out of Plymouth Bay with a full payload of exports. The Pilgrims expected the abundance of cargo not only to appease the Merchant Adventurers but to encourage them to send supplies and provisions in return. If they could survive another winter, they would reap the rewards in the spring.

In the meantime, the new Strangers disrupted not only their food supply but their way of life. On Christmas Day, Bradford organized villagers to work in the woods and fields. The latest arrivals to New Plymouth objected, arguing "it went against their consciences to work on that day."[10] Bradford said that if indeed it was a matter of conscience, he would not force them to work until they better understood the colony's dire condition.

When Bradford and the rest of the villagers returned for lunch, they found the Strangers playing openly in the streets, partaking in games such as "stool-ball." Bradford was furious. He walked up to them and took away their bats and balls. He told them "that was against his conscience, that they should play, and others work; if they made the keeping of it matter of devotion, let them keep their houses, but there should be no gaming, or revelling in the streets."[11] They never played again.

⸎

With slow, deliberate steps, a Narragansett warrior walked out of the woods and toward the gates of New Plymouth. His arms stretched out before him with a gift in his hands: long straight arrows, adorned with flint-knapped points and bound tight with a snakeskin.

The messenger entered the village and walked onto its main street. All eyes turned toward the man and his unusual parcel, but none knew how to respond.

Squanto immediately declared the curious package to be a sinister message and a challenge. The warrior carried his bundle on behalf of the Narragansett tribe, the feared regional power that supposedly conspired with Corbitant to plot against Massasoit, and eventually the Pilgrims. The Narragansetts had not joined the Pilgrims' peace treaty, nor did they align politically with Massasoit. They saw the Pilgrims as invaders of the region and their cherished hunting grounds.

The Pilgrims sent the Narragansett messenger off with a return volley: a snakeskin filled with gunpowder and bullets.

"[I]t was no small terror to the savage king," Bradford learned of their bullet bouquet, "insomuch as he would not once touch the powder and shot or suffer it stay in his home and country. . . ."[12]

Standish and Squanto viewed the Narragansett message as clear provocation and suggestive of a forthcoming attack. They immediately implemented more drastic defensive measures. The New Plymouth government mobilized all villagers available to begin building a stockade: an eight-foot wooden wall—nearly a mile in circumference—around the entire village. By the end of March 1622, New Plymouth's residents had constructed the wall with three gates, which they guarded at night.

With the wall completed, the Pilgrims turned their attention toward preventing a battle. They preferred a diplomatic solution and would try the approach again. Hobbamock had intelligence that the Narragansetts had aligned with the Massachusetts tribe to plot an ambush. Hobbamock warned them that they might be sailing into a dangerous situation, but they nonetheless prepared the shallop for a mission to the Massachusetts tribe to stave off an attack.

Hobbamock had other concerns to address with Bradford. He claimed to witness Squanto in the woods talking with men he did not recognize—men not from within their alliances. Hobbamock worried that this could be somehow correlated to the Narragansett and Massachusetts threat.

Squanto categorically denied Hobbamock's allegations. The Pilgrims sided with Squanto. He had proven his trust and friendship to the Pilgrims, but this friendship had sparked a jealous rivalry between the native men. Bradford and the New Plymouth leaders thought it merely Hobbamock's envy.

The Pilgrims planned to proceed with the mission to the Narragansetts despite Hobbamock's warnings. Standish took the lead, as the men loaded the shallop and shoved off from the harbor.

The shallop had not sailed far from the village when an Indian friend of Squanto raced into New Plymouth, frantic and bleeding from the face. He claimed the village would soon be under attack because the Narragansetts had recruited Corbitant and Massasoit to attack the Pilgrims.

The warning, however unusual, caused immediate alarm.

The mission to the Massachusetts tribe had left New Plymouth vulnerable. With their military leader and best armed forces on board the shallop, the Pilgrims knew the enemy had an opportunity. They could take no risks.

Several men rushed to the hilltop artillery platform overlooking Cape Cod. With the shallop still within earshot, they fired the cannon to sound a recall. Within minutes the shallop tacked for a return to the harbor.

Hobbamock assured Bradford and the New Plymouth leaders that Massasoit would not break his treaty. He had heard nothing about an attack, and since he still served as Massasoit's trusted adviser, surely the sachem would have informed him.

Skeptical and searching for answers himself, Hobbamock sent his wife to Massasoit's village to investigate. At New Plymouth, everyone waited on edge. The hours passed painfully slowly, with every unusual noise seeming to predicate the impending attack.

Nothing came.

⸙

Hobbamock's wife returned from Sowams with news. She found Massasoit at home under no emergency or duress. Her inquiry about the attack shocked him—he had not interacted with Corbitant or the Narragansetts and vowed never to break his treaty.

Massasoit, however, had a guess at the culprit: Squanto.

Hobbamock's wife learned that Squanto had orchestrated similar bouts of panic among other villages in the region. Leveraging his friendship with the Pilgrims, Squanto had told various Indian leaders that he could control war and have the Pilgrims bring it upon anyone he wished. He made many believe that the Pilgrims kept the plague buried in the ground, and they could bring it out at their command. These stories terrified the Indians and elevated Squanto to a position of perceived power. Out of fear, many of the Indians would bring Squanto gifts to placate him, and Squanto enjoyed the attention.

Squanto had kept this maneuvering out of Bradford's view. Hobbamock's revelation shocked the governor and the Pilgrims, who "began to see that Squanto sought his own ends and played his own game by putting the Indians in fear, and drawing gifts from them to enrich himself."[13]

Soon an envoy of braves from Sowams arrived at New Plymouth. They had a specific demand from Massasoit: Squanto's head.

Massasoit's demand vexed Bradford. Squanto was, indeed, at New Plymouth, and under the terms of their treaty with Massasoit, they might be required to turn over an enemy of Massasoit. The Pilgrims, however, did not want to lose Squanto—their mouthpiece, translator, and adviser. They had no one else to fill his void. Although Hobbamock had proven himself trustworthy, he lacked Squanto's skill at English and his understanding of English custom. Their trust of Hobbamock could only go so far, knowing that ultimately his loyalty lay with Massasoit.

More importantly, the evidence against Squanto was not yet clear enough to accuse him of treachery paramount to a death sentence. The English had the custom of a trial, and Massasoit had already rendered a guilty verdict. Perhaps they had it wrong. Maybe Hobbamock sought to end his rivalry with Squanto in an elaborate scheme. Or perhaps a simple miscommunication had led to an overreaction. Whatever the cause, Bradford wanted to better understand the situation before placing Squanto in Massasoit's hands.

On the contrary, the Pilgrims could not risk disavowing Massasoit. Should he turn against them, the entire balance of power in the region would shift out of their favor. They would have no ally among the Indians and most assuredly would appear vulnerable to an attack. Defensive measures aside, the Pilgrims remained bound by the peace treaty and thus had a duty to surrender Massasoit's enemies. Squanto had clearly become his enemy.

Massasoit had anticipated their response. The sachem recognized their dilemma and sent his warriors with an offer. If the Pilgrims would not relinquish Squanto quickly, Massasoit's men would buy the wanted man with beaver skins. They even brought Massasoit's knife to complete the task.

"It was not the manner of the English to sell men's lives at a price," Bradford told them, "but when they had deserved justly to die, to give them their reward."[14]

Begrudgingly, Bradford sided with the treaty and sent for Squanto. He gathered Massasoit's men, and within a few minutes, New Plymouth guards escorted Squanto to them. Bradford prepared to hand him over.

A ship! At the instant when Bradford planned to hand over Squanto, New Plymouth's watch called out the sighting.

A ship had entered Cape Cod Bay in front of New Plymouth. The Pilgrims watched as it crossed the bay, then disappeared behind a headland. The town had only recently endured the terror of the rumored French vessel. Despite the relief of seeing an English flag flying over the *Fortune*, the fear of a French ship had not vanquished. This new sighting immediately reignited old fears and stalled the prisoner exchange.

Bradford postponed Squanto's transfer for the time being. He wanted to address the immediate security of the colony first. The governor's deferral enraged Massasoit's men, who saw his delay as a thinly veiled excuse to protect Squanto. They irately departed New Plymouth, empty-handed.

The boat soon arrived at New Plymouth. Once again it

comforted everyone to see an English flag flying over the small vessel—another shallop.

When seven sailors came ashore, the Pilgrims learned that the small boat had launched from a larger fishing vessel named the *Sparrow*. Their comfort did not last long, however, as the surprise visit quickly grew unfriendly. The English sailors came equipped with demands. First and foremost, the Pilgrims must assist the sailors and "supply with such necessaries as you can spare and they want."[15] They had no provisions to offer New Plymouth and refused to share any of their haul in fish. Second, they had arrived with a message from Thomas Weston, the Merchant Adventurers' agent.

Weston had sent the *Sparrow* to "get up what we are formerly out" by recouping some of his organization's extensive investment in the Pilgrims.[16] If Weston could not trust the Pilgrims to repay him, he would take matters into his own hands. And the sailors informed the Pilgrims that this would not be the last unpleasant visit at his behest.

Weston, in his defense, had heard nothing from the Pilgrims nor received any reward. The *Fortune*, which he had sent to retrieve his commodities and return quickly, had grown overdue, leaving him with no return on investment since the *Mayflower* voyage nearly two years before.

Unbeknown to Weston or the Pilgrims, five weeks after departing New Plymouth, the *Fortune*'s captain had sailed into what he thought was the English Channel. Instead of being welcomed home by fellow English sailors, a French warship approached with guns ready. The captain had made a common error, mistaking a long peninsula on the west coast of France for the Lizard Peninsula in England. He had mistakenly sailed south into France's Bay of Biscay, undershooting the English Channel by 350 miles.

The French ship had boarded the *Fortune*. Under normal circumstances, French authorities would not seize an English commercial vessel, but France had heightened its naval security in an effort to quell a rebellion. Concerned that English vessels assisted the rebels, they had ordered the seizure of all foreign vessels in French waters.

The French navy had locked up the *Fortune*'s captain and kept the crew under guard while they searched the boat for contraband. They found nothing threatening, but the French governor took an interest in its cargo, confiscating the valuable beaver skins as well as its guns. Despite appropriating almost everything else, the French overlooked the manuscript and letters. With the *Fortune* pillaged, the authorities finally released the ship. It would limp into the port at London, a month after the *Sparrow*'s departure.

With no knowledge of the *Fortune*'s seizure, Weston grew anxious not only for a financial return on the debt the Merchant Adventurers had incurred but for any news at all. His letter, carried by the *Sparrow* and dated January 1622,[17] offered a sarcastic curt rebuke of the Pilgrims: "So faithful, constant and careful of your good are your old and honest friends, that if they hear not from you, they are like to send you no supply, etc."[18]

Weston also hinted at how the Merchant Adventurers might recoup their investment: "By the next ship, we intend to send more people on our own account, and to take a patent; lest your people should be as inhuman as are some of the adventurers, and should not permit us to dwell with them, which would be such extreme barbarism that I will not let myself think [it]."[19]

The Pilgrims did as Weston directed, housing and feeding the seven English fishermen. In addition to Weston's letter, the Englishmen also brought a letter from Captain John Huddleston.

The Pilgrims had not met Huddleston personally but recognized his name as that of an English fisherman in Maine.

"To all good friends at New Plymouth, these, etc.," Huddleston's letter opened. He continued:

> Friends, Countrymen, and Neighbours, I salute you and wish you all health and happiness in the Lord. I make bold to trouble you with these lines, because unless I were inhuman I could do no less. Bad news spreads itself too far; but still, I may inform you that I and many good friends in the south colony of Virginia, have sustained such a loss as the lives of 400 persons would not suffice to make good. Therefore I hope, although not knowing you, that the old rule which I learnt at school may be sufficient: that is,—Happy is he whom other men's ills doth make to beware! And now, and again and again whishing all those that willingly would serve the Lord all health and happiness in the world, and everlasting peace in the world to come, I rest.[20]

Despite its near obliteration, Jamestown had clung to a scintilla of life. But it had survived and begun to grow. The expanding tobacco industry had consumed more and more of the Virginia wilderness surrounding Jamestown. Eventually the Indians of the Powhatan confederacy found the colony's incessant sprawl a threat to their livelihood and besieged the town. Jamestown proper received an early warning, sparing its colonists, but the Powhatan attacked villages along the James River on March 22, 1622. By the end, the death toll of "the Virginia massacre" had risen to 347 colonists.

In the wake of the Virginia massacre, threats made against New Plymouth gave the Pilgrims more reason to be anxious.

Weston's intimidation coupled with Huddleston's admonition left the Pilgrims feeling uneasy. And they still had serious concerns about surviving until the next harvest.

"All this," Bradford wrote, "was but cold comfort to fill their hungry bellies."[21]

With respect to their defensive strategy, Huddleston's warning bolstered their tactics and motivated their construction efforts. The Pilgrims needed more protective facilities and proceeded intently with plans to build a fort of "good timber."[22] A fort would not only reinforce their defenses but provide a vantage point. From its peak, a flat roof with cannon mounts, they could see farther into the countryside and the bay.

In the early summer of 1622, Winslow set out on another diplomatic mission, taking the shallop up the coast to Maine to meet Huddleston and beg him for provisions. Huddleston obliged and gave as much as he could spare. They packed the shallop as tightly as they could manage, but even a shallop's load of food amounted to only a small portion per person when distributed at New Plymouth.

Midsummer, two more ships, the *Charity* and the *Swan*, sailed into Plymouth Bay. The Pilgrims hoped these vessels might be carrying their long-awaited provisions. Neither boat brought anything but further burden on the town.

One ship carried a letter from Weston explaining that he had quit the Merchant Adventurers. His letter continued that he would no longer support the Pilgrims and advised them to break their agreement with the Merchant Adventurers, just as he had done.

Weston's letter then asked for the Pilgrims' help. The two ships carried almost sixty men. They had not come to join New Plymouth, but to start their own colony on the shores of Cape

Cod Bay. Weston had even secured the patent. He wanted the Pilgrims to provide room and board for the men until they could establish the new colony.

Directly contradicting Weston, they also received a letter from Cushman in London. Cushman advised the Pilgrims not to trust Weston or the men he sent.

Bradford and the Pilgrim leaders discussed how to proceed. They trusted Cushman, one of their own, much more than Weston. Still, the Pilgrims believed it their duty, or moral obligation, to fulfill their contract with the Merchant Adventurers. The alternative, as Bradford put it, was "neither lawful nor profitable." Despite opposing Weston's letter, they would not turn away visitors, but "they were an unruly company and had no good government over them,"[23] Bradford grumbled.

On top of their intractable behavior, Weston's men took advantage of New Plymouth at every opportunity. They stayed in the village during the best season of the year, when the colony had less work to do and fewer hardships to endure. They not only expected food, but stole it—taking corn directly out of the Pilgrims' fields. When the men finally moved north to establish their colony, Wessagusset,[24] twenty-five miles to the north, they left their sick in New Plymouth to be housed and healed. The Pilgrims, who had recently endured destitution and death, felt as though Weston's men had escaped North America's rite of passage—that anyone who wanted to settle in this New World must learn to cope and survive.

By the end of summer in 1622, the Pilgrims hoped that a strong harvest might correct their food deficit and shore up the colony for winter. As the harvest festival arrived again, they celebrated with a plentiful meal, but a crop that would fall short of expectations. The "Indian corn" had proved more difficult to grow than the Pilgrims anticipated, even with Squanto's guid-ance. Adding to the low yield, the unexpected demands of the English sailors and Weston's men had taken a toll on their stores.

As the Pilgrims took stock of foodstuff inventory in the wake of the harvest festival, it became immediately clear that their situation would again be dire. They were short on food and found themselves, yet again, on the brink of destitution. Not only had they nothing to eat, but they possessed nothing to trade. They had run out of beads and knives, the staple trade goods in demand by the Indians. Now the Pilgrims could only harvest local resources, which native people could do more efficiently.

Perhaps this was finally the end.

❧

"Behold now another providence of God," Bradford exclaimed, "a ship comes into the harbour."[25]

As the *Discovery* slowly made its way through the chan-nel, the Pilgrims watched with hope. The ship had sailed from London intent on trading along the American coastline. Accordingly, it arrived with a cargo of items that could reinvigo-rate New Plymouth's efforts to trade. The *Discovery* carried large stores of beads and knives, and the ship's proprietors wanted it to return to England with a full load of beaver skins.

The Pilgrims could gather beaver skins—one of the few valued resources they could acquire. The crew of the *Discovery*, however, proposed an exorbitant rate that bordered on extortion. Desperate for this fleeting opportunity, the Pilgrims traded anyway.

Weston's men in Wessagusset soon caught wind of the *Discovery*'s arrival. Before long, they arrived in their small boat, the *Swan*, and offered to embark on a joint trading expedition to Indian villages farther south with whom they had not yet traded. The Pilgrims agreed.

From New Plymouth, the *Swan* and the shallop sailed south toward the Cape. Once again, Standish led the expedition, and Bradford included Squanto by necessity as their only interpreter. A short way into their voyage, a massive storm arose, forcing the boats back to New Plymouth. Standish grew ill from the rough seas, rendering him unable to lead. Bradford took command and put Squanto at his side to navigate. The boats continued south, eventually sailing into waters beyond Squanto's knowledge. Increasingly dangerous conditions forced them to anchor at the nearest safe harbor, but perhaps far enough south to begin trading.

With no villages in sight at their landing place, Bradford sent Squanto out to find the nearest village. He had the task of alerting people of the boats' arrival and encouraging them to come out and trade.

In short order, Indians began arriving at the beach in large numbers. They came, as Winslow put it, "welcoming our governor according to their savage manner, refreshing them very well with store of venison and other victuals which they brought to them in great abundance."[26]

Returning from one of the villages, Squanto began to feel hot and sluggish. He soon began bleeding profusely from the nose, "which the Indians take for a symptom of death," Bradford acknowledged. He collapsed. Squanto's condition worsened over the next couple of days and he called for Governor Bradford. He "begged the Governor to pray for him, that he might go to the Englishman's god in heaven."[27] Despite the Pilgrims' care and comfort, Squanto did not improve, and he closed his eyes for the final time.

"His death was a great loss," Bradford mourned.[28] The expedition continued trading, acquiring what corn and beans they could from various Indian villages. They returned to New Plymouth with little show and great disappointments to share.

Despite the symptoms, Squanto's death aroused suspicion. His friendship with the Pilgrims had made him an enemy of Indian tribes up and down the coast, and assassination by poison had been used as a weapon among warring tribes in the region. Massasoit still wanted Squanto's head for his attempted rebellion. If anyone had the means for an assassination, Massasoit did. He was a great warrior who knew Squanto would not retreat from his quest for power. Corbitant also wanted Squanto dead. Failing to kill Squanto earlier had embarrassed him and forced him into an uncomfortable treaty.

Perhaps nothing nefarious had taken place after all. Squanto may have caught "Indian fever," as they called it, interchangeably smallpox or leptospirosis. He had been captured by Captain Hunt prior to the widespread epidemic in North America and returned from Europe shortly after the epidemic subsided. He may not have been immune but simply avoided it. Such a conclusion coalesced with rumors of the plague returning near Wessagusset, possibly ignited by the arrival of Weston's men.

Soon after Squanto's death, Bradford could see the end nearing in Wessagusset. "This was the end of those who once boasted of their strength,—all able, healthy men," Bradford commented, "—and what they would do in comparison with the people here, who had many women and children and weak ones among them. . . . God can make the weak to stand: let him also that standeth heed lest he fall!"[29]

Although the Pilgrims had not supported the idea of Wessagusset, its conception bound them together. Wessagusset did not have the fortune of an alliance with Massasoit, nor the consequential multitribe treaty. A weakened Wessagusset was vulnerable, and a triumph over this European settlement would embolden its victors.

Should Wessagusset fall, so, too, might New Plymouth.

Chapter Twelve

Provocation

MARCH 1623

WESSAGUSSET

S tandish stood face-to-face with Wituwamat, a warrior of the Massachusetts tribe.

"[T]hey died crying, making sour faces more like children than men," Wituwamat sinisterly boasted to Captain Standish about killing Englishmen and Frenchmen.[1]

Whether he had actually killed Europeans, Standish could not be certain, but many of the chiefs and warriors had learned how to aggravate the English captain.

In the wake of Squanto's death and Bradford's failure to secure more corn for New Plymouth, Standish continued reaching out to tribes with offers to trade. On one such mission, he met Wituwamat. The encounter left Standish on guard. Corroborating Wituwamat's threats, Standish had noticed a pattern of growing hostility toward the Pilgrims. Standish himself had been the victim of at least two incidents of petty theft—only trinkets and beads—but still crimes he had not previously witnessed. He also noticed that the welcomes the Pilgrims received in villages had become lukewarm. He believed something had changed.

Standish watched as Wituwamat ceremoniously made a presentation to the chief of the village where Standish came to trade. Wituwamat took a dagger from around his neck and gave it to the chief, accompanied by a lengthy speech in their language. After the presentation, Standish secretly learned the translation. Wituwamat wanted to recruit this village to attack Wessagusset and New Plymouth.

The Massachusetts tribe had thirty or more warriors, roughly equal to the number of men remaining at Wessagusset. The tribe felt confident they could overpower the men at Wessagusset but knew that New Plymouth's militia would immediately declare war on them. Success would, therefore, require conquering both villages. Attacking New Plymouth would be a much more onerous task, and the Massachusetts wanted to guarantee victory. To do so, they needed to secure the alliance of other tribes.

Standish returned the news to New Plymouth. Wessagusset would fall quickly if attacked, this much the Pilgrims knew. The colony had fallen into disarray and starvation. They would be too disorganized and lethargic to mount a sufficient defense.

"It may be thought strange that these people should fall to these extremities in so short a time," Bradford said of Wessagusset's condition, "being left completely provided when the ship left them . . . "[2]

The situation had grown so desperate at Wessagusset that the men went to humiliating lengths to survive.

"[M]any sold their clothes and bed coverings," Bradford explained, "others, so depraved were they, became servants to the Indians, cutting them wood and fetching them water for a capful of corn; others fell to plain stealing, both night and day, from the Indians, of which they complained grievously. In the end some starved and died with cold and hunger."[3]

The men of Wessagusset resorted to gathering whatever food they could find, typically groundnuts and shellfish. The Indians, seeing their destitute condition, turned to insult. As the men of Wessagusset would prepare food, "[Indians] would take it out of their pots and eat it before their faces," Bradford explained, and if the men objected "[the Indians] were ready to hold a knife at their breasts."[4]

Wessagusset's leaders took extraordinary measures to assuage their native neighbors. When one of the European men stole from the Indians, the Wessagusset group hung him as a public show of justice.

Eventually fear forced the Wessagusset men to take shelter behind the walls of their palisade, locking themselves inside. They slipped out a letter to New Plymouth, asking whether they should preemptively attack the Indians and force them to sell their corn.

The letter from Wessagusset, along with the report from Standish, left the Pilgrims uneasy. Regional stability hung in the balance, and perhaps the tide had now turned against European settlements. The Pilgrims decided that New Plymouth would have to act, but the Pilgrims needed the cooperation of their friend Massasoit.

❦

"[N]ews came to Plymouth that Massasoit was likely to die," according to Winslow. This news arrived unexpectedly, and inconveniently, just as they prepared to ask their closest ally to fulfill his commitment to the treaty.

"Now it being a commendable manner of the Indians," Winslow explained, "when any, especially of note, are dangerously sick, for all that profess friendship to them to visit them in their extremity, either in their persons, or else to send some acceptable persons to them; therefore it was thought meet, being a good and warrantable action, that as we had ever, professed friendship, so we should now maintain the same, by observing this their laudable custom."[5]

The Pilgrims dispatched Winslow and Hobbamock, outfitted with a medicinal mixture of herbs, to Sowams. They set a quick pace, not knowing how much longer Massasoit might have. While they were passing through an area under Corbitant's authority, a group of Indians stopped the New Plymouth envoy and told them that Massasoit had already died and his body had been buried that day.

"My loving sachem, my loving sachem!" Hobbamock wailed. "Many have I known, but never any like thee."[6]

Hobbamock turned to Winslow and said: "[W]hilst I lived, I should never see his like amongst the Indians; saying, he was no liar, he was not bloody and cruel, like other Indians; in anger and passion he was soon reclaimed; easy to be reconciled towards such as had offended him; ruled by reason in such measure as he would not scorn the advice of mean men; and that he governed his men better with few strokes, than others did with many; truly loving where he loved."[7]

Hobbamock feared that the Pilgrims had lost their only faithful friend among the Indians. As the men walked, he continued memorializing the chief with long speeches and "unfeigned sorrow, as it would have made the hardest heart relent."[8]

Their journey suddenly seemed irrelevant, but Winslow lobbied to continue. Considering that Corbitant made the most likely candidate to succeed Massasoit, they should at least attempt to build a friendlier relationship with him. Winslow knew the mission would become increasingly dangerous, given that he and Hobbamock had attacked Corbitant.

"He might now fitly revenge," Winslow noted, "yet esteeming it the best means, leaving the event to God in his mercy. . . ."[9]

If nothing else, they would continue to Sowams to at least pay their respects and meet Massasoit's successor. Given the circumstances with Wessagusset, they needed to reinforce their alliance with the Wampanoag confederacy and encourage Massasoit's successor to honor the treaty.

Half an hour before sunset, they happened upon a messenger from Sowams. Massasoit had not died, but the chief would surely pass before they could reach him. Hobbamock and Winslow decided to push forward as fast as possible.

As Winslow and Hobbamock approached Sowams, they could hear the cries and wails reverberating from the village. They found a large crowd gathered inside Massasoit's house. Hobbamock and Winslow could barely push their way into the room. The multitude danced and howled, orbiting a mass of activity at the center. As people noticed them, the large, undulating circle began to part. In the middle, they found Massasoit—still alive but gravely ill. Around him sat several women, rubbing his arms, legs, and thighs to keep him warm. He had lost his sight and retained barely enough energy to speak.

"Art thou Winslow?" Massasoit whispered.

"Yes," Winslow replied.

"Oh Winslow, I shall never see thee again," the chief murmured.

Through Hobbamock's translation, Winslow gave the chief a message from Bradford: "[T]he Governor, hearing of his sickness, was sorry for the same; and though, by reason of many businesses, he could not come himself, yet he sent me with such things for him as he thought most likely to do him good in this his extremity."[10]

Winslow took out the herb mixture he had carried from New Plymouth. He placed a dollop of the remedy onto the tip of his knife and slipped it into Massasoit's mouth. Winslow followed the herb mixture with mouthfuls of fruit juice, which Massasoit could swallow.

The people in the house began to cheer. Massasoit had not swallowed anything in two days. Within half an hour, his condition began to improve noticeably, and his sight began to return.

Over the next day, the sachem's health waivered precariously but gradually improved with sleep and food. Winslow stayed at his side, nursing him back to health and encouraging him. After a day of rest, Massasoit gained the energy to walk again.

Massasoit admitted that another sachem had visited him the day before regarding the plot against Wessagusset. This sachem had told Massasoit that the English had deceived him. If the Pilgrims were truly his friends, they would have visited him during his sickness. The sachem had tried to persuade Massasoit to disavow his alliance, though Massasoit would not give Winslow specifics on who or what he plotted.

"Now I see the English are my friends and love me," Massasoit told Winslow, "and I will never forget their kindness."[11]

With Massasoit's health improving, Hobbamock and Winslow prepared to return to New Plymouth. Before they could leave, Massasoit called for Hobbamock to meet with him privately. Winslow stepped away.

Massasoit had disturbing news. The people of Nauset, Paomet, Succonet, Mattachiest, Manomet, Agowaywam, and the isle of Capawock had joined together to plan an attack on Wessagusset and New Plymouth. Although these tribes had earnestly solicited Massasoit, he had refused to join them. Massasoit advised Hobbamock to kill the Massachusetts men who had planned the assault.

"If, upon this intelligence," Massasoit told Hobbamock, "[the Pilgrims decide not to attack], tell them, when their country-men at Wessagusset are killed, they being not able to defend themselves, that then it will be too late to recover their lives; . . . [therefore, the Pilgrims should] take away the principals, and then the plot would cease."[12]

Finally, Masssasoit told Hobbamock to share his advice with Winslow so that he could inform Governor Bradford.

Once the men had trekked beyond the earshot of Sowams, Hobbamock shared Massasoit's message. As soon as they arrived at New Plymouth, Hobbamock and Winslow gathered Bradford and New Plymouth's leaders. Winslow revealed to him the details of the Massachusetts plot against New Plymouth, and that Massasoit wanted them to know. He revealed that seven tribes had agreed to join the Massachusetts in the attack against Wessagusset and New Plymouth.[13]

"This did trouble [us]," Bradford admitted, "and [we] took it in serious deliberation."[14]

At a meeting on March 23, New Plymouth's leaders decided to strike first.

Winslow described the plan: "Captain Standish should take so many men as he thought sufficient to make his party good against all the Indians in the Massachusetts bay and to take them in such traps as they lay for others, therefore he should pretend trade, but first go to the English and acquaint them with the plot."[15]

On board the shallop, Standish took eight men to Wessagusset. They found the *Swan* anchored in the harbor and decided to board. The Wessagusset men had left the vessel empty and defenseless. Standish was shocked to find it unguarded. Back on board the shallop, they fired several musket rounds to announce their presence to Weston's men. A few minutes later, several Englishmen wandered onto the beach.

Standish asked for Wessagusset's deputy governor, informed him of the plot, and described the Pilgrims' plan. Standish told the deputy governor, when the Indians inquired as to the Pilgrims' purpose, to explain the visit as a simple trading mission. The deputy governor should then invite the Indians to come to Wessagusset with furs, and the captain would trade with them. Then, Standish explained, at the right moment, he would strike against the Indians who plotted against them.

As the plan began to unfold, Standish drew more attention than expected. His prickly demeanor, fiery red hair, and short stature made him a recognizable figure in the region. The people knew him as a warrior, and he struggled to hide his intentions. His expressions suggested an ulterior motive.

As one Indian who came to trade told his fellow Massachusetts, "[I] saw by his eyes he was angry in his heart."[16]

Within a short time, several Massachusetts warriors came to town to investigate, including Wituwamat and another powerful warrior named Pecksuot. When they found Standish, they took to taunting him.

"You may be a great captain, but you are a little man," Pecksuot said to him, "I am not a great chief, yet I am a man of great strength and courage."[17]

In front of Standish, the warriors began to whet and sharpen the points of their knives. Standish contained himself. He continued to trade for the rest of the day, then quietly ended it.

The next morning, he resumed bartering again. When the warriors returned, Standish invited Pecksuot and Wituwamat, along with a young boy, into a separate room. In the room,

Standish had eight men in hiding. As he shut the door behind the warriors, Standish lunged at Pecksuot, grabbing the knife the warrior had strung around his neck. The captain's men broke cover and charged Wituwamat and the boy. The warriors put up a fight but quickly fell to the blows of their nine Pilgrim attackers.

"It is incredible how many wounds these [warriors] received before they died," Winslow wrote, "not making any fearful noise, but catching at their weapons and striving to the last."[18]

Upon leaving the room, Standish cut off Wituwamat's head as evidence and ordered the execution of every Massachusetts warrior found in town—including the boy. When the men could find only two warriors, they proceeded out of the town gates and into the forest. Beyond the town, they came across a band of Massachusetts Indians who fled at the sight of them. The Pilgrims gave chase as the Indians fired arrows back toward them. The Massachusetts took cover deep in a dense, wooded swamp where Standish knew he had no ability to fight.

Standish gathered Weston's men in Wessagusset to make plans for their evacuation. They could no longer safely stay there, as neither the fledgling town nor the men possessed the fortitude to withstand near certain retribution. New Plymouth would welcome them, Standish told them, if they wished to come. They did not. The men desired to return to England and decided, instead, to reboard the *Swan* and sail for Maine. From there they could join a fishing vessel bound for England.

Returning to New Plymouth, Standish received a joyous welcome home. He triumphantly carried his spoil of war into town—the head of Wituwamat—and impaled it on a spike at New Plymouth's fort, a common practice for the victor of the battle. In addition to celebrating the victory, Bradford lamented the prospects of Wessagusset. With their retreat to the *Swan*,

European settlers had now officially abandoned the plantation—another failed New World colony to further discourage their friends and suppliers.

"Thus this plantation is broken up in a year," Bradford declared indignantly, "and this is the end of those who being all able men, had boasted of their strength and what they would bring to pass."[19]

Beyond Wessagusset and New Plymouth, the Pilgrim offensive reverberated through the region's Indian tribes. Many tribes deserted their settlements and houses, removing themselves to swamps, fearing that the Pilgrims would attack them.

News of Standish's attack even made it to Europe, where Pastor John Robinson in Leiden had less than a joyous reaction. He wrote earnestly and authoritatively to New Plymouth: "Concerning the killing of those poor Indians, of which we heard at first by report . . . where blood is once begun to be shed, it is seldom staunched of a long time after. . . . Necessity of this, especially of killing so many, I see not. . . . I am afraid lest, by these occasions, others should be drawn to affect a kind of ruffling course in the world."[20]

Had there been any lingering doubts about the Pilgrims' military prowess, the Pilgrims had now subdued them and secured their position of power more prominently in the region. Although it brought them a greater sense of security, and arguably more leverage upon which to trade, New Plymouth still had not established a reliable food supply.

Since they could only kill a small number of deer and fowl, they relied instead on the shallop's daily haul of sea bass. A poor catch sent people out to the beach to dig for clams. The village remained on the edge of starvation, little better off than the first winter.

Chapter Thirteen

Thanksgiving

New Plymouth had now grown to require a structural change to its government. The Pilgrims' experiment in simple, communal living had carried them through two harsh winters, but as they began to settle into a routine, they found it no longer fit.

"The failure of this experiment of communal service," Bradford wrote, "which was tried for several years, and by good and honest men proves the emptiness of the theory of Plato and other ancients, applauded by some of later times; that the taking away of private property, and the possession of it in community, by a commonwealth would make a state happy and flourishing; as if they were wiser than God."[1]

The Pilgrims found that their experiment in shared property bred "confusion and discontent." New Plymouth's young, single men complained that they labored for other men's wives and children without proportionate compensation. Older men, some even sick or elderly, protested that they were expected to perform as much work as their abler, younger counterparts. Some women, too, were required to work dressing meat and washing clothes in service to the community. They criticized this as a form of slavery.

The Pilgrims had held New Plymouth's property in common, as well as the chores and duties of the community. The size of New Plymouth, however, and its ever-arriving waves of newcomers had finally outgrown its family-survival ethos. Few of them still shared the common bond of the *Mayflower* voyage, the signing of the compact, the first tree felled. Without this foundation, the community began to fracture.

Age became the most prominent fault line. The younger people of New Plymouth felt disenfranchised by their elders. The young believed they unequally bore the burden of the community workload—laboring in the fields while the older generation lived off their efforts. Their elders had toiled for nearly three years, in sickness and starvation, to found New Plymouth. They believed they had earned the right to step back from the most laborious tasks.

The growing unrest with communal living forced the Pilgrims to divide up the farmland as well. They divided the land by the number of individuals in the community. Each person received an equal portion of land, assigned in plots to families. Each family would now be responsible for its own food supply, rather than relying on the community farm.

One important communal duty could not be divided up: fishing. Fishing required the use of the shallop and skilled labor, and they could not simply build a boat for each family. Thus, it was decided that their fishing enterprise would be held in common, with each person paying a tax for its upkeep and bounty.

The new structure brought noticeable change to New Plymouth. "This was very successful," Bradford wrote. "It made all hands very industrious, so that much more corn was planted than otherwise would have been by any means the Governor or any other could devise, and saved him a great deal of trouble, and gave far better satisfaction. The women now went willingly into the field, and took their little ones with them to plant corn; which before would allege weakness and inability; and to have compelled them would have been thought great tyranny and oppression."[2]

In addition to structural changes that came to New Plymouth in 1623, new visitors arrived as well. Weston would make a surprise visit, only to find he had completely lost his investment in Wessagusset. Others arrived in New Plymouth's harbor hoping to capitalize on the disorganization in North America. One such visitor presented himself as the admiral of New England and demanded that the Pilgrims purchase licenses to fish in New England's waters. The Pilgrims would have none of it.

During the year, New Plymouth would receive ninety-three new arrivals into the colony, twenty-nine of whom came from Leiden. Much to their disappointment, however, the arrivals did not include their pastor, John Robinson.

These arrivals still found themselves profoundly disappointed at the sight of New Plymouth. While the structural changes had made some of the Pilgrims more industrious, the village remained a shantytown. The actual state of New Plymouth contrasted sharply to the stories Europeans heard of North America. In *Mourt's Relation*, Winslow had painted a promising portrait of New England—an embellished effort to attract their friends and family in Leiden. And in a few more months, he would send over another work, *Good Newes from New-England*, further painting a fictitious image of prosperity in New Plymouth.

"These passengers," Bradford observed, "when they saw their low and poor condition ashore, were much daunted and dismayed. . . . Some wished themselves in England again; others fell a-weeping, fancying their own misery in what they saw now in others; some pitying the distress they saw their friends had been long in, and still were under. In a word, all were full of sadness."[3]

The only rejoicing happened between old friends now reunited. For all the others, the moment was depressing. The new arrivals found the Pilgrims in poor condition. Their clothing had worn to shambles leaving some of the Pilgrims "little better than half naked."[4] Beyond their apparel, they looked sickly, gaunt, and weathered. The Pilgrims wanted to welcome them properly but had almost nothing to share with them beyond a piece of fish or a cup of water.

The influx of arrivals had doubled the size of New Plymouth, and since they had arrived after the planting season, they did not have time to prepare or plant enough land. Naturally, those who had been living at New Plymouth worried, yet again, about their overtaxed food supply. Bradford asked the arrivals to rely primarily on supplies they brought from the ship, then divided the newcomers among the village's thirty-two houses.

On top of their hardships and inflating head count, the weather had not cooperated throughout the most critical part of the growing season. A dangerously hot and dry summer brought "a great drought," as Bradford put it. New Plymouth had not seen a drop of rain between the third week in May and mid-July. The crops had withered in sun-scorched fields, some well beyond the ability to recover.

"[T]he great hopes of a large crop, the Lord seemed to blast, and take away the same," Bradford wrote, "and to threaten further and more sore famine unto them by a great drought . . . Upon which they set apart a solemn day of humiliation, to seek the Lord by humble and fervent prayer, in this great distress."[5]

It was a sweltering July day as they gathered in the sun, dedicating an entire day to petition God for relief. Bradford described it:

For all the morning, and greatest part of the day, it was clear weather and very hot, and not a cloud or any sign of rain to be seen, yet toward evening it began to overcast, and shortly after to rain with such sweet and gentle showers as gave them cause of rejoicing and blessing God. It came without either wind or thunder or any violence, and by degrees in that abundance as that the earth was thoroughly wet and soaked therewith. Which did so apparently revive and quicken the decayed corn and other fruits, as was wonderful to see, and made the Indians astonished to behold.

And He was pleased to give them a gracious and speedy answer, both to their own and the Indians' admiration that lived amongst them."[6]

The Pilgrims had no doubt they witnessed a miracle. They had questioned God and wondered why he would allow them such disappointment and heartache. Bradford wrote: "And afterwards the Lord sent them such seasonable showers, with interchange of fair warm weather as, through His blessing, caused a fruitful and liberal harvest, to their no small comfort and rejoicing. For which mercy, in time convenient, they also set apart a day of thanksgiving."[7]

This "day of thanksgiving" captured the Pilgrims' appreciation for God's blessings. Before the rains, New Plymouth hurtled toward starvation—a path they had been on several times, but again appeared hopeless. They had watched as colonies across North America starved and failed. Between the new arrivals from Europe and the extreme drought, it appeared that New Plymouth would indisputably suffer the same fate.

But with the rain and the lifting of the drought, the Pilgrims now had much to celebrate and combined the day of thanksgiving with another joyful event—the wedding of Governor

Bradford.[8] Bradford had lost his first wife in unusual circumstances soon after the *Mayflower*'s arrival at Cape Cod. In the intervening years, he had struck up correspondence with Alice Southworth, a widow in England. She joined the *Anne* on its voyage to New Plymouth that summer.

The "day of thanksgiving" swelled to a great celebration. They cooked twelve deer and gathered grapes, plums, and nuts. They invited Massasoit, who gladly accepted, and contributed a turkey and several deer. Joining him was his ample entourage: five wives, four other chiefs, and 120 warriors. Massasoit's group danced and sang, creating quite a spectacle for the Pilgrims.

The day of thanksgiving made for a great success.

❦

The fall of 1623 and its bountiful harvest would signify a turning point for New Plymouth and New England generally. At the end of the season, the Pilgrims finally had resources at hand to export to Europe. The *Anne* made a return trip to England with a full cargo, carrying beaver pelts, oak, and cedar, as well as Edward Winslow to provide political representation for New Plymouth in England.

With New Plymouth finally enjoying a glimmer of sustainability and the growing expatriation of Europeans to the colony, the settlement could no longer quietly slip by English officials.

The son of Fernando Gorges, for one, arrived in New Plymouth alleging to possess the official commission to serve as governor of New England. He claimed his domain contained New Plymouth, and he thereby relieved Governor Bradford of his duties. The younger Gorges quickly found New Plymouth reprehensible to a man of his English nobility, and only weeks later he returned to England, leaving the colony back in the steady hands of Bradford.

A stream of visitors and new arrivals followed during the next few years. Many came to New England hoping to prospect on its natural resources; others joined a growing contingent seeking a better quality of life than Europe could offer. But nearly all ran afoul of the Pilgrims' myopic vision for the New World.

Among the first to challenge the Pilgrims' ideologies was Thomas Morton, an English lawyer equally attracted to the lawlessness of North America as to its bountiful resources. As an adviser on the law of the seas, Morton enjoyed the permissive lifestyle of seamen, which ran in abrupt conflict to England's pressures of Puritanism. Eventually he came into the service of Ferdinando Gorges, who pointed him to the New World. He soon followed the siren call of entrepreneurial opportunity and Puritan-free adventure, forming an expedition to plant a colony in North America. In 1624, Morton and his men settled in a placed called Mount Wollaston[9] and adopted a lifestyle far different from the Pilgrims.

"[T]hey fell to utter licentiousness," Bradford wrote, "and led a dissolute and profane life. Morton became lord of misrule, and maintained, as it were, a school of Atheism. As soon as they acquired some means by trading with the Indians, they spent it drinking both wine and strong drinks to great excess, and, as some reported, ten shillings worth in a morning!"[10]

To the consternation of Bradford, Morton erected a maypole at Mount Wollaston. Borrowed from pagan traditions, the maypole worried Bradford as a premonition of things to come in the New World. Morton's men made the maypole their epicenter for "drinking and dancing about it for several days at a time, inviting the Indian women for their consorts, dancing and frisking together—like so many fairies, or furies rather—to say nothing of worse practices. It was as if they had revived the celebrated feasts of the Roman goddess Flora, or the beastly practices of the mad Bacchanalians.[11]

"They changed the name of the place," Bradford continued, "and instead of calling it Mount Wollaston, they called it Merry Mount, as if this jollity would last forever."[12]

As much as the immorality of Merry Mount troubled the Pilgrims, they grew gravely concerned about Morton's activities that extended beyond drinking and pagan rituals. Morton began amassing large quantities of fur, primarily by selling arms to the Indians. He not only sold them muskets, but also taught them how to shoot.

Merry Mount presented several dangers to New Plymouth and other developing colonies along the New England coast. Morton's inflow of muskets changed the balance of power between European settlers and Indian tribes. Muskets served as the chief military advantage for settlers, and the sale of arms radically increased their vulnerability. Merry Mount also became a refuge for embittered hired servants. Many newcomers joined wealthy settlers as servants, exchanging several years of labor for expenses paid. These servants would arrive in New England with their voyage costs paid, and then abscond to Merry Mount without fulfilling their contracts.

The Pilgrims decided that the security threat had grown too severe. When diplomatic efforts to engage Morton failed, they decided they would take Morton by force.

Standish, naturally, led the military operation. Arriving at Merry Mount, the Plymouth force found little resistance from Morton's inebriated men.

"They were so drunk that their guns were too heavy for them," Bradford said.[13]

Morton, like his men, was too drunk to fight. He tried to

fire his gun but could not aim. Standish rushed Morton, disarmed him, and tackled him to the ground. Standish removed him from Merry Mount to New Plymouth and then placed him alone on a nearby island to sober up in isolation. Morton subsequently complained that Standish gave him no gun, food, or shelter. According to Morton, Standish only returned to the captive a month later, when a ship had readied to sail for England. Standish placed him on the outbound vessel.

⁓

In England, King James had grown seriously ill, suffering from arthritis and kidney problems. His son and heir apparent, Charles I, began assuming control in his father's growing absence from public affairs. When King James died in 1625, Charles took over without interruption.

The pressure King James had put on the Separatists to conform to the Church of England dramatically increased and, under Charles, was applied to everyone in England, including the Puritans. Even greater religious pressure came with the appointment of William Laud as archbishop of Canterbury. Laud had a vision for elevating the Church of England to a more powerful global force, on par with the Catholic Church.

Archbishop Laud wanted to cultivate uniformity in the Church of England, following a strict set of practices approved by King Charles. Laud saw any nonconformists, such as the Puritans and Congregationalists, as direct threats that needed to be eliminated. Even Huguenot refugees, who had fled to England after religious intolerance in France forced them abroad, caught the ire of Laud. They, too, Laud declared, must conform to the Church of England's required practices.

Archbishop Laud's practices were strict, aligning more

closely to Rome's edicts than to the growing Protestant influence in Europe. His requirements went further than what even the Puritans, who believed they could eventually change the church from within, could handle. Laud wanted to destroy Puritanism altogether, and anyone who refused to conform would be subject to fines or imprisonment. Despite protests, Charles unquestioningly deferred to Laud with respect to matters of religious toleration.

In January 1629, Charles opened the house session of Parliament. An ensuing quarrel led Charles to immediately dissolve Parliament, ushering in an era of personal rule. With Laud at the helm of state religion, intolerance of nonconforming practices could proceed unchecked.

For the Puritans—now a large population of commoners—the brazen rule of King Charles forced a critical deliberation: fight or flee? Despite a growing sentiment for revolution, it seemed unlikely that a rebellion against the Crown would be successful. Instead, most Puritans began to look abroad. With much of Europe straining under similar religious tension, the Puritans had few options for refuge. Like the Scrooby congregation two decades earlier, some went to Holland. To others, the New World appeared more and more attractive. England's land charters made it increasingly easy to settle, and for now, the land was far enough beyond the reach of Charles and his agents that they could practice as they wished.

∽⁂∽

New Plymouth was a triumph in Europe. Despite its long-desperate condition, the colony's unlikely survival overshadowed the failures at Roanoke, Popham, Jamestown, Wessagusset, and Merry Mount. Increasing in prominence through Winslow's manuscripts, the Pilgrims served as inspiration for those who felt persecuted. Accordingly, the heavy hand of Archbishop Laud encouraged many Puritans to consider the transatlantic crossing.

The area around Massachusetts Bay, forty miles north of New Plymouth, became flush with new arrivals. What began as a small fishing village on Massachusetts Bay caught the attention of Puritan leaders and investors. Soon, the Massachusetts Bay Company was born. Its organizers worked effectively to recruit settlers, and with the mass exodus of Puritans from England, it found little shortage of skilled labor or money.

The Massachusetts Bay Company wanted to build a community on Puritan ideals, but upon the foundation of the Church of England. Consequently, many Anglican practices came along too. Church attendance, for instance, was mandatory—for everyone, Puritan or otherwise.

Not everyone who arrived in New England under the umbrella of the Massachusetts Bay Company claimed Puritanism. Indeed, many Separatists joined the flight from King Charles and Laud. For the Separatists stirring quietly among the Puritan majority, New World Puritanism felt much like a reprise of English intolerance.

Puritan leaders feared that the Separatists might draw unwanted attention from England. The Puritan church organized at Massachusetts Bay looked enough like the Church of England that they could implement Puritan practices without notice. However, a large Separatist community breaking the uniformity of religious practice, in English-claimed territory no less, might be enough to draw sanctions or, at worst, revoke their charter.[14]

New Plymouth itself struggled with the growing pains of a changing culture. Those who had weathered the difficult early years of New Plymouth resented the new arrivals. The "Oldcomers" as they called themselves, had arrived on the earliest ships, including the *Mayflower*, surviving both famine and illness.

The latest arrivals always received the title "Newcomers," and the previous batch of Newcomers would diffuse into Oldcomers. This tradition continued until 1627 when New Plymouth's population rose to about 180 and the Oldcomers drew a line. After 1627, no longer would anyone receive the honorific title of "Oldcomer."

The Pilgrims had typically dealt with misconduct as a family affair, opting for reconciliatory and nontraditional punishment. That, too, would change. John Billington, Sr., one of the *Mayflower* Pilgrims, made enemies with one of the Newcomers. When Billington and his adversary crossed paths in the forest one day, Billington drew his musket and fired. Billington's shot hit the man in the shoulder, mortally wounding him. Murder within the Pilgrim brethren shocked the pious community. They arrested Billington and placed him before a twelve-man jury. Upon "plain and notorious evidence," the jury found him guilty and recommended a sentence of death.[15]

The ordeal signaled a coming-of-age moment for New Plymouth. The Pilgrims could no longer be insulated from such heavy matters, nor resolve them among friends. New Plymouth now had to subscribe to a greater civil plan—a body politic. The Pilgrims consulted John Winthrop, the governor of the Massachusetts Bay Company, for another opinion. He had a simple recommendation to end the Billington saga: hang him.

In a departure from New Plymouth's ethos of survival and preservation, the village followed Winthrop's advice. Billington's execution brought a great sadness upon New Plymouth, particularly among the Oldcomers.

In 1630, New Plymouth also received a new patent for the colony, officially giving the town control of a significant portion of land from the south shore of Boston Bay.[16] This was good news—but with a catch. The patent, unfortunately, did not possess the Great Seal, which would have designated it a "royal patent." Since the Pilgrims had not settled in their designated location under the umbrella of the Virginia Company, this nonroyal patent would give a temporary, seven-year window to establish their colony and reapply for the seal. The result recognized New Plymouth as a plantation, but not as a separate legal jurisdiction. In the meantime, the plantation would remain under the jurisdiction of the Council of New England, which held a royal patent.[17]

On February 5, 1631, Roger Williams stepped off a ship and onto the docks of the Massachusetts Bay Colony's Boston harbor. He and his wife, Mary, were among a new and growing wave of religious refugees joining the flight to New England to avoid the wrath of King Charles and Archbishop Laud.

Williams, twenty-eight, had progressive theological ideas on topics ranging from believers' baptism to the separation of church and state, with an interest in promoting wide religious toleration. His broad-minded theology stemmed, perhaps, from his youth in England where he had witnessed persecution and executions because of relatively minor theological differences. While completing his formal education at Cambridge, he became a Puritan, forgoing permanent placement as a clergyman in the Church of England.

Coinciding with Williams's arrival in America, the minister of the Boston Church had to travel back to England. In the minister's absence, the Boston Church asked Williams to step into the pulpit. Before he would agree, he had a peculiar, but adamant, request. He asked that the church's members publicly repent for taking communion with the Church of England while they lived in England.

Williams's mandate stoked a heated debate in the Boston

Church over the scope of repentance. The dispute quickly caught the attention of Massachusetts Bay Colony officials, who attempted to defuse the matter. Williams sharply rebuked the colony, challenging whether civil officials had the authority to speak into religious matters.

The controversy created a contentious environment for him at the Boston Church. When it became clear he would not prevail, he left Boston for a church in Salem. Nevertheless, the controversy followed him to his new post, and with increasing political pressure, he had to look elsewhere yet again.

Eventually Williams found his way to the church in New Plymouth. Its Separatist ideals offered the theological foundation he had searched for in New England, and the Pilgrims welcomed him into their church. With so many Puritans flooding into New England, they found it refreshing to find a young leader committed to challenging Anglican traditions. Williams and his wife moved to New Plymouth, sharing in the labor of the village, farming, and living by humble means. In the church, his teachings were "highly approved."[18]

After a year in New Plymouth, Williams began asking questions that challenged the philosophy of the community: Did the Pilgrims have any right to the land on which they settled?

The Pilgrims presented their patent to him. But Williams probed deeper: Did the king have any right to grant the patent at all? The king had not purchased the land from the Indians, Williams argued. He stole it. Therefore, New Plymouth rightfully belonged to the Indians.

Governor Bradford and the leaders in New Plymouth did not know what to make of his questions. Williams refused to let them go. The provocative inquiry soon grew into heated exchanges, putting Williams's future in New Plymouth on the line.

"[H]e this year fell into some strange opinions," Bradford

wrote, "and from opinion to practice which caused some contro-versy between the church and him, and in the end some discontent on his part, by occasion whereof he left them somewhat abruptly."[19]

Upon being dismissed from the New Plymouth church, Williams transferred to the church at Salem despite his former employer's cautions. His new position at Salem did not proceed smoothly. His ideas quickly ran afoul of his new church and the local government.

"He is to be pitied and prayed for," Bradford said, "and so I shall leave the matter, and desire the Lord to show him his errors, and reduce him into the way of truth, and give him a settled judg-ment and constancy in the same, for I hope he belongs to the Lord."[20]

Brewster and the leaders at the New Plymouth church did not object to Williams's departure. He returned to Salem, but he could not shake his controversial reputation. No church or city wanted him, and soon he found legal action brought against him. A court at the Massachusetts Bay Colony determined that Williams should be removed from Massachusetts and sent back to England.

Privately, the governor of the Massachusetts Bay Colony wrote to Williams advising that if he wanted to stay in the New World, he should look beyond the English settlement to Indian territory.

With five followers, Williams crossed Narragansett Bay to the south and found the Narragansett chief.[21] The chief gave land to Williams on which to develop and found a town. He named his settlement "Providence" and founded a Baptist church there.

Williams wanted religious freedom to stand as the core tenet for his community, thus establishing complete religious toleration.

With the influx of Puritans, New England had swelled in population. New Plymouth, with its now-established farming practices, reaped the benefits of supply and demand. Where it had once relied on the fur trade for income, it could now earn more money from large-scale farming.

New Plymouth's sudden growth and the demand for its agricultural products began slowly disintegrating the community. Since their arrival, the residents had remained largely self-contained. Other than establishing remote, sparsely inhabited outposts to better facilitate the fur trade, the village had focused on its own self-development. Now, with the growing potential to trade with neighboring communities, many residents of New Plymouth wanted to expand their production, acquiring land beyond New Plymouth for farming and grazing livestock.

With this sprawl, the community began to fracture. The residents moving outward intended to continue worshipping at New Plymouth, but as their commutes grew longer and winter weather became treacherous, new satellite churches sprang up in more convenient, outlying locations.

New Plymouth's leaders kept an eye on England, too, as religious tensions flared. The exodus to New England led King Charles to close English ports to prevent the departure of more Puritans. The emigration of Puritans to New England ground to a halt, and some Puritans even chose to return to England to join in the fight. The Puritan Revolution in England had begun and would lead to the eventual abolition of the monarchy. To Bradford and those who had suffered in England, these were great victories.

"Full little did I think that the downfall for the Bishops with their courts, canons and ceremonies had been so near when I began these scribbled writings," Bradford wrote. "Do you not now see the fruits of your labours, O ye servants of the Lord that have suffered for the truth?"[22]

Then, suddenly, New Plymouth's burgeoning agriculture industry crashed. The dramatic decrease in Puritan emigrants allowed agricultural production in New England to catch up to demand. Massachusetts no longer needed to buy surplus food from New Plymouth.

By 1644, New Plymouth had fallen back to subsistence living: fishing and farming for survival. The appeal of more prosperous colonies, like Boston, captivated many Pilgrims and particularly the youth. Consequently, the flight of Pilgrims from New Plymouth increased, and the community became a desolate shell of its former self.

In addition to these changes, the community also lost its elder-in-chief. Brewster died in 1643, leaving a spiritual void in New Plymouth.

"The Church began seriously to think whether it were not better jointly to remove to some other place than to be thus weakened and as it were insensibly dissolved," Bradford lamented.[23]

A congregational discussion ensued. A significant number of New Plymouth's residents said that if the church did not move, then they would.

They agreed to consider resettling in the Nauset region, about fifty miles southeast of New Plymouth, and farther out onto the Cape. It would further isolate them from the magnetic pull of Massachusetts Bay. The Pilgrims had visited the Nauset area several times, for it was the place of the "first encounter" upon the *Mayflower*'s arrival.

New Plymouth sent a search party to identify a new settlement site. They chose a location that appeared to offer good soil and was set at the point where the forearm of Cape Cod turned north.

By June 1646, they began clearing land at Nauset and building houses.[24] Many of New Plymouth's residents joined the move, and soon the old community was largely abandoned. Immediately after the move, the Pilgrims realized the soil was not as rich as they had thought and the space would not support all the Plymouth Pilgrims.

"They began too late to see the error of their previous policy," Bradford admitted, "for they found they had already given away the best and most convenient places to others, and now were in want of such situations themselves."[25]

Bradford wrote of New Plymouth:

Thus was this poor church left like an ancient mother, grown old and forsaken of her children—though not of their affections, yet in regard of their bodily presence and personal helpfulness. Her ancient members being most of them worn away by death, and these of later times being, like children, transferred into other families, she, like a widow left only to trust in God. Thus she that had made many rich, herself became poor.[26]

Epilogue

1644

PLYMOUTH COLONY

William Bradford sat by the fire in a corner of his small home; his gray hair draped down to his shoulders. A kettle hung by a chain over the blaze, boiling water for dinner. He stood up, put on his coat, and stepped out on New Plymouth's main dirt road.

Bradford had organized another gathering of the youth at New Plymouth's fort. His first dialogue with the youth had been helpful, but many questions still lingered. They wanted to meet again, and with Bradford's deep concern for New Plymouth, he readily obliged.

The "ancient men" of the New Plymouth church gathered in the meeting house to join them. The young men of New Plymouth opened the meeting once again. "Gentlemen, we hope you will pardon our boldness, in that we have importuned you to give us meeting once more in this kind, for our instruction and establishment in the truth."[1]

The young men wanted to discuss recent controversies that had arisen about the role of church and state. Bradford welcomed the inquiry—one of the formative questions in the founding of New Plymouth.

"We [hope] that you may see the worth of these things, and not negligently loose [*sic*] what your fathers have obtained with so much hardship," Bradford responded. "[M]aintain these privileges which not man, but the Lord Jesus, the King of the Church, has purchased for you. You see how when they were lost in the former ages, both what evil and misery followed thereupon, and how long and with what difficulty it was, before they could in any purity be recovered again."

Bradford expounded on the dangers they had witnessed when the state controlled the church. The bishops and church leaders had been overcome by their thirst and ambition for power. Through their quest for control of the people, they lost sight of their higher purpose.

"[I]t has cost much blood and sweat in the controversies," Bradford continued. But yet the church could be redeemed.

"It will require much prayer, zeal, holiness, humility, vigilance and love, and peace, with a spirit of meekness, that liberty be not abused. . . . Stand fast in the liberty where Christ has made us free. You have been called into liberty; only use not liberty for an occasion to the flesh, but by love serve one another."

Bradford wanted to do more than host dialogues with New Plymouth's youth. He wanted to preserve the journey of the Pilgrims for generations to come, to survive him and whatever may come to pass. Since before their *Mayflower* voyage, Bradford had held on to documents and letters and kept his journals. Now was the time to organize them.

Of Plymouth Plantation became his opus, a chronicle of New Plymouth and an admonition for how he saw the future. "My object is that their children may see with what difficulties their fathers had to wrestle in accomplishing the first beginnings," Bradford wrote, "and how God ultimately brought them through."[2]

Among his collection of documents, he had included a

letter written by the Pilgrims' stalwart pillars of faith, John Robinson and William Brewster: "We verily believe and trust that the Lord is with us, unto Whom and Whose service was given ourselves in many trials; and that He will graciously prosper our endeavors according to the simplicity of our hearts therein."[3]

Adjacent to this letter, Bradford wrote the following addendum at a later date, presumably long after the Pilgrims' arrival, in the twilight of New Plymouth:

O sacred bond,—whilst inviolably preserved! How sweet and precious were its fruits! But when this fidelity decayed, then their ruin approached. Oh that these ancient members had not died (if it had been the will of God); or that this holy care and constant faithfulness had still remained with those that survived. But, alas, that still serpent hath slyly wound himself to untwist these sacred bonds and ties. I was happy in my first times to see and enjoy the blessed fruits of that sweet communion; but it is now a part of my misery in old age to feel its decay, and with grief of heart to lament it. For the warning and admonition of others, and my own humiliation, I here make note of it.[4]

THANKSGIVING

The Pilgrims did not create a Thanksgiving holiday, nor intend that future fall institution. The singular event was a one-off expression of gratitude. However, combined with their "harvest festival" the year before, the events have become intermixed in American mythology.

Although the Pilgrims did not specifically mention

consuming turkey, they likely had it among their fowl. They did not eat cranberries, though had they known, they could have found them.

"Thanksgiving" in the spirit of the Pilgrims became a common tradition throughout New England. In 1827, Sarah Josepha Hale, a prominent writer credited with the authorship of "Mary Had a Little Lamb," published a novel featuring this fall tradition. She then lobbied state and federal officials to create a national day of thanks. By 1854, thirty states had adopted her suggestion.

In 1863, on the heels of the Battle of Gettysburg, President Abraham Lincoln took an interest in Hale's suggestion. He imagined this national day of thanks as an event to help heal wounds. Secretary William Seward quickly drafted Lincoln's proclamation, formally institutionalizing Thanksgiving as a national holiday on the last Thursday in November.

WILLIAM BRADFORD

Bradford served several terms as governor of New Plymouth over the course of thirty-six years. He died in 1657 at the age of sixty-seven. Bradford left a legacy of one of Plymouth's most prominent and important figures. His writings, particularly *Of Plymouth Plantation*, remain the most useful historical documents chronicling the Pilgrims' journey.

MILES STANDISH

Standish remained the Pilgrims' military adviser until around 1640. He retired to Duxbury across Plymouth Harbor. He claimed he had inheritance rights to a large estate in England but never received it. He died in 1656.

EDWARD WINSLOW

With diplomatic skills honed in the New World, Winslow was elected governor of New Plymouth in 1633, followed by several more rotations through the governor's office. He traveled regularly between New Plymouth and England to represent the colony's interests. In 1646, he permanently moved to London to serve in Oliver Cromwell's government. Winslow died of yellow fever in 1655 on an expedition to the East Indies as chief commissioner.

MASSASOIT

Massasoit died around 1660, only three years after Governor Bradford. Massasoit's son succeeded him as the leader of the Wampanoag confederacy. The friendship between these tribes and New Plymouth was built on a foundation of trust and mutual respect, due largely to the loyal dedication of Massasoit, Bradford, and Winslow. With the passing of Bradford and Massasoit, the absence of Winslow, and the changing demographics of New Plymouth, the friendship between New Plymouth and the Wampanoag deteriorated.

New Plymouth's continued expansion led to a growing appetite for land and the capture of Massasoit's son. After the altercation, Massasoit's son grew ill and died. His brother, Matacom, also known as King Philip, took control and led his people into a war to preserve their confederacy. King Philip led attacks on Plymouth Colony's outlying settlements, eventually threatening Boston and including a raid on New Plymouth. The colonists responded with a series of destructive attacks that killed King Philip and brought an end to the war.

NEW PLYMOUTH

The unattained royal charter would have set the stage for New Plymouth to become the fourteenth founding state of the United States. Instead, Plymouth was later absorbed by Massachusetts in 1691, ending its designation as a separate "colony" and eventually dropping "new" from its name.

Acknowledgments

I am deeply thankful for the team at Thomas Nelson who faithfully stewarded this book. I am, once again, grateful to Janene MacIvor. She is a patient, thoughtful, and excellent editor. I am indebted to Brian Hampton who saw the value in this project and gave me the opportunity to write it. I am thankful for Webster Younce who guided the project in its infancy and shaped a better manuscript. I appreciate the marketing and publicity efforts of Stephanie Tresner and Sara Broun and the expertise in cover design of Belinda Bass. Thank you for all you do to get this story out into the world.

I remain indebted to Sealy Yates. This book would likely not exist without his attention and friendship.

I am thankful for my family who encourages my writing projects: my grandparents, Bob and Pat Ludlow; my parents, Kim and Sarah Milbrandt; and my sister and her husband, Eliza and Eric Raum.

Finally, I am grateful to my wife, Lisa, and daughter, Lilly. Lisa is incredibly patient with my much-consuming book projects, particularly when I have deadlines and long evenings at the keyboard. While Lilly may not yet be old enough to read, she is a reason to write. Hopefully this book serves as another guidepost for her life and reminder of the many things for which we should be thankful.

Timeline of Major Events

1588—Henry Barrow's trial

1593—Separatists Barrow and Greenwood executed in England; religious persecution of Separatist churches

1605—Squanto captured in North America and brought to England

1606—Scrooby Separatist congregation begins meeting in England

1607—Scrooby congregation decides to leave for Holland; Jamestown founded in North America

1608—Ship captain turns in fleeing Pilgrims (including William Bradford), who are jailed; finally escape to Holland after an additional year

1609—Scrooby congregation settles in Leiden, Holland

1610—Jamestown abandoned due to hardship and disease

1614—Squanto returns to North America; recaptured by Hunt and returned to Europe

1618—Squanto arrives in Newfoundland, then sails to England with Dermer

1619—Squanto and Dermer begin peace missions; Scrooby congregation feels challenges in Holland and discusses leaving for the New World

1620—Pilgrims depart for New World in July; Pilgrims
arrive in November; Mayflower Compact signed

1621—Construction of plantation begins; half of Pilgrims
die over winter; Bradford elected governor; Squanto
meets Pilgrims; peace treaty signed between Massasoit
and Pilgrims; Pilgrims celebrate harvest (commonly
misidentified as first Thanksgiving); attack on
Corbitant

1622—Arrival of *Discovery*; Squanto dies on trade mission

1623—Healing of Massasoit; attack on Massachusetts
tribe; First "Thanksgiving" held

List of Mayflower Passengers in 1620

From William Bradford, *Of Plymouth Plantation, 1650* (http://www.pilgrimhall.org/list_passengers.htm).

The names of those which came over first, in the year 1620, and were by the blessing of God the first beginners and in a sort the foundation of all the Plantations and Colonies in New England; and their families.

Mr. John Carver, Katherine, his wife, Desire Minter, and two manservants, *John Howland, Roger Wilder. William Latham*, a boy, and a maidservant and a child that was put to him called *Jasper More*.

Mr. William Brewster, Mary, his wife, with two sons, whose names were *Love* and *Wrestling*. And a boy was put to him called *Richard More*, and another of his brothers. The rest of his children were left behind and came over afterwards.

Mr. Edward Winslow, Elizabeth his wife and two menservants called *George Soule* and *Elias Story*; also a little girl was put to him called *Ellen, the sister of Richard More.*

William Bradford and *Dorothy his wife*, having but one child, a son left behind who came afterward.

Mr. Isaac Allerton and *Mary his wife*, with three children, *Bartholomew, Remember* and *Mary.* And a *servant boy John Hooke.*

Mr. Samuel Fuller and a *servant called William Button.* His wife was behind, and a child which came afterwards.

John Crackston and *his son John Crackston.*

Captain Myles Standish and *Rose his wife.*

Mr. Christopher Martin and *his wife* and *two servants, Solomon Prower* and *John Langmore.*

Mr. William Mullins and *his wife and two children, Joseph and Priscilla*; and a *servant, Robert Carter.*

Mr. William White and *Susanna his wife* and one *son called Resolved*, and *one born a-shipboard called Peregrine*, and *two servants named William Holbeck and Edward Thompson.*

Mr. Stephen Hopkins and *Elizabeth his wife*, and *two children called Giles and Constanta*, a daughter, both by a former wife. And two more by this wife called *Damaris and Oceanus*; the last was born at sea. And *two servants called Edward Doty and Edward Lester.*

Mr. Richard Warren, but his wife and children were left behind and came afterward.

John Billington and *Ellen his wife*, and *two sons, John and Francis.*

Edward Tilley and *Ann his wife*, and *two children that were their cousins, Henry Sampson and Humility Cooper.*

John Tilley and *his wife*, and *Elizabeth their daughter.*

Francis Cooke and his *son John*; but his wife and other children came afterward.

Thomas Rogers and *Joseph his son*; his other children came afterward.

Thomas Tinker and *his wife and a son.*

John Rigsdale and *Alice his wife.*

James Chilton and *his wife*, and *Mary their daughter*; they had another daughter that was married, came afterward.

Edward Fuller and *his wife*, and *Samuel their son.*

John Turner and *two sons*; he had a daughter came some years after to Salem, where she is now living.

Francis Eaton and *Sarah his wife*, and *Samuel their son*, a young child.

Moses Fletcher, John Goodman, Thomas Williams, Digory Priest, Edmund Margesson, Peter Browne, Richard Britteridge, Richard Clarke, Richard Gardiner, Gilbert Winslow.

John Alden was hired for a cooper at Southampton where the ship victualed, and being a hopeful young man was much desired but left to his own liking to go or stay when he came here; but he stayed and married here.

John Allerton and *Thomas English* were both hired, the latter as master of a shallop here, and the other was reputed as one of the company but was to go back (being a seaman) for the help of others behind. But they both died here before the ship returned.

There were also other two seamen hired to stay a year here in the country, *William Trevor*, and one *Ely*. But when their time was out they both returned.

These being about a hundred souls, came over in this first ship and began this work, which God of His goodness hath hitherto blessed. Let His holy name have the praise.

Mayflower Compact

In the name of God, Amen. We, whose names are under-written, the loyal subjects of our dread Sovereigne Lord, King James, by the grace of God, of Great Britaine, France and Ireland king, defender of the faith, etc. having undertaken, for the glory of God, and advancement of the Christian faith, and honour of our king and country, a voyage to plant the first colony in the Northerne parts of Virginia, doe by these presents sol-emnly and mutually in the presence of God and one of another, covenant and combine ourselves together into a civill body pol-itick, for our better ordering and preservation, and furtherance of the ends aforesaid; and by virtue hereof to enacte, constitute, and frame such just and equall laws, ordinances, acts, constitu-tions and offices, from time to time, as shall be thought most meete and convenient for the generall good of the Colonie unto which we promise all due submission and obedience. In witness whereof we have hereunder subscribed our names at Cape-Codd the 11. of November, in the year of the raigne of our sovereigne lord, King James, of England, France and Ireland, the eigh-teenth, and of Scotland the fiftie-fourth. Anno Dom. 1620.

- John Carver
- William Bradford
- Edward Winslow
- William Brewster
- Issac Allerton
- Myles Standish
- John Alden
- Samuel Fuller
- Christopher Martin
- William Mullins
- William White
- Richard Warren
- John Howland
- Stephen Hopkins
- Edward Tilley
- John Tilley
- Francis Cooke
- Thomas Rogers
- Thomas Tinker
- John Rigsdale
- Edward Fuller
- John Turner
- Francis Eaton
- James Chilton
- John Crackston
- John Billington
- Moses Fletcher
- John Goodman
- Degory Priest
- Thomas Williams
- Gilbert Winslow
- Edmund Margeson
- Peter Browne
- Richard Britteridge
- George Soule
- Richard Clarke
- Richard Gardiner
- John Allerton
- Thomas English
- Edward Doty
- Edward Lester

Author's Lineage

Miles Standish	Edward Doty
Josiah Standish	Samuel Doty
Mary Standish	Joseph Doty
Elizabeth Cary	George Doty
Samuel Whitman	Sarah Doty
Mahitable Whitman	Sally Clark
Abner Curtis Bates	Jane Osborne
Marcus Whitman Bates	Horace J. Ludlow
Marcus Frederick Bates	Burr Ludlow
Ruth Bates	H. Bedford Ludlow
Robert Ludlow	Robert Ludlow
Sarah Milbrandt	Sarah Milbrandt
Jay Milbrandt	Jay Milbrandt

Bibliography

"About the Pilgrims—Religion." Pilgrim Hall Museum. http://www
.pilgrimhallmuseum.org/ap_religion.htm.

Abbott, John Stevens Cabot. *Miles Standish: The Captain of the
Pilgrims.* New York: Dodd Mead, 1898. https://archive.org/details
/milesstandishcap00abbo.

———. *Miles Standish: The Puritan Captain.* Boston: B. B. Russell,
1875. https://archive.org/details/milesstandishpur00abboiala.

Amar, Akhil Reed. *America's Constitution: A Biography.* New York:
Random House, 2005.

Ames, Azel. *The May-flower and Her Log, July 15, 1620–May 6, 1621.*
Boston and New York: Houghton Mifflin and Company, 1901.
https://archive.org/details/mayflowerherlogj00amesuoft.

Amory, Hugh and David D. Hall. *A History of the Book in America.*
Cambridge: Cambridge University Press, 2000.

Arber, Edward, ed. *The Story of the Pilgrim Fathers.* London: Ward and
Downey, 1897. https://archive.org/details/storyofthepilgri000478mbp.

Archbishop of Canterbury in the Times of Q. Elizabeth and K. James I.
Printed for R. Chiswell, 1699. https://archive.org/details
/lifejohnwhitgif00paulgoog.

Baker, Peggy M. "Searching for the Promised Land: The Travels and Travails of Richard Clyfton." Pilgrim Hall Museum. http://www.pilgrimhallmuseum.org/pdf/Richard_Clyfton_First_Pastor_Pilgrims.pdf.

Banks, Ronald F., ed. *A History of Maine: A Collection of Readings on the History of Maine 1600–1974*, 3rd ed. Dubuque, IA: Kendall /Hunt, 1974.

Barr, Andrew. *Drink: A Social History of America*. New York: Carroll & Graf Publishers, 1999. https://www.nytimes.com/books /first/b/barr-drink.html.

Blackhorse, Amanda. "Blackhorse: Do You Prefer 'Native American' or 'American Indian'? 6 Prominent Voices Respond." Indian Country Media Network, May 22, 2015. http://indiancountrytodaymedianetwork.com/2015/05/21/blackhorse -do-you-prefer-native-american-or-american-indian-6 -prominent-voices-respond.

Blaeu, Joan. "Delfshaven." 1649, map.

Burgess, Walter Herbert. *The Pastor of the Pilgrims: A Biography of John Robinson*. New York: Harcourt, Brace & Howe, 1920. https://archive.org/details/pastorofpilgrims00burg.

Burrage, Henry S. *Gorges and the Grant of the Province of Maine, 1622: A Tercentenary Memorial*. Portland, ME: State of Maine, 1923.

Carleton, Dudley. *Letters from and to Sir Dudley Carleton During His Embassy in Holland*. London: 1775. https://archive.org/details /lettersfromtosir00carl.

Clink Museum, visited January 5, 2014.

Clink Prison: History Guide. London: Clink Prison Museum, 2011.

Collections of the Massachusetts Historical Society. Boston: Massachusetts Historical Society, 1832.

Congregational Magazine, The (formerly The London Christian Instructor), vol. 9 (1845). https://books.google.com/books/about /The_Congregational_magazine_formerly_The.html?id =Rw8EAAAAQAAJ.

Cook, Minnie G. "The Susan Constant and the Mayflower." *The William and Mary Quarterly* 17, no. 2 (1937): 229–37. http://www.jstor.org/stable/1925278.

Daniels, Bruce C. *New England Nation: The Country the Puritans Built.* New York: Palgrave Macmillan, 2012.

Davis, Daniel K. *Miles Standish: Military Leader at Plymouth Colony.* New York: Chelsea House, 2013.

Deetz, Patricia Scott, and James Deetz. "Population of Plymouth Town, Colony & County, 1620–1690." http://www.histarch.illinois.edu/plymouth/townpop.html.

Defoe, Daniel. *Moll Flanders.* Reprint ed. Los Angeles: Norilana Books, 2006.

Drake, Samuel G. *Drakes Book of the Indians of North America*, 1833.

———. *History of the Early Discovery of America and Landing of the Pilgrims.* Boston: Higgins and Bradley, 1854. https://archive.org/details/landingofthepilg00drakrich.

Emsley, Clive, Tim Hitchcock, and Robert Shoemaker. "Schools—The Journey from Newgate to Tyburn." Old Bailey Proceedings Online. http://www.oldbaileyonline.org/static/JourneyTyburn.jsp.

Fenn, William Wallace. "John Robinson's Farewell Address." *Harvard Theological Review* 13, no. 3 (1920): 236–51. http://www.jstor.org/stable/1507747.

Firth, Charles Harding. *Oliver Cromwell and the Rule of the Puritans in England.* London: G. P. Putnam Sons, 1904.

"Fleet Prison," Luminarium: Encyclopedia Project. http://www.luminarium.org/encyclopedia/fleetprison.htm.

Gorges, Ferdinando. *A Brief Relation of the Discovery and Plantation of New England.* London: John Haviland Publishers, 1620.

———. *Sir Fernando Gorges and His Province of Maine.* Boston: Publications of the Prince Society, 1890.

Hall, Edwin. *The Puritans and Their Principles.* New York: Baker and Scribner, 1846. https://archive.org/details/puritansandthei01hallgoog.

Historic Jamestowne. "What Happened to the Three Ships?" National Park Service. https://www.nps.gov/jame/learn /historyculture/what-happened-to-the-three-ships.htm.

Hollar, Vaclav. *Port Delftshaven.* 1620, painting.

Hopkins, Samuel. *The Puritans, or the Church, Court and Parliament of England during the Reigns of Edward VI and Queen Elizabeth*, vol. 3. Boston: Gould and Lincoln, 1861. https://www .forgottenbooks.com/en/readbook/ThePuritansandQueen Elizabeth_10163651#0.

Johnson, Ben. "Newgate Prison Wall," Historic UK. http://www .historic-uk.com/HistoryMagazine/DestinationsUK/Newgate -Prison-Wall/.

Johnson, Madeleine. "The Pilgrims Should Have Been Thankful for a Spirochete." *Slate*, November 20, 2012. http://www.slate .com/articles/health_and_science/medical_examiner/2012/11 /leptospirosis_and_pilgrims_the_wampanoag_may_have_been _killed_off_by_an.html.

Jones, Augustine. *The Life and Work of Thomas Dudley: The Second Governor of Massachusetts.* Boston: Houghton, Mifflin and Company, 1899.

"Life Inside Newgate Prison, London, UK," BBC. http://www.bbc .co.uk/dna/place-london/plain/A987861.

Lossing, Benson J. *The Pictorial Field-Book of the Revolution*, vol. 1. New York: Harper and Brothers, 1860. https://archive.org /details/pictorialfieldb00lossgoog.

Maranzani, Barbara. "Abraham Lincoln and the 'Mother of Thanksgiving.'" History in the Headlines, History Channel, October 3, 2013. http://www.history.com/news/abraham -lincoln-and-the-mother-of-thanksgiving.

Marr, John S., and John T. Cathey. "New Hypothesis for Cause of Epidemic Among Native Americans, New England, 1616–1619." *Emerging Infectious Diseases* 16, no. 2 (2010). https://wwwnc.cdc .gov/eid/article/16/2/09–0276_article.

Masefield, John. *Chronicles of the Pilgrim Fathers.* New York: E. P. Dutton, 1910.

Metaxas, Eric. "The Miracle of Squanto's Path to Plymouth." *Wall Street Journal,* November 24, 2015.

Morton, Nathaniel. *New England's Memorial.* Reprint. Boston: Congregational Board of Publication, 1855. https://archive.org /details/newenglandsmemor00m.

Motley, John Lothrop. *The History of the United Netherlands,* vol. 3, *1590–1600.* London: John Murray, 1867.

Native Sun News Editorial Board, "Native American vs. American Indian: Political Correctness Dishonors Traditional Chiefs of Old." Native Times. http://www.nativetimes.com/index.php /life/commentary/11389-native-american-vs-american-indian-political-correctness-dishonors-traditional-chiefs-of-old.

"Newgate Prison: A History of Infamy." duhaimelaw.org. http:// www.duhaime.org/LawMuseum/LawArticle-602/Newgate -Prison-A-History-of-Infamy.aspx.

Papers of the New Haven Colony Historical Society, vol. 5. New Haven, CT: Printed for the Society, 1894. https://archive.org/details /papersnewhavenc03socigoog.

Paule, George, and Richard Cosin. *The Life of John Whitgift, Archbishop of Canterbury in the Times of Q. Elizabeth and K. James I.* Printed for R. Chiswell, 1699.

Plimoth Plantation and the New England Historic Genealogical Society. "Plymouth Colony Timeline." https://www.plimoth .org/sites/default/files/media/pdf/historical_timeline.pdf.

Porter, Stephen. *The London Charterhouse.* Stroud, UK: Amberley Publishing, 2009.

Preston, Richard Arthur. *Gorges of Plymouth Fort.* Toronto: University of Toronto Press, 1953.

Purchas, Samuel. *Purchas His Pilgrimes.* Glasgow: University of Glasgow Press, 1906.

Robinson, Gregory, and Robin R. Goodison. "Sarah versus Susan."
    The William and Mary Quarterly 16, no. 4 (1936): 515–21. http://
    www.jstor.org/stable/1920592.

Robinson, John. "Farewell Letter to the Pilgrims." Pilgrim Hall
    Museum. http://www.pilgrimhallmuseum.org/pdf/John
    _Robinson_Farewell_Letter_to_Pilgrims.pdf.

———. "Farewell Sermon." Pilgrim Hall Museum. http://www
    .pilgrimhallmuseum.org/pdf/John_Robinson_Farewell_Sermon
    .pdf.

Rosier, James. *True Relation of Waymouth's Voyage, 1605.* Digital
    reprint. Madison: Wisconsin Historical Society, 2003. http://
    www.americanjourneys.org/pdf/AJ-041.pdf.

Schmidt, Gary D. *William Bradford: Plymouth's Faithful Pilgrim.*
    Grand Rapids: Wm. B. Eerdmans, 1998.

Shepard, James. *Governor William Bradford and His Son, Major
    William Bradford.* New Britain, CT: Herald Print, 1900. https://
    archive.org/details/governorwilliamb00shep.

Smith, John. *A Description of New England.* London: Printed
    by Humfrey Lownes for Robert Clerke, 1616. http://
    digitalcommons.unl.edu/cgi/viewcontent.cgi?article
    =1003&context=etas.

———. *The Generall Historie of Virgina, New-England, and the
    Summer Isles*; vol. 2. London: 1629. Republished, Franklin Press:
    1819.

———. *The Generall Historie of Virginia, New England & the Summer
    Isles, Together with The True Travels, Adventures and Observations,
    and A Sea Grammar,* vol. 2. London: Macmillan and Co., 1907.

Stedman, Edmund C., and Ellen M. Hutchinson, eds. *A Library of
    American Literature: From the Earliest Settlements to the Present
    Time,* vol. 1. New York: Charles L. Webster & Co., 1888–90.
    https://archive.org/details/ofamericalibrary01stedrich.

Steele, Thomas. "The Biblical Meaning of Mather's Bradford." *The
    Bulletin of the Rocky Mountain Modern Language Association* 24,
    no. 4 (1970): 147–54. http://www.jstor.org/stable/1346721.

Stephens, Archibald John. *The Statutes Relating to the Ecclesiastical and Eleemosynary Institutions of England, Wales, Ireland, India, and the Colonies: With the Decisions Thereon*, vol. 1. London: J. W. Parker, 1845. https://archive.org/details/statutesrelatin00unkngoog.

Thompson, Ralph E., and Matthew R. Thompson. *The First Yankee: David Thomson, 1592–1628*. Portsmouth, NH: Peter E. Randall, 1997.

Tirado, Michelle. "The Wampanoag Side of the First Thanksgiving." Indian Country Media Network, November 23, 2011. http://indiancountrytodaymedianetwork.com/2011/11/22/wampanoag-side-first-thanksgiving-story-64076.

"Tisquantum ('Squanto')." Caleb Johnson's MayflowerHistory.com. http://mayflowerhistory.com/tisquantum/.

Toensing, Gale Courey. "What Really Happened at the First Thanksgiving? The Wampanoag Side of the Tale." Indian Country Media Network, November 23, 2012. http://indiancountrytodaymedianetwork.com/2012/11/23/what-really-happened-first-thanksgiving-wampanoag-side-tale-and-whats-done-today-145807.

Wampanoagtribe.net

Wenska, Walter P. "Bradford's Two Histories: Pattern and Paradigm in *Of Plymouth Plantation*." *Early American Literature* 13, no. 2 (1978): 151–64. http://www.jstor.org/stable/25070879.

Winship, George Parker. *Sailors Narratives of Voyages Along the New England Coast, 1524–1624*. Boston: Houghton Mifflin & Co., 1905. https://archive.org/details/sailorsnarrative00wins.

"Words of John Robinson." Old South Leaflets, No. 143. http://lf-oll.s3.amazonaws.com/titles/558/0063_Bk.pdf.

Notes

AUTHOR'S NOTE

1. Language has been a challenge in writing this book. Most of
   the original sources come from the beginning of the seventeenth
   century. The antiquated English is dense and often tedious to
   interpret. While I strove for fastidious accuracy, I occasionally
   took the liberty of modernizing English for readability when
   necessary. Generally, changes were made only to spelling or
   grammar (i.e., *belongeth* to *belongs*). In certain circumstances, the
   meanings of words have changed, and I rarely, but occasionally,
   changed them to better reflect the intentions of the writer (i.e.,
   jealous meant "apprehensive" rather than "envious" in the early
   seventeenth century). One of the characteristics of Bradford's
   writing, due in part to its literature period, is that he wrote
   almost exclusively in third person. He, for example, typically
   referred to "we" or "the Pilgrims" as "they." After careful
   consideration, I decided to further translate his use of the
   third person to first person. The primary purpose of this work
   is to tell the story in a readable, engaging manner, and while
   using Bradford's third person might most accurately reflect the
   original source, it is a stumbling block toward the primary goals

of this book. My changes were carefully considered and do not, I believe, materially change the source content. When possible, I retained the original language in the endnotes, for those who wish to read or cite it. Additionally, when possible, I used published translations, such as William Bradford's *Of Plymouth Plantation* (Mineola, NY: Dover, 2006).

PREFACE

1. Song arranged by Samuel Francis Smith in 1831.
2. *Records Relating to the Early History of Boston*, vol. 16, 173–74, https://books.google.com.sl/books?id=2MMr1ZZDfOgC&lr=&as_brr=0&source=gbs_navlinks_s.
3. Francis Dillon, *The Pilgrims: Their Journeys & Their World* (New York City: Doubleday, 1975).

PROLOGUE

1. Bradford lived from 1590 to 1657. He became governor in 1621 and held that post throughout most of his adult life.
2. William Bradford, *Of Plymouth Plantation*, ed. Samuel Eliot Morison (New York: Knopf, 2002), 316.
3. Found in Nathaniel Morton, *New England's Memorial* (Boston: Congregational Board of Publication, 1855), 171–72, https://archive.org/details/newenglandsmemor00m.
4. Bradford styles this as a transcript. The dialogues were likely not exact transcripts of the conversation, but a literary tool similar to Plato's and Socrates's great dialogues in Athens. They would likely have reflected real group conversations between the youth and elders of Plymouth. I took the liberty of organizing Bradford's dialogue into a conversation for readability.
5. William Bradford, "A Dialogue, or Sum of a Conference," https://static1.squarespace.com/static/50a02efce4b046b42952af27/t/50a93d01e4b0ef49c45e18d0/1353268481219/FirstConference.pdf.
6. Bradford used the term *aspersed*, which I changed to *hated* for readability.

CHAPTER 1: THE CLINK

1. Leland H. Carlson, ed., *Elizabethan Non-conformist Texts,
Volume IV: The Writings of John Greenwood 1587–1590, Together
with the Joint Writings of Henry Barrow and John Greenwood,
1587–1590* (New York: Routledge, 1962), appendix C, 247–69.

2. This amount is equal to about £17, or $25 in today's currency.
Calculation made at http://measuringworth.com.

3. See "A Book which Showeth the Life and Manners of all True
Christians; and How Unlike They Are unto Turks and Papists
and Heathen Folk. Also the Points and Parts of all Divinity
that is, of the Revealed Will and Word of God Are Declared by
Their Several Definitions and Divisions, in Order as Followeth,"
in Leland H. Carlson and Albert Peel, eds., *Elizabethan Non-
conformist Texts, Volume II, The Writings of Robert Harrison and
Robert Browne* (New York: Routledge, 2014), 221–395.

4. George Punchard, *History of Congregationalism from about A.D. 250
to the Present Time*, vol. 3 (New York: Hurd and Houghton, 1867),
49, https://books.google.com/books?id=QiwYAAAAYAAJ.

5. Ibid., 50.

6. Benjamin Brook, *The Lives of the Puritans: Containing a
Biographical Account of Those Divines Who Distinguished
Themselves in the Cause*, vol. 2 (London: James Black, 1813), 25,
https://books.google.com/books?id=18c5AAAAcAAJ.

7. Ibid., 26–28.

8. Leland H. Carlson, ed., *Elizabethan Non-conformist Texts:
Volume III, The Writings of Henry Barrow, 1587–1590* (London:
Allen & Unwin, 1962), 105, note 3.

9. Carlson, ed., *Elizabethan Non-Conformist Texts, Volume IV*, 249.

10. He would remain in office as lord treasurer from 1572 to 1598.

11. Brook, *Lives of the Puritans*, 38.

12. The original text used the word *conference*. I have chosen to
replace it with the word *hearing* to better describe their intention.
Barrow and Greenwood wanted a public hearing, or trial, rather
than the closed-door tribunals they received.

13. Barrow might have read from the Bishop's Bible, authorized by

the Church of England and first published in 1568. It preceded the King James Bible.

14. Brook, *Lives of the Puritans*, 34.

15. James Spedding, Robert Leslie Ellis, and Douglas Denon Heath, eds., "Certain Observations Made upon a Libel," *The Works of Francis Bacon: Volume 8: The Letters and the Life 1* (Cambridge: Cambridge University Press, 2011), 165–66. Removed material: "had not Brown their leader written a pamphlet, wherein, as it came into his head, he inveighed more against logic and rhetoric, than against the state of the church, which writing was much read; and . . ."

16. Punchard, *History of Congregationalism*, 77.

17. Ibid., 80.

18. *Historical Papers: Congregational Martyrs, First Series* (London: Elliot Stock, 1861), 170, https://books.google.com/books?id =PAJeAAAAcAAJ.

19. Ibid., 174.

20. Punchard, *History of Congregationalism*, 82–83.

21. Ibid., 83.

22. Ibid., 83–84.

CHAPTER 2: THE SLAVE

1. Martin Pring, *The Voyage of Martin Pring* (Madison: Wisconsin Historical Society, 1906), 346. The author translated Pring's Old English to modern English. Pring was the captain of the *Speedwell*.

2. Squanto's story has not received its due attention. A chief reason is that his story was never chronicled in full. While Squanto was clearly articulate in several languages, we have no evidence that he wrote. To our knowledge, he kept no journal, and he wrote no letters. Squanto's story, therefore, must be derived from both the letters and annals of those with whom his path crossed. One of the curious aspects of Squanto's life, which has clouded his history, is his name. We know him as Squanto. Those who came into contact with him spelled his name phonetically. The

diversity in spelling his name is matched only by the diversity of those he met. It appears as "Tasquantum," "Tisquantum," "Squantum," "Squanto," "Sassacomoit," and "Assacumet." This has muddied the Squanto trail. While I regard "Tasquantum" as likely more accurate, I have chosen to refer to him as "Squanto" in this book. Squanto is the name by which most readers will know him, and I want the reader to quickly connect with the character. Over generations, Squanto has grown into a legend. Writers have added to the legend or imagined what he might have done or said. I have done my best to keep the story as accurate as possible, relying on verifiable, original sources. Any errors are mine.

3. Age is approximate since we do not have record of Squanto's birth date.

4. Pring, *Voyage*, 348.

5. Ibid., 347. See also Matthew R. Thompson, *Tasquantum, 1589–1622, The Pilgrims' Interpreter: A Biography* (Salem: Privately printed, 1980), 3.

6. After setting sail in mid-August, the *Speedwell* reached its harbor in England on October 2, completing its six-month expedition.

7. Historical theories differ about whether Squanto actually made his way to Maine. See: http://historyofmassachusetts .org/squanto-the-former-slave/. In *True Relation of Waymouth's Voyage, 1605*, Rosier identifies five men taken by Weymouth. How these names were documented is unknown. Presumably Rosier did his best to capture a phonetic spelling, whether taken directly or secondhand. It is also unclear if the Kennebec men gave full names, partial names, or aliases. It would not be unusual to have been known by more than one name or title. Later Gorges specifically names Squanto as one of the five Kennebec men. Some historians have suggested that Gorges erred in naming Squanto. These historians suggest that when Gorges wrote his *Narration* fifty-two years later, he was likely mistaken or remembered incorrectly. I am suspicious of this claim and tend to trust Gorges. First, he had no apparent reason to place Squanto at the kidnapping other than recounting the

truth. Gorges had intimate knowledge of these men. He lodged them in his house and spent considerable time with them working on maps. Theirs was not a casual acquaintance. Such an error would have been obvious and, if not caught by an editor or proofreader, then it would have undermined the credibility of Gorges's memory. Squanto would have been known publicly at this point. They were public spectacles, known to Londoners and the government elite. These men had been the only Native Americans in England and perhaps the first to step foot on the European continent. Additionally, William Bradford and Edward Winslow's book, *Mourt's Relation*, had been published in 1620; if an error was made at all, surely it would be corrected. In *The Book of Indians*, Samuel Drake worked carefully to achieve accuracy with his history. Drake writes: "To return to Tisquantum. There is some disagreement in the narratives of the contemporary writers in respect to this chief, which shows, either that some of them are in error, or that there were two of the same name—one carried away by Weymouth, and the other by Hunt. From a critical examination of the accounts, it is believed that was but one, and that he was carried away by Weymouth, as Sir Ferdinando Gorges relates. . . . It is impossible that Sir Ferdinando should have been mistaken in the name of those he received from Weymouth. The names of these carried off by Hunt are not given, nor but few of them, nor were they kidnapped until nine years after Weymouth's voyage. It is, therefore, possible that Squantum, having returned home from the service of Gorges, went again to England with some other person, or perhaps even with Hunt. But we are inclined to think that there was but one of the name, and his being carried away an error of inadvertence."

8. James Rosier, *True Relation of Waymouth's Voyage, 1605*, Wisconsin Historical Society, American Journeys, 387, http://www.americanjourneys.org/pdf/AJ-041.pdf.

9. Successful navigation of the Northwest Passage would not be completed until 1906 by Norwegian explorer Roald Amundsen.

10. Rosier, *True Relation of Waymouth's Voyage, 1605*, 357.

11. The *Archangel* was sixty tons and carried twenty-eight crew members.

12. Rosier was hired in 1605 to serve as the chronicler of Weymouth's voyage.

13. Rosier, *True Relation of Waymouth's Voyage*, 372.

14. Ibid., 377.

15. Ibid., 378–79.

16. Sir Ferdinando Gorges names three of the captives: Manida, Skettwarroes, and Tasquantum (see Sir Ferdinando Gorges, "A Briefe Narration of the Originall Undertaking of the Advancement of Plantations into the Parts of America," in *Sir Fernando Gorges and His Province of Maine* [Boston: The Prince Society, 1890], 8). Rosier names the five as: "1) Tahanedo, a Sagamo or Commander, 2) Amoret, 3) Skicowaros, 4) Maneddo, gentlemen; 5) Saffacomoit, a servant" (see Rosier, *True Relation of Waymouth's Voyage*, 394). Drake names them as Squanto, Manida, Skettwarrots, Dehamda, and Assacumet. Gorges called Tahanedo, "Dahamda." Drake writes, "Although Gorges does not say Dahamda was one brought over at this time, it is evident that he was, because, so far as we can discover, there were no other natives, at that time in England, but these five" (see Drake, *The Book of the Indians of North America*, 5). Tahanedo returned to America with Martin Pring in 1606. We can link the names Manida and Maneddo, as well as Skettwarroes and Skicowaros. Skicowaros was one of two Kennebecs to move in with Lord Chief Justice John Popham. Popham was deeply involved with his own colonization efforts in the New World, and Skicowaros returned with Popham's colonists. Amoret is occasionally interpreted as Assacumet. Likewise, Saffacomoit is sometimes written as Sassacomoit, then interpreted as Assacumet. One of these men is indeed Assacumet, who will play an important role later in the story. If one is not Squanto, then we have no further record of this man.

17. Rosier, *True Relation of Waymouth's Voyage*, 391.

18. Ibid.
19. Plymouth Fort served as his home and battle station in time of war, but with England's current time of peace, Gorges lived in a manor house with his family.
20. Ferdinando Gorges, *A Briefe Narration of the Originall Undertakings of the Advancement of Plantations into the Parts of America* (London: E. Brudenell, 1658), 9.
21. Ibid., 50.
22. The sailors called the Antilles Islands the "West Indies."
23. Samuel Purchas, *Purchas His Pilgrimes* (Glasgow: University of Glasgow Press, 1906), 285.
24. Ibid., 285–86.
25. This incident took place on November 10, 1606, approximately 100 miles east-southeast of St. Augustine, Florida. St. Augustine was Spain's northernmost outpost in the Americas.
26. Purchas, *Purchas His Pilgrims*, 288. The text specifically identified rapiers, swords, and half pikes.
27. Ibid., 292.

CHAPTER 3: DISSENTERS

1. Originally built by the Romans, it became known as the Old North Road, and eventually the Great North Road.
2. Charles Harding Firth, *Oliver Cromwell and the Rule of the Puritans in England* (London: G. P. Putnam Sons, 1904), 11, https://archive.org/details/olivercromwellan015097mbp.
3. "Doctor Cotton Mather's Life of Governor William Bradford," in Edward Arber, ed., *The Story of the Pilgrim Fathers, 1606–1623 A.D.* (London: Ward and Downey, 1897), 39, https://archive.org/details/cu31924025962964.
4. He possessed a Geneva Bible published in 1592, http://www.pilgrimhallmuseum.org/ap_religion.htm. The Geneva Bible was translated around 1560 by a group of Protestant scholars who fled from England to Geneva, Switzerland. The Geneva Bible was particularly important in that it was mechanically produced for the general public. The Geneva Bible included annotations

and study aids written by its Protestant drafters, of which Anglican theologians disapproved.

5. William Bradford, "Scrooby and Gainsborough," in Arber, *Story of the Pilgrim Fathers*, 69.

6. Peggy M. Baker, "Searching for the Promised Land: The Travels and Travails of Richard Clyfton," Pilgrim Hall Museum.

7. William Bradford, "A Dialogue, or Sum of a Conference," https://static1.squarespace.com/static/50a02efce4b04 6b42952af27/t/50a93d01e4b0ef49c45e18d0/1353268481219 /FirstConference.pdf.

8. Baker, "Searching for the Promised Land."

9. Twenty pounds in 1605 is roughly $4,000 USD in 2016, according to MeasuringWorth.com.

10. Bradford, "Scrooby and Gainsborough," 69.

11. Ibid., 68.

12. Ibid., 69. Bradford wrote additionally: "Yet these, and many other sharper things which afterwards befell them, were no other than they looked for: and therefore were [they] the better prepared to bear them by the assistance of GOD'S grace and SPIRIT."

13. Ibid., 70.

14. William Bradford, "The Flight into Holland" in Arber, *Story of the Pilgrim Fathers*, 88.

15. Ibid.

16. Ibid., 89.

17. William Bradford, *Of Plymouth Plantation*, (Mineola, NY: Dover, 2006), 7.

18. Ibid.

19. John Lothrop Motley, *History of the United Netherlands, Vol. 3, 1590–1600* (London: John Murray, 1867), 94. Bradford's text says the captain "swore his country's oath, 'Sacramente.'" Derived from Latin, *sacramentum*, meaning *oath*, originated in Roman law. Pledges of allegiance, or oaths, were a common practice for the Dutch military in the late 1500s following the Dutch Revolt against the Roman Catholic Church. According

to *The History of the United Netherlands, 1590–1600*, "The oath of allegiance, extracted from soldiers as well as officers, mentioned the name of a particular providence to which they belong, as well as the States-General."

20. Bradford, *Of Plymouth Plantation*, 7.
21. Ibid., 8.
22. Ibid.
23. Bradford, "Flight into Holland," 91.
24. Ibid.
25. Ibid., 90–91.
26. Ibid., 92.
27. Ibid., 93.

CHAPTER 4: RETURN TO SLAVERY

1. There is considerable debate about whether Smith's vessel was named *Susan Constant* or *Sarah Constant*. *Susan* was the name given in Samuel Purchas's *Pilgrimes*, but there is evidence that he misspelled it. I have continued with *Susan Constant* since it is the most common name by which the vessel is recognized.

2. The expedition had voyaged no farther than the Azores before Smith's leadership created conflict. Other sailors accused him of mutinous action, forcing them to lock him up for the remaining thirteen weeks of the journey.

3. See Historic Jamestowne, "What Happened to the Three Ships?" National Park Service, https://www.nps.gov/jame/learn /historyculture/what-happened-to-the-three-ships.htm. The expedition brought a third vessel, *Discovery*, along for further exploring and intended to leave it at Jamestown. It is possible that this *Discovery* is the same *Discovery* used on the Martin Pring voyage in 1603. According to the U.S. National Park Service, "Brown, in his Genesis of the United States, states that these two ships 'were the same vessels which returned from Cherry Island, August 15, 1606. . . . It is possible that the *Discovery* was the *Discovery* of Pring's voyage to our northern coast in 1603.'"

4. John Smith, *A Description of New England* (Washington: P. Force, 1837), 1, https://books.google.com/books?id=yu1HAQA AMAAJ&pg=PA1&lpg=PA1&dq=%22fish+and+furres%22&s ource=bl&ots=bSoeYpsBzi&sig=zuVMthCOigUOKmqTSeaLa o3r-Kc&hl=en&sa=X&ved=0ahUKEwjlofHGyInSAhXM8 CYKHfzmAZsQ6AEIMjAD#v=onepage&q=%22fish%20 and%20furres%22&f=false.

5. Smith called him Dohanidda.

6. Smith published *A Description of New England* in 1616, which first applied the term New England widely.

7. Smith would sail for North America again in March 1615. This expedition would have instructions to found a colony for the purpose of fishing and trading with the Indians. Soon after departing England, his boat sailed into a violent storm. His ship lost its mast and suffered such severe damage that it was forced to return to harbor. Smith received a different vessel and set sail again for North America. Near the Western Islands, his ship was commandeered by a French pirate and Smith was taken prisoner. His ship escaped in the night, but Smith did not escape with it. He eventually was set free and returned to England.

8. Fernando Gorges, "A Brief Relation of the Discovery and Plantation of New England," in Henry S. Burrage, *Gorges and the Grant of the Province of Maine, 1622* (Portland, ME: Printed for the State, 1923), 144.

9. John Smith, *The Generall Historie of Virginia, New-England, and the Summer Isles* (London: I.D. and I.H. for Michael Sparkes), 205. Smith also wrote of Hunt, "most dishonestly, and inhumanely, for their kind usage of me and all our men, carried them with him to Malaga, and there for a little private gain sold those silly salvages for rials of eight," 204.

10. James Phinney Baxter, ed., *Sir Ferdinando Gorges and His Province of Maine*, vol. 2 (Boston: The Prince Society, 1890), 20.

11. See William Shakespeare, *Henry VIII*, act 5, sc. 4, "[O]r have we some strange Indian with the great tool come to court, the women so besiege us?"; and *The Tempest*, act 2, sc. 2, "[W]hen

they will not give a doit to relieve a lame beggar, they will lay out ten to see a dead Indian."

12. Gorges, "A Brief Relation," in Burrage, *Gorges and the Grant*, 144.
13. Ibid., 144–45.
14. It's possible that Squanto learned, or observed, some farming techniques here. The Newfoundland colony had made some efforts to cultivate the land, which perhaps included using fish as fertilizer.
15. Nathaniel Morton, "New England's Memorial," in *Chronicles of the Pilgrim Fathers* (London, J. M. Dent & Sons, 1920), 40.

CHAPTER 5: A NEW WORLD AWAITS

1. Dillon, Francis, *The Pilgrims: Their Journeys & Their World* (New York: Doubleday, 1975).
2. Ibid., 90.
3. William Bradford, *Of Plymouth Plantation* (Mineola, NY: Dover, 2008), 9.
4. Ibid.
5. Ibid.
6. Ibid.
7. Near the end of 1616, Brewster established the book publishing business with a financing partner, Thomas Brewer.
8. The press used the address of Choir Alley in Latin-Vicus Choralis, an alley now referred to as the Pilgrims Press.
9. *The Letters from and to Sir Dudley Carleton During His Embassy in Holland* (London: n.p., 1775), 380.
10. Arber, ed., *The Story of the Pilgrim Fathers*, 212.
11. Letters from and to Sir Dudley Carleton, 380.
12. Dutch authorities did attempt to arrest Brewster's business partner.
13. Ferdinando Gorges, "A Brief Relation," in Henry S. Burrage, *Gorges and the Grant of the Province of Maine, 1622* (Portland, ME: printed for the State, 1923), 145.
14. "Dermer's Letter to Thomas Purchas, 1619" in Burrage, *Gorges and the Grant*, 129.
15. Referred to as Nummastaquyt, eventually Namasket, Massachusetts.

16. *Papers of the New Haven Colony Historical Society*, vol. 5 (New Haven, CT: Printed for the Society, 1894), 282. "When I arrived in my savage's native country, finding all dead, I travelled a long day's journey westward, to a place called Nummastaguy, where, finding inhabitants, I dispatched a messenger a day's journey farther west to Pocanoket, which bordereth on the sea, whence came to see me, two Kings, attended with a guard of fifty men, who being well satisfied with my savage and I discoursed with them . . . ," 282.

17. Arber, *Story of the Pilgrim Fathers*, 40. Full text: ". . . they would have killed me when I was at Namassaket, had not he entreated hard for me" (https://archive.org/details/storyofthepilgri 000478mbp).

18. "Dermer's Letter to Thomas Purchas, 1619," in Burrage, *Gorges and the Grant*, 131. "Departing hence, the next place we arrived at was Capawock (Martha's Vineyard), an island formerly discovered by the English, when I met with Epinow, a savage that had lived in England, and speaks indifferent good English, who four years since, being carried home, was reported to have been slain with divers of his countrymen by sailors, which was false. With him I had much conference, who gave me very good satisfaction in every thing almost I could demand. Time not permitting me to search here, which I should have done for sundry things of special moment, the wind fair, I stood away, shaping my course as the coast led me, till I came to the most westerly part, where the coast began to fall away southerly," 131–32.

19. Dermer does not specifically identify where he will stay in his letter to Thomas Purchas on December 27, 1619, from the plantation of Captain John Martyn, a councilman of Jamestown colony. We can infer that he likely spent that winter at Jamestown.

CHAPTER 6: ESCAPE

1. William Bradford, *Of Plymouth Plantation* (Mineola, NY: Dover, 2008), 12.

2. Ibid.

3. Francis Dillon, *The Pilgrims* (New York: Doubleday, 1975), 97–98. "The Dexters also made a careful check of the number of Pilgrims in Leyden, and at first the number is between four and five hundred, or on breakdown: known or presumable Pilgrims, 298; those more less loosely associated with them, 281; which gives a total of 579; but 106 names occur in both lists, so the Pilgrim colony equaled 473 men, women, and children. Thirty of them became citizens of Leyden before 1620."

4. Bradford, *Of Plymouth Plantation*, 12.

5. Ibid., 13.

6. Ibid.

7. Ibid., 12.

8. Ibid., 13.

9. Ibid., 14.

10. Ibid.

11. Ibid.

12. Ibid.

13. Ibid.

14. Books available to them: Sir Walter Raleigh's *Discoverie of the Large Rich and Beautiful Empire of Guiana* (1596), Whitaker's *Good News from Virginia* (1613), Purchas's *Pilgrims*, and Hakluyt's *Voyages of the English Nation*.

15. Bradford, *Of Plymouth Plantation*, 15.

16. Ibid.

17. Ibid.

18. Ibid.

19. Dillon, *The Pilgrims*, 110. John Carver was not part of the Scrooby congregation. He came from a town ten miles from Scrooby and emigrated to Holland under his own means. He does not appear in the Pilgrim records before 1616.

20. Bradford, *Of Plymouth Plantation*, 17–18.

21. Dillon, *The Pilgrims*, 110. Dialogue between the King's chief secretary, Sir Robert Nanton, and King James: Nanton: "(He asks His Majesty) to give way to such people, who could not comfortably live under the government of another State, to

enjoy their liberty of Conscience under his gracious protection in America, where they would endeavor the advancement of His Majesty's Dominions and the enlargement of the Gospel by all due means." James: "This is a good and honest motion. What profit might arise in the part they intend?" Nanton: "Fishing." James: "So God have my soul 'tis an honest trade. 'Twas the Apostles' own calling."

22. Edward Winslow, "How the Pilgrims Sailed from Delet Haven," in Edmund Clarence Stedman and Ellen McKay Hutchinson, eds., *A Library of American Literature: From the Earliest Settlements to the Present Time*, vol. 1 (New York: Charles L. Webster & Co., 1889), 131.

23. Ibid.

24. Ibid., 131–32.

25. Dillon, *The Pilgrims*, 111. In a letter dated May 8, 1619, we learn Brewster was still in England and went to conclude negotiations with Virginia Company. At this point, he had to go into hiding.

26. Bradford, *Of Plymouth Plantation*, 16.

27. Taken in the name of Mr. J. Wincot, who intended to go with them but never did.

28. Bradford, *Of Plymouth Plantation*, 22.

29. Dillon, *The Pilgrims*, 112.

30. Bradford, *Of Plymouth Plantation*, 22.

31. Benson J. Lossing, *The Pictorial Field-Book of the Revolution*, vol. 1 (New York: Harper and Brothers, 1860), 442.

32. John Smith, Generall Historie (chap. 4, n. 9), 263. ". . . but nothing would bee done for a plantation, till about some hundred, of your Brownists, of England, Amsterdam, and Leyden, went to New Plimouth whose humorous ignorances, caused them for more than a yeare, to endure a wonderfull deale of misery, with an infinite patience; saying my books and maps were much better cheape to teach them, than myself; many others have used the like-good husbandry, that have played soundly in trying their selfe-willed conclusions; but those in time doing well, divers others have in small handfuls undertaken

to goe there, to be severall Lords and Kings of themselves, but most vanished to nothing. . . ."

33. Ibid.

34. Bradford, *Of Plymouth Plantation*, 23.

35. The name appears to be used loosely, sometimes "The Merchant Adventurers," "The Adventurers," or "Merchants and Adventurers."

36. Dillon, *The Pilgrims*, 115.

37. Ibid., 116.

38. Ibid. Among the Puritans were Christopher Martin and his family. The Martins had run afoul of the Church of England, which drove them to seek an opportunity to leave England. Martin had intended to travel with the Virginia Company until this opportunity with the Merchant Adventurers became available. He treated the Separatists poorly, and they had little respect for him. He appointed himself governor of the *Speedwell* but was ousted in favor of John Carver once on board the *Mayflower*.

39. Bradford, *Of Plymouth Plantation*, 32.

40. There are no official records of the *Mayflower*'s length, and ship sizes had not yet been standardized by the time it was built. The estimate of 100 feet by 25 feet is based on recorded cargo from the ship's log and a volume estimate made by Bradford. The size is also similar to other merchant ships of the day.

41. Prior to Captain Jones, there are no substantial records of the *Mayflower*, including when it was built and from where it was launched. The *Mayflower* had perhaps sailed to Greenland on a whaling expedition.

42. Nathaniel Morton, "New England's Memorial," in *Chronicles of the Pilgrim Fathers* (London: J. M. Dent & Sons, 1910; repr. Boston: Congregational Board of Publication, 1855), 170. https://archive.org/details/newenglandsmemor00m. Little is known about Miles Standish, but his personal and family history has been the subject of much debate. One of the only original sources for information comes from an obituary

written for Standish in 1669 by Nathaniel Morton, Plymouth Colony's secretary: "He was a gentleman, born in Lancashire, and was heir apparent unto a great estate of lands and livings, surreptitiously detained from him; his great grandfather being a second or younger brother from the house of Standish. In his younger time he went over into the low countries, and was a soldier there, and came acquainted with the church at Leyden, and came over into New England, with such of them as at the first set out for the planting of the plantation of New Plymouth, and bare a deep share of their first difficulties, and was always very faithful to their interest" (170).

43. John Stevens Cabot Abbott, *Miles Standish: The Puritan Captain* (Boston: B. B. Russell, 1875), 35–36. Standish was likely born in 1584 in Lancashire, England. He claimed to be the rightful heir to a large estate but had been defrauded of his inheritance. According to Standish biographer John Abbott, the annual income from the estate was estimated at around half a million. The Standish family split apart upon religious lines—Catholic and Protestant. Standish was of the line to inherit the fortune, but someone maliciously scratched out important birth records, thereby redirecting the fortune away from him.

44. Bradford, *Of Plymouth Plantation*, 32.

45. Ibid., 32.

46. Samuel G. Drake, *The History and Antiquities of the City of Boston* (Boston: Luther Stevens, 1856), 33.

47. Bradford, *Of Plymouth Plantation*, 53–54.

48. Ferdinando Gorges, *Briefe Narration* (London: E. Brudenell, 1658), 31.

49. Bradford, *Of Plymouth Plantation*, 54.

50. Ibid., 32.

51. Ibid.

52. John Robinson's Farewell Sermon, Pilgrim Hall Museum, http://www.pilgrimhallmuseum.org/pdf/John_Robinson _Farewell_Sermon.pdf.

53. Bradford, *Of Plymouth Plantation*, 33.

54. Vaclav Hollar, *Port Delftshaven*, 1620, painting; Joan Blaeu, "Delfshaven," 1649, map.

55. Bradford, *Of Plymouth Plantation*, 33.

56. Oude of Pelgrimvaderskerk would eventually come to be called "Pilgrim Father Church."

57. Bradford, *Of Plymouth Plantation*, 33.

CHAPTER 7: STORMS ON THE OCEAN

1. Bradford, *Of Plymouth Plantation*, 41.

2. The present value of the currency from the seventeenth century is extremely difficult to calculate and one of the hardest questions a historian can be asked. A rough estimate may be somewhere around $20,000 in 2014. See discussion and calculations at http://www.history.org/foundation/journal /summer02/money2.cfm.

3. Bradford, *Of Plymouth Plantation*, 33.

4. Sixty firkins of butter, or approximately a weight of 4,000 pounds.

5. Bradford, *Of Plymouth Plantation*, 34.

6. Azel Ames, *The Mayflower and Her Log, July 15, 1620–May 6, 1621* (Boston: Houghton, Mifflin and Company, 1907), 332.

7. Ibid., 239.

8. Bradford, *Of Plymouth Plantation*, 38.

9. Ames, *The Mayflower and Her Log*, 263.

10. Bradford, *Of Plymouth Plantation*, 38.

11. Mariners at Plymouth Harbor determined the *Speedwell* to be "overmasted"—carrying too large and too heavy of a mast for a ship of its size. At full sail, the mast put too much pressure on the hull, causing the *Speedwell*'s joints to bow and leak. The *Speedwell* could be retrofitted to the proper mast, but such an undertaking would be too arduous if they were to settle in the New World before winter. The *Speedwell* would indeed be later retrofitted and put into many more years of good service.

12. Bradford would allege that members of the crew later confessed to the conspiracy.

13. Bradford, *Of Plymouth Plantation*, 39.
14. Ibid., 38.
15. Dillon, *The Pilgrims*, 123. "[H]aving been kindly entertained and courteously used by divers friends there dwelling." Bradford and Winslow, *Mourt's Relation, Part I*, http://www.histarch .illinois.edu/plymouth/mourt1.html.
16. By total space, this would have given each passenger eighteen feet of personal space. Naturally, not all this space would have been available for use.
17. The *Mayflower* passengers, as a collective, were no longer truly "pilgrims." Only those from Leiden made the trip for predominantly religious reasons. The English may have had peripheral religious convictions for the voyage, but they saw the opportunity for its commercial value rather than its freedom.
18. Bradford's wife joined him on the voyage, as did Brewster's wife and two children.
19. Bradford, *Of Plymouth Plantation*, 41.
20. Morton, *New England's Memorial*, 25. "[F]or their intention was the Hudson's river, but some of the Dutch having notice of their intentions and having thoughts about the same time of erecting a plantation there likewise, they fraudulently hired the said Jones, by delays, while they were in England, and now under pretence of the danger of the shoals . . . to disappoint them in their going thither." Morton added in the margins, "I have had late and certain intelligence."
21. Bradford, *Of Plymouth Plantation*, 43.
22. Ibid., 60.
23. Ibid., 44.

CHAPTER 8: THE NEW WORLD

1. Geologic History of Cape Cod, Massachusetts. United States Geological Survey, http://pubs.usgs.gov/gip/capecod/glacial .html.
2. November 11, 1620. There is some discrepancy about the date due to calendar differences. Could be November 20.

3. Bradford, *Of Plymouth Plantation*, 49.

4. Ibid., 49–50.

5. William Bradford and Edward Winslow, *Mourt's Relation: A Journal of the Pilgrims at Plymouth, 1622, Part I*, Plymouth Colony Archive Project, http://www.histarch.illinois.edu /plymouth/mourt1.html.

6. Bradford, *Of Plymouth Plantation*, 45.

7. Bradford and Winslow, *Mourt's Relation, Part I*, http://www .histarch.illinois.edu/plymouth/mourt1.html.

8. Ibid.

9. Ibid.

10. Ibid.

11. The Mayflower's first mate was John Clarke. Over time, the *e* was dropped and the island is modernly known as "Clark's Island."

12. This is one of the few assumptions I am making. Bradford does not record who told him. I suspect it would have been William Brewster, Bradford's spiritual guide from Scrooby, who would be the one to break the news to him. From Bradford and Winslow, *Mourt's Relation* we know the members of the party to be: Standish, Carver, Bradford, Winslow, John and Edward Tilley, John Howland, two mariners, Hopkins, Warren, Doty, Clarke, and Copin from the *Mayflower*, and three or more sailors.

13. According to Dillon, *The Pilgrims*, 147: "Nowhere does he ever mention her again. His silence has suggested to most commentators that Dorothy May may have committed suicide, then and until our own times considered one of the gravest crimes in the eyes of God and man. The verdict should be 'not proven,' though conditions and prospects on the *Mayflower* were desperate enough to drive any sensitive woman into temporary insanity."

CHAPTER 9: A LONG AND DIFFICULT WINTER

1. Bradford, *Of Plymouth Plantation*, 50.

2. Ibid.

3. Bradford and Winslow, *Mourt's Relation*, 51. There is some debate about whether he said "Welcome, Englishmen!" as the phrase is commonly portrayed. *Englishmen* does not exist in the Bradford or *Mourt's Relation* text. Only *Mourt's Relation* notes the word *welcome*. The longer phrase is drawn from Thomas Prince, *A Chronological History of New England*, vol. 3 (Boston: Cummings, Hilliard and Company, 1826), which claims to draw on Bradford's long lost notes.

4. *Patuxet* means "Little Bay" and was given to both the name of the place that became New Plymouth and the tribe who lived there.

5. "Letter from Emmanuel Altham to Sir Edward Altham, September 1623," in "Who Were the Native People," Pilgrim Hall Museum, http://www.pilgrimhallmuseum.org/ap_who _were_native.htm: "He is as proper a man as ever was seen in this country, and very courageous. He is very subtle for a savage, and he goes like the rest of his men, all naked but only a black wolf skin he wears upon his shoulder. And about the breadth of a span he wears beads about his middle."

6. Bradford and Winslow, *Mourt's Relation, Part I*, http://www .histarch.illinois.edu/plymouth/mourt1.html.

7. Ibid.

8. Ibid. "We sent to the king a pair of knives, and a copper chain with a jewel at it. To Quadequina we sent likewise a knife and a jewel to hang in his ear, and withal a pot of strong water, a good quantity of biscuit, and some butter, which were all willingly accepted. Our messenger [Winslow] made a speech unto him, that King James saluted him with words of love and peace, and did accept of him as his friend and ally, and that our governor desired to see him and to truck with him, and to confirm a peace with him, as his next neighbor. He liked well of the speech and heard it attentively, though the interpreters did not well express it. After he had eaten and drunk himself, and given the rest to his company, he looked upon our messenger's sword and armor which he had on, with intimation of his desire to buy it, but on the other side, our messenger showed his unwillingness to part

with it. In the end he left him in the custody of Quadequina his brother, and came over the brook, and some twenty men following him, leaving all their bows and arrows behind them. We kept six or seven as hostages for our messenger."

9. Modern-day Barrington, Rhode Island.

10. Bradford, *Of Plymouth Plantation*, 52.

11. Ibid., 55.

12. Ames, *The Mayflower and Her Log*. The *Mayflower* arrived in England in May of 1621, and Captain Jones was in London on May 6. The *Mayflower* underwent repairs, and Jones returned to transporting wine from French ports. Within the year, he grew ill and passed away on March 5, 1622. Little is known of the *Mayflower* after Jones's death. It is unlikely that it made another voyage, and some historians believe it was scrapped for wood.

13. Dillon, *The Pilgrims*, 160.

14. Michelle Tirado, "The Wampanoag's Side of the First Thanksgiving," Indian Country Today Media Network, November 23. 2011, https://indiancountrymedianetwork.com /news/the-wampanoag-side-of-the-first-thanksgiving-story/. "[Plimoth Plantation's] literature tells that before 1616, the Wampanoag numbered 50,000 to 100,000, occupying 69 villages scattered throughout southeastern Massachusetts and eastern Rhode Island. The plague, however, killed thousands, up to two-thirds, of them."

15. Madeleine Johnson, "The Pilgrims Should Have Been Thankful for a Spirochete," *Slate*, November 20, 2012, and John S. Marr and John T. Cathey, "New Hypothesis for Cause of Epidemic among Native Americans, New England, 1616–1619," *Emerging Infectious Diseases* 16, no. 2 (February 2010), 281–86.

16. Bradford and Winslow, *Mourt's Relation*, *Part II*, http://www .histarch.illinois.edu/plymouth/mourt2.html.

17. Bradford and Winslow, *Mourt's Relation*, *Part II*, http://www .histarch.illinois.edu/plymouth/mourt2.html.

18. John Billington is the son of John Billington, Sr. His brother is Francis Billington.

19. Bradford and Winslow, *Mourt's Relation*, *Part III*, http://www
.histarch.illinois.edu/plymouth/mourt3.html.

20. Ibid.

CHAPTER 10: WAR

1. Bradford and Winslow, *Mourt's Relation*, *Part IV*, http://www
.histarch.illinois.edu/plymouth/mourt4.html.

2. *The New England Historical and Genealogical Register*, vol. 3–4,
218, https://books.google.com/books?id=_oweAQAAMAAJ.

3. Ibid.

4. Bradford, *Of Plymouth Plantation*, 57.

5. Ibid.

6. Ibid.

7. Bradford and Winslow, *Mourt's Relation*, *Part IV*, 75–76, http://
www.histarch.illinois.edu/plymouth/mourt4.html.

8. Drake, *Drakes Book of Indians*, 29. Signatories of the treaty
were: Ohquamehud, Nattawahunt, Quadaquina, Cawnacome,
Caunbatant (Corbitant), Huttmoiden, Obbatinnua,
Chikkatabak, Apannow (Epenow).

9. Michelle Tirado, "The Wampanoag Side of the First
Thanksgiving."

10. Winslow, *Mourt's Relation*, *Part VI*, http://www.histarch.illinois
.edu/plymouth/mourt6.html.

11. Bradford, *Of Plymouth Plantation*, 58.

CHAPTER 11: THE HOPE OF PEACE

1. Bradford, *Of Plymouth Plantation*, 58.

2. Ibid.

3. Ibid.

4. Ibid.

5. Andrew Barr, *Drink: A Social History of America* (New York:
Carroll & Graf, 1999), 252, https://www.nytimes.com/books
/first/b/barr-drink.html.

6. The captain did offer to take them farther south to Virginia.

7. Cushman also brought New Plymouth's legal charter for the
plantation from the New England Company.

8. "Letter from Thomas Weston, July 6, 1621," in Bradford, *Of Plymouth Plantation*, 59.

9. The manuscript was titled *A Relation or Journal of the Beginnings and Proceedings of the English Plantation Settled at Plymouth, New England*. This is known today as *Mourt's Relation*. It is believed to be written by Bradford and Winslow.

10. Bradford, *Of Plymouth Plantation*, 62.

11. Ibid.

12. Ibid., 61.

13. Bradford, *Of Plymouth Plantation*, 63.

14. Winslow, *Good Newes*, 15.

15. Bradford, *Of Plymouth Plantation*, 63–64.

16. Dillon, *The Pilgrims*, 171.

17. At this time the English colonies operated by the Julian calendar, under which New Year's Day was recognized as March 25. In original manuscripts and unedited translations, these dates are noted as 1621. I have translated the dates into the Gregorian calendar.

18. Bradford, *Of Plymouth Plantation*, 63.

19. Ibid., 64.

20. Ibid., 70.

21. Ibid., 64.

22. Ibid., 70.

23. Ibid., 69.

24. Now the city of Weymouth.

25. Bradford, *Of Plymouth Plantation*, 71.

26. Winslow, *Good Newes*, 25.

27. Bradford, *Of Plymouth Plantation*, 72.

28. Ibid.

29. Ibid., 74.

CHAPTER 12: PROVOCATION

1. Winslow, *Good Newes*, 28.

2. Bradford, *Of Plymouth Plantation*, 73.

3. Ibid.

4. Winslow, *Good Newes*, 44.

5. Ibid., 31.

6. Ibid., 32.

7. Ibid. Winslow appears to be providing a translation in various parts of this section. He is directly attributing these words to Hobbamock, but he likely paraphrased rather than recorded an accurate quote.

8. Ibid.

9. Ibid.

10. Ibid., 28.

11. Ibid., 37.

12. Ibid., 32.

13. Some scholars, such as George F. Willison, believe Winslow fabricated this story to justify Standish's militaristic actions against the Indians. (See Dillon, 178.) Such scholars cite the fact that Winslow apparently felt safe walking through villages of these tribes and willingly spending considerable time in them on the return to Plymouth. In my view, it is dangerous to infer such conclusions from Winslow's actions. Winslow had become Plymouth's most seasoned and effective diplomat. Without clear circumstantial evidence to the contrary, we can only affirmatively rely on his record.

14. Bradford, *Of Plymouth Plantation*, 74.

15. Winslow, *Good Newes*, 38.

16. Ibid., 41.

17. Ibid., 42.

18. Ibid., 42–43.

19. Bradford, Of *Plymouth* Plantation, 74.

20. Walter Herbert Burgess, *The Pastor of the Pilgrims: A Biography of John Robinson* (New York: Harcourt Brace, 1920), 280, https://books.google.com/books?id=Ijt5AAAAMAAJ.

CHAPTER 13: THANKSGIVING

1. Bradford, *Of Plymouth Plantation*, 76.

2. Ibid.

3. Ibid., 81.

4. Ibid., 82.

5. Ibid., 131.

6. Ibid., 131–32.

7. Ibid.

8. Dillon, 161. The Pilgrims' view of marriage: "The Separatists never recognized marriage as a sacrament, 'being but a civil thing.'"

9. Modern-day Quincy, Massachusetts.

10. Bradford, *Of Plymouth Plantation*, 129.

11. Ibid.

12. Ibid.

13. Ibid., 131.

14. The first winter at the Massachusetts Bay Company was also difficult. On March 28, 1631, Governor Dudley wrote: "The next year, 1629, we sent divers ships over, with about three hundred people. . . . Our four ships which set out in April [1630] arrived here in June and July, where we found the Colony in a sad and unexpected condition, above eighty of them being dead the winter before; and many of those alive weak and sick . . . the remainder of a hundred and eighty servants we had the two years before sent over coming to us for victuals to sustain them, we found ourselves wholly unable to feed them . . . many died weekly, yea, almost daily . . . not much less than a hundred, (some think many more) partly out of dislike of our government, . . . returned back again [to England]. . . . Others also, afterwards hearing of men of their own disposition, which were planted at Pascataway, went from us to them. . . . And of the people who came over with us, from the time of their setting sail from England in April, 1630, until December following, there died by estimation about two hundred at the least. . . . I should also have remembered, how the half of our cows and almost all our mares and goats, sent us out of England, died at sea in their passage hither. . . . It may be said of us almost as of the Egyptians, that there is not a house where there is not one dead, and in some houses many." See Augustine Jones, *The Life*

and Work of Thomas Dudley: The Second Governor of Massachusetts.
Boston: Houghton, Mifflin and Company, 1899, p. 440.

15. Bradford, *Of Plymouth Plantation*, 148.

16. *Charter of the Colony of New Plymouth Granted to William Bradford and His Associates*, 1629.

17. The Council of New England would fold within a few years, and New Plymouth would proceed for twenty-five years with little oversight from England. The matter of the patent would seemingly be forgotten and, in practice, unnecessary. Meanwhile their mother country would see many political changes and would largely overlook New Plymouth. By the time the matter received attention again, it was too late to resolve. A royal charter would have made them the fourteenth founding state. Instead, Plymouth was later absorbed by the state of Massachusetts.

18. Bradford, *Of Plymouth Plantation*, 164.

19. Alexander Young, *Chronicles of the Pilgrim Fathers* (New York: E. P. Dutton, 1910), 108.

20. Ibid.

21. Canonicus was the chief sachem of the Narragansett tribe. Williams grew close to Narragansett leaders, even becoming a student of the Narragansett language.

22. Bradford, *Of Plymouth Plantation*, 4.

23. Ibid., 215.

24. The name Nauset was changed to Eastham in 1651.

25. Bradford, *Of Plymouth Plantation*, 214.

26. Ibid., 148.

EPILOGUE

1. Third Dialogue was written in 1652. A second dialogue has never been found, nor is there any reference to it in Pilgrim historical documents. It may not exist or may have been lost.

2. Bradford, *Of Plymouth Plantation*, 32.

3. "Letter from Robinson and Brewster to Edwin Sandys," December 15, 1617, in Bradford, *Of Plymouth Plantation*, 17–18.

4. Ibid., 18.

Index

About the Author

J ay Milbrandt is the author of *The Daring Heart of David Livingstone* and a professor at Bethel University in Minnesota. He formerly directed the Global Justice Program and served as Senior Fellow in Global Justice with the Nootbaar Institute at Pepperdine University School of Law. He has traveled throughout the world as a lawyer, managing global initiatives in Africa and Southeast Asia, and consulting with organizations engaged in human rights and legal development efforts.

JayMilbrandt.com